社交媒体视域下
中国国内移民适应研究

RESEARCH ON THE ADAPTATION OF CHINESE INTERNAL
MIGRANTS FROM THE PERSPECTIVE OF SOCIAL MEDIA

孟娇娇　著

上海三联书店

Acknowledgements

I owe a great deal of thanks to many people for finishing this book. First and foremost, I would like to express my deepest appreciation to my dear PhD supervisor Professor Steve J. Kulich at Shanghai International Studies University. He is a theorist of intercultural communication(IC) and practitioner making great efforts to develop IC as a discipline in China. He is a helpful mentor who guided me throughout my academic journey with his wisdom, profound academic achievements, patience, encouragement, and generous support. His valuable suggestions, professional guidance, and timely help made it possible for me to finish this book.

My special gratitude goes to my PhD co-supervisor Professor Dharm P.S. Bhawuk at University of Hawaii. Professor Dharm P.S. Bhawuk gave me many valuable suggestions on both conceptual and methodological issues in the present study. He helped review the items of my scales and make some critical comments on the present study.

My deep appreciation goes to Professor Yan Bing Zhang at University of Kansas. Professor Yan Bing Zhang inspired me with her expert knowledge of doing quantitative studies, and helped lay the conceptual framework for this study from the very beginning. She reviewed each item of the scales and gave suggestions on statistical analysis of the data.

My sincere thanks are expressed to Professor Zhang Hongling at Shanghai International Studies University, Professor Yan Jinglan at East China University of Science and Technology, Professor Dai Xiaodong at Shanghai Normal University, Professor Zhang Yanli at Shanghai International Studies University, and Professor Gao Yihong at Peking University for their suggestions and comments on this study.

I further express my appreciation to teachers and PhD students at SISU Intercultural Institute (SII) for their support and encouragement. My special thanks go to my colleague Hu Yijun for doing the arduous work of translating the English questionnaire, to my colleague Zhao Haiyan for the back translation, and to my colleagues who helped review the items of the scale.

Finally, my heartfelt gratitude goes to my family. I would like to thank my parents-in-law and my parents for their support. I am deeply indebted to my husband Shaojie for his help on my academic research and his devotion to the family. And I am deeply grateful to my two lovely children Tiantian and Yangyang for their patience and encouragement.

Foreword

Since being formalized in 1970 (see Kulich, 2012; Prosser, 2012) the field of intercultural communication (IC) is robust and developing rapidly (Kulich, Weng, Tong, & DuBois, 2020). In a similar fashion, adaptation has been one of the primary and expanding topics in this evolving field. This makes sense as more and more people are having adapted to a growing range of culture situations and issues worldwide. And while IC may have previously been considered to focus on the comparative study of patterns across countries ("big C" Culture in the tradition of E. T. Hall's domains or Hofstede's and Trompenaars' national dimensions) the field is increasingly considering interactions between "small c" cultural groups within or across nations (distinctive religious, ethic, socio-economic, gender, or other distinctive cultural identity grouping). From the previous focus on types of international immigration, the focus is shifting to include dynamics of internal migration. Therefore this book addresses an important trend in the literature: *Research on the Adaptation of Chinese Internal Migrants from the Perspective of Social Media*. And as the title suggests, it also addresses an important gap, that of the role of social media as an influence on migrant identities or tool affecting the adaptation process.

This book shows how China's implementation of the reform and opening-up policy forty years ago has led to an ever-increasing flow of internal migration. Whether this has been seen in trends of rural to urban migration or migration from smaller urban centers to larger urban metropolis, groups of people are moving and seeking to find their identities in new surroundings. Having to set up life in a new context requires adaptation, and it can be argued that each region or city has its own cultural characteristics. If source and target culture can be shown to have a number of distinct "cultural characteristics" (different cultural patterns, values, identities, styles, etc.), migration from one cultural context to another is then an intercultural phenomenon. This book posits that intercultural adaptation theories CAN be used to study internal migration and that the IC-based theoretical applications can frame meaningful hypotheses that generate informative results and IC-relevant findings.

The book begins explaining the context of China's growth and development and how the 14th Five Year Plan urges the exploration of a new human-centered approach of urbanization. As China's urbanization moves toward a new stage of quality development, it is my own and the author's conviction that intercultural communication/relation studies can provide pertinent answers on how to better help China's internal migrants integrate into the cities of settlement to further development. Thus, this book appropriately explores the adaptation of internal migrants in China and examines related factors, and originally examines the importance and effects of social media use in this process.

The book then undertakes an extensive review of leading theories and empirical research on adaptation and acculturation. Based on these and considering ways of adapting them to intergroup/intercultural contexts within nations, the book proposes a structural model explaining factors affecting internal migrants' adaptation, with a focus on the ways through which social media use affects their adaptation. Three variables are specifically identified as the potential indicators that affect internal migrants' adaptation(acculturative stress, life satisfaction, and local cultural identification). Among these, social support is identified as a mediator of the relations between social media use and the other important adaptation variables. To test this model and the related hypotheses, a sample of Shanghai internal migrants are recruited to participate in this mixed-method research design. Most instructive for the reader is the discussion of findings, and the related suggestions on what specifically can facilitate the more successful adaption of internal migrants in new urban contexts, especially those relocating in modern city centers like Shanghai.

I recommend the book for its theoretical significances in two main areas. First, much of IC research has focused on face-to-face communication. In fact, many consider IC to be an extension of interpersonal communication studies(thought there are branches that focus on IC educational exchange and IC mass media). Though the traditional modes of communication continue, the growing and extensive use of social media is postulated to be changing patterns of human communication(cf. Shuter, 2012). It is therefore necessary that all areas in the study of intercultural communication be expanded to include social media and consider how it may be affecting or changing what we thought we knew, even in established areas of research like adaptation studies, and re-evaluate how workable past theorizing is in these new contexts and with this new virtual means of communication. Second, as noted by Gudykunst and Kim(2003), the term "intercultural" does not necessarily mean national differences, but includes various situations at intergroup, interethnic, and interracial levels. Unlike the mainstream of intercultural adaptation studies focusing on immigrants, international students, refugees etc., this book undertakes the new perspective of not only studying internal migrants(which a few studies have examined in Western contexts) but in the much-understudied contexts of China. This adds to the existing literature both on intercultural adaptation by examining with-nation adaptation and on China, which is significant for better understanding its rich regional diversity as well as its increasing influence as a nation of growing urbanization and emerging global economic power.

The book can also be recommended for its practical value. The author collected a large sample for the quantitative survey and postulated a theoretical model based on the carefully designed hypotheses. By employing structural equation modeling (SEM), a type of multivariate analysis, and considering the interrelationships of specific factors, the author tested the proposed model for its ability to accurately describe Chinese internal migrants' adaptation in general and specifically which factors most affect their positive adaptation. Based on the rich and solid research findings, we can gain new understanding into some aspects and applications of the adaptation process faced by internal migrants in China. The proposed indicators for measuring adaptation of international migrants in China and the sales adopted or developed provide a helpful reference for similar studies and applications relevant to Chinese internal migrants' adaptation.

I was privileged to watch this project develop from its early proposal stage, to consulting with co-advisors like Dharm P. S. Bhawuk of the University of Hawaii, Yan Bing Zhang of the University of Kansas, Hongling Zhang, Alex S. English, Ruobing Chi, Weng Liping of SISU, and other esteemed professors on the proposal, pre-defense, and defense committee. Because of the invaluable suggestions made at each stage, the diligence of the author to revise and update many aspects of her project design, selection of appropriate scales, the proposed model, re-evaluation of the data, reflection, and much re-analysis, responding, and rewriting, this book captures the best intentions of the author and our institute's research program.

Therefore, I am pleased to recommend this book as a valuable resource that responds to concerns facing the nation on promoting new approaches to urbanization and better social integration of internal migrants. The author proposes suggestions on ways to facilitate and enhance the adaptation of internal migrants in China and how to make better use of social media to promote their adapting to local societies. Such an academic work can add to the body of work that provides an informative basis for the government and institutions concerned to consider how to practically formulate policies on migration-related issues and human-centered urbanization in ways that will hopefully enhance the well-being and shared destiny of all.

Shanghai, July 21, 2021
Steve J. Kulich 顾力行

President(2019-2021) of the International Academy of Intercultural Research(IAIR)
Director of the SISU Intercultural Institute(SII)
Shanghai International Studies University(SISU)

Preface

China has been experiencing a significant increase of internal migration with the rapid development of urbanization since its implementation of the reform and opening-up policy. Given the regional differences in terms of culture and economic development brought about by variations across China's vast territory, internal migrants are often faced with some challenges in adapting to their new locations. Internal migrants' adaptation is not only important to their physical and psychological wellbeing, but also important for the harmony of society as a whole. Social media has significantly changed many patterns of human communication, to the degree that intercultural communication theories need to be further expanded in the context of social media use. Yet, relatively little research has been done to examine the effects of social media use on migrants' adaptation. Therefore, this book seeks to examine adaptation of internal migrants in China and the mechanism of how social media use affects their adaptation.

The book first reviewed existing theories in the fields of migration, intercultural adaptation, communication etc., and examines empirical findings on intercultural adaptation and on the adaptation of internal migrants in China. Second, based on the literature review, a structural model describing Chinese internal migrants' adaptation and factors affecting their adaptation was proposed, with a focus on the ways through which social media use affects internal migrants' adaptation. More specifically, three variables were identified as indicators of internal migrants' adaptation (acculturative stress, life satisfaction, and local cultural identification), and social support was identified as a mediator of the relations between social media use and these adaptation variables. Third, internal migrants in Shanghai were sampled, and a questionnaire was developed to collect the data. Structural equation modeling(SEM) was used to test the hypothesized structural model. In the quantitative analysis, exploratory factor analysis(EFA) was conducted on the self-developed social support scales for internal migrants. Next, confirmatory factor analysis(CFA) was conducted to develop the measurement models of the latent variables. Then, based on the factor scores of the latent variables, the Independent Samples *t* Test was conducted to examine the effects of some demographic variables on adaptation. Last, path coefficients were examined to test the direct effects specified in the hypothesized model, and the mediation effects were examined using the Bootstrap method.

The book has proposed and tested a hypothesized structural model to examine the adaptation of internal migrants in China and the effects of social media use on the adaptation of internal migrants. Findings in the present study not only supplement theories of intercultural adaptation in the social media communication context but also expand the extant literature on the adaptation of internal migrants in China. The self-developed social support scale specifically related to internal migrants as well as the measurements used for assessing internal migrants' adaptation have reference value for related studies. Based on the research findings, a few suggestions are put forward to facilitate the adaptation of internal migrants in China, which can serve as an aid for government or institutions concerned to formulate policies on migration-related issues.

List of Figures

List of Tables

Contents

Chapter One

Introduction

In an increasingly globalized world, human mobility has become a more common phenomenon than ever. Countless people move "in search of security or better livelihood: from villages to towns, from one region to another in their home country, or between countries or continents"(Castles, 2000, p.269). With the increasing influx of migrants, migration has become an important research topic in social science studies.

Two types of migration are distinguished in migration literature: international migration and internal migration. International migration refers to people's movement across nation-state borders while internal migration refers to people's movement within one country(Castles, 2000). Traditionally, international migration has received more focus, however, increased attention has shifted towards internal migrants due to their significant growth throughout the past few decades, especially "in the colossal BRIC countries" (Sun, 2019, p.1).

Internal migration in China is a significant social phenomenon and has received a great deal of interest from various disciplines such as sociology, demography, and social psychology. The present study focuses on the adaptation of internal migrants and the role of social media use in their adaptation process. This chapter provides an overview of the present research, including research background, research questions, research procedures, significance of the study, research methodologies applied, and organization of the book.

1.1   Research Background

1.1.1   Growing Concern About Adaptation of Internal Migrants

China is a country with a large number of internal migrants. Since China released its restrictions on the Hukou(or household registration) system in the late 1980s, China's population mobility has grown in volume, with a large number of people seeking temporary employment or permanent residence in places outside their hometown(Hao & Tang, 2018; Zhao, Liu, & Zhang, 2018).① Over the past four decades, China's internal migration population has been growing steadily. According to the statistics, China's internal migration population reached a number of 236 million by the end of 2019, which accounted for 16.86% of the total population(see Figure 1.1).

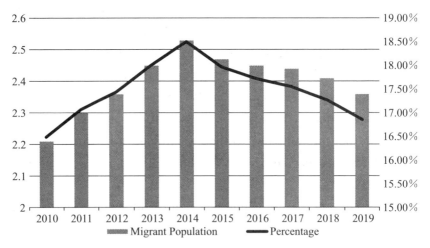

Figure 1.1   Migration Population in China from 2010 to 2019

Source: Wind Database.

---

① China's Hukou system was established in 1958. It assigns each person to a place of residence and categorizes the population into two types: urban vs. rural. When it was established, it served as a means to regulate the rural to urban population movement(Chen, 2011).

As China is a large country characterized by its vast territory, there are some differences across different regions in some aspects such as institutional system, economic development, and cultural values and norms. Therefore, as internal migrants move to new places and relocate themselves, they are likely to experience challenges brought about by changes in the sociocultural environment and may find it difficult to fit into the local environment (Chen, 2011). Extant literature has indicated some problems that internal migrants have encountered in their adaptation process. For example, Wang (2009) found that internal migrants experience culture shock in terms of lifestyles, cultural values, and social norms and rituals. Beyond that, internal migrants have some confusion about their cultural identification. These migration-related issues have negative effects on internal migrant's mental health, causing some negative psychological outcomes (e.g., depression, anxiety, social isolation) (Wong, He, Leung, Lau, & Chang, 2008).

What are the difficulties or stress internal migrants have experienced in their adaptation process? What are the factors affecting internal migrants' adaptation at both individual and environmental levels? What are the important issues that need to be addressed to facilitate their adaptation process? The present study was initiated as an attempt to answer these questions.

1.1.2 The Need to Examine the Effects of Social Media Use on Adaptation of Internal Migrants

Social media has become an important tool of communication in our daily lives. It has dramatically changed the patterns of human communication by enabling people to "exchange messages, share knowledge, and interact with each other" (Sawyer & Chen, p.12) regardless of time and geographic boundaries.

China's social media use has boomed in recent decades. According to a 2018 report from CZWZC (China Internet Network Information

Center), social media has become one of the main types of media used among Chinese netizens(See Figure 1.2). WeChat and Tencent QQ had a utilization ratio of 85.8% and 67.8% in 2016 respectively.

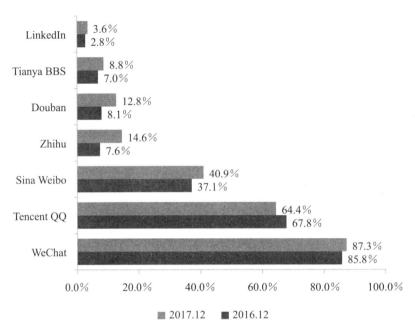

Figure 1.2   The Ratio of Social Media Use of Chinese Netizens

Source: "China Statistical Report on Internet Development", CINIC(China Internet Network Information Center).

Communication is an indispensable part of adaptation studies (Kim, 2001). Previous intercultural adaptation literature primarily focuses on the impact of face-to-face communication and mass communication in migrant's adaptation process(Dalisay, 2012; McKay-Semmler & Kim, 2014; Moon & Park, 2007). With the increasing popularity of the use of social media among people, an increasing amount of research has examined its role in international migrant's adaptation process. Extant literature suggests that international migrants use social media to obtain information about their receiving culture, in addition to maintaining contact with their previous social networks(Sawyer & Chen, 2012). Moreover, there is research evidence that social media facilitates international migrants' seeking of social support, increasing their perception of the availability of social support as well as their satisfaction with the social support received(Chen & Choi, 2011; Chen & Yang, 2015; Forbush & Foucault-Welles, 2016).

Compared with intercultural adaptation literature, social media use of internal migrants was not widely examined in domestic literature. The available literature examining internal migrants' social media use focuses on describing the patterns of their social media use, the purposes of their social media use, and their satisfaction with social media use(Jia, 2012; Zhou & Lv, 2011). Limited efforts, in contrast, have been exerted on exploring how and why social media use affects the adaptation process of internal migrants in China. In response to the wide use of social media among internal migrants, it is necessary to examine how internal migrants' social media use affects their adaptation process.

Therefore, the importance of exploring factors affecting internal migrants' adaptation, together with the necessity of investigating the impact of social media use on their adaptation serve as the impetus for the present study.

1.2   Research Questions

The main objective of the present study is to examine the adaptation of internal migrants in China and investigate the effects of social media use on their adaptation. The main research questions are:

1. How can the adaptation of internal migrants be assessed?

2. What are the important factors affecting the adaptation of internal migrants? And how are these factors associated with internal migrants' adaptation?

3. How does social media use combine with these factors to affect the adaptation of internal migrants?

1.3   Research Procedures

Based on the aforementioned research questions, the author carried out the following procedures to conduct the present research:

First, building on a review of theories and empirical research, the author identified three key variables to assess the overall adaptation of internal migrants: acculturative stress, life satisfaction, and local cultural identification.

Second, drawing upon the existing literature, the author identified certain individual factors affecting adaptation process and outcomes, including social support, two personality variables (extroversion and neuroticism), and internal migrant's length of stay in their current residence.

Third, based on existing research evidence, the author proposed a hypothesized structural model featuring internal migrants' adaptation and factors affecting their adaptation, with a focus on the ways through which social media use affects their adaptation.

Last, the author selected internal migrants in Shanghai as the research sample and conducted a quantitative study to test the hypothesized structural model.

1.4   Significance of the Study

1.4.1   Theoretical Significance

According to DeWind and Holdaway(2005), international migration and internal migration "have many things in common in terms of their causes and origins, the process involved, and their impact and outcomes"(p.28). Extensive efforts have been exerted to explain intercultural adaptation of international migrants. Despite internal migration take place within country borders, however, as Castles(2000) argued, it may involve people who are more culturally distinct than those who cross short nation-state distances and who are culturally similar. Therefore, like international migrants, internal migrants may encounter some problems in their adaptation to the local residence.

According to Kim (2012), the concept of culture has been broadened from national culture to include "subcultures of smaller groups from domestic ethnic or racial groups and other sociological groups along the lines of gender, sexual orientation, psychical ability or disability, and geographic areas, among others"(p.357). Due to China's vast territory, there exist some regional variations in terms of values, social norms and practices. The term "intercultural" does not necessarily mean national differences, but includes various situations at intergroup, interethnic, and interracial levels (Gudykunst & Kim, 2003). Kim(2012) argued that all social encounters are potentially "intercultural" because of the heterogeneity in the "experiential backgrounds of interactants" (p.357). Therefore, the present study borrows some intercultural adaptation theories(Berry, 1997; Kim, 2001) and concepts (e.g., acculturative stress) to examine within-nation adaptation of internal migrants in China. It helps extend intercultural adaptation theories to internal migration studies. Meanwhile, the research results of the present study supplement the existing intercultural adaptation literature.

In addition, responding to the reality that social media has become an indispensable tool of communication, the existing intercultural adaptation theories, which are built on the context of face-to-face communication or mass communication, need to be reexamined(Shuter, 2012). By relating social media use and the adaptation of internal migrants, the present study adds to the existing literature on the effects of social media use on adaptation, which will supplement intercultural adaptation theories.

1.4.2   Practical Significance

The present study adopted a quantitative method to examine

the adaptation of internal migrants and the effects of social media use on their adaptation. The present study contributes to a better understanding of internal migrants' adaptation. The research findings will provide a basis for the government and policymakers to formulate measures to facilitate the adaptation of internal migrants.

1.5   Research Methodologies Applied

A quantitative survey method was adopted in the present study. First, the author reviewed the theories in the fields of migration, intercultural adaptation, and communication, and the empirical studies in intercultural adaptation and the adaptation of internal migrants in China. Based on the literature review, the author identified the main study variables related to the current topic and proposed a hypothesized structural model to illustrate the factors affecting the adaptation of internal migrants.

Then, the author selected internal migrants in Shanghai as the research sample, developed questionnaires on their social media use and adaptation, and conducted an online survey to collect data. The statistical technique of structural equation modeling (SEM) using Mplus 7.4 was conducted to test the hypothesized model.

SEM is a technique to simultaneously test the dependence relationships among a set of variables in a structural model. SEM comprises two models: the measurement model and the structural model. The measurement model examines the factorial validity of the measuring instrument, i.e., whether the observed variables best represent the latent constructs or not (Byrne, 2010). The structural model is also called the path model, and it examines the relationships among the latent constructs (Nachtigall, Kroehne, Funke, & Steyer, 2003).

Two basic techniques of factor analysis were used to develop the measurement models of the latent constructs in the hypothesized structural model: Exploratory factor analysis (EFA) and Confirmatory factor analysis(CFA). EFA was conducted to derive the facto-rial structure on the self-developed perceived social support scales, and CFA was conducted to validate the factorial structures of the latent variables. Then, factor score of the latent variables were cal-culated based on the CFA models and was used to examine the effects of demographic variables on the adaptation of internal mi-grants using the Independent Samples t Test. Last, path coeffi-cients were examined to estimate the direct effects among the varia-bles in the structural model. Bootstrap method was used to test the mediation effects in the hypothesized structural model.

1.6   Organization of the Book

The book is divided into eight chapters. Chapter One introduces the research background, the research questions, the research procedures, significance of the study, and the organization of the book.

Chapter Two is the literature review. It first provides an over-view of the theories relevant to the present study, including migra-tion theories, intercultural adaptation theories, theories related to social media and social support. Then, it reviews topic-related stud-ies in intercultural adaptation of international migrants and domes-tic studies on the adaptation of internal migrants in China. Finally, building on the literature review, it summarizes the literature re-view and presents a conceptual framework for the empirical study.

Chapter Three presents the research hypotheses among the var-iables and proposes a hypothesized structural model of factors af-fecting their adaptation, focusing on the impact of social media use on adaptation.

Chapter Four introduces the research methodology. It first in-troduces the target sample of the research. Second, it describes measurement of the variables. Third, it introduces questionnaire design procedures, including the composition of the questionnaires, the panel validity establishment, the translation and back translation of the questionnaire, and the pilot study. Forth, it describes the collection of the data, including the sample size estimation and the data collection procedures. Last, it introduces the statistical methods used for data analysis.

Chapter Five is the preliminary analysis of the data. This chapter first presents an overview of the survey questionnaires, and then describes the survey respondents' characteristics. Then, it presents the respondents' social media use types and use frequency. Last, it describes the data screening, including the test of the multivariate outliers, correlations, multicollinearity, and the reliability of the scales.

Chapter Six focuses on the data analysis of the measurement models. First, it introduces the methods of factor analysis. Second, it introduces the process of the development of the measurement models of the latent variables in the hypothesized structural model. Third, it presents the test of the validity and reliability of the overall CFA model. Fourth, it presents the common method variance (CMV) test of the overall CFA model. Last, it introduces the Independent Samples t Test on the factor score to examine the effects of demographic variables on the adaptation variables.

Chapter Seven is the data analysis of the structural model. It first introduces the respecification of the hypothesized structural model based on the CFA of the measurement models. Second, it introduces the structural model fitting process. Third, it presents the test of the hypothesized direct effects. Fourth, it describes the robustness test. Fifth, it presents the estimation results of the structural model through item parceling. Last, it presents the test of mediation effects using Bootstrap method.

Chapter Eight is the discussion and conclusions. It first provides an overview of the present study, and then discusses the main research findings and implications of the research findings. Following that, it presents the contributions of the present study. Last, it puts forwards the research limitations and directions for future research.

Chapter Two

Literature Review

The present study examines the adaptation of internal migrants in China and the effects of social media use on their adaptation. This chapter consists of four sections. The first section provides an overview of theories on related topics, including migration, intercultural adaptation, social media, and social support, with an aim of describing the theoretical bases for the present study. Second, it reviews topic-related research on intercultural adaptation of international migrants. Third, it reviews the literature on the adaptation of internal migrants in China. Finally, it summarizes the literature review and puts forward a conceptual framework for the present study.

2.1 A Review of Related Theories

2.1.1 Migration Theories

2.1.1.1 Definition of Migration

Migration is an important social phenomenon in the process of the development of human history. Lee(1966) defined migration as "a permanent or semi-permanent change of residence"(p.49). He pointed out four important dimensions of migration: (1) the repellant factors associated with the area of origin, (2) the attractive factors of the destination, (3) some intervening obstacles(e.g., physical barriers), and (4) personal factors that affect the migration process(e.g., personal sensitivities, personalities, intelligence, and knowledge of the destination).

Depending on the intended destination, two types of migration can be distinguished from each other: international and internal migration. International migration refers to the movement of human beings across borders of nation-states, while internal migration refers to the movement of human beings within one country, usually "from one area(province, district or municipality) to another" (Castles, 2000, p.269).

In addition to the distinction drawn between international migrants and internal migrants, Berry and Sam(1997) classified migrants into other broad groups: permanent migrants vs. temporary migrants and voluntary migrants vs. involuntary migrants(See Table 2.1). Permanent migrants(e.g., immigrants) and temporary migrants(e.g., sojourners) differ in their length of stay in the culture of settlement and their intention to stay permanently. Voluntary migrants(e.g., immigrants and sojourners) are those who move to the host society in order to realize a range of self-fulfilling purposes through employment or education, whereas involuntary migrants (e.g., refugees and asylum seekers) are those who are avoiding political instability, persecution, economic depression, or other life disasters(Berry, 1997; Richmond, 1993).

Table 2.1   Types of Migrants

Length of Stay	Voluntariness of Contact	
	Voluntary	Involuntary
Permanent	Immigrants	Refugees
Temporary	Sojourners	Asylum Seekers

Source: Adapted from Berry & Sam, 1997, p.295.

However, it is important to note that migration requires a certain minimum length of residence in the host place—usually 6 months or a year(Castles, 2000). Typical migration involves immigrants or long-term temporary migrants who usually move for work, business, or education purposes(Castles, 2000). For the purpose of the present study, migrants are defined as those who moved from their place of origin to the place of destination and who have been residing there for at least 6 months. Tourists and short-term business travelers were not considered in the present study.

2.1.1.2 Origins of Migration

Scholarly attention to migration can be traced back to as early as 1885 when Ravenstein published his paper "The Laws of Migration." Since the 1960s, a number of scholars have attempted to provide the theoretical explanations of the origins of international and internal migration from different perspectives. This section presents some classical theories on the origins of migration.

2.1.1.2.1 The Push and Pull Theory

The Push and Pull theory(Lee, 1966; Ravenstein, 1885) is among the earliest explanations of the factors propelling migration and has inspired further studies on the origins of migration. It builds on Ravenstein's(1885) ideas, as presented in "The Law of Migration." In examining migration patterns in the United Kingdom, Ravenstein(1885) observed that migration regularly followed certain patterns, such as "The majority of migrants go only a short distance," "Migration proceeds step by step," "Migrants proceeding long distances generally go by preference to one of the great centers of commerce or industry," and "The natives of towns are less migratory than those of rural areas"(pp.189—199). In a further study, Ravenstein(1989, as cited in Arango, 2000) noted that:

> Bad or oppressive laws, heavy taxation, an unattractive climate, uncongenial social surroundings, and even compulsion(slave trade, transportation), all have produced and are still producing currents of migration, but none of these currents can compare in volume with that which arises from the desire inherent in most men to "better" themselves in material respects.(p.284)

Ravenstein's pioneering studies provided some insights into

patterns of and reasons for migration, and were used as a foundation for further studies by several other scholars. Lee(1966) provided a systematic explanation of the push and pull factors in migration. He pointed out that the decision to migrate was affected by
certain "plus" factors, which attracted people to the place of destination, and "minus" factors, which repelled the people from the
place of origin. According to the Push and Pull Theory(Lee, 1966;
Ravenstein, 1885), migration can be considered as an interplay between some "push"(or repellant) factors in the place of origin and
some "pull"(or attractive) factors in the place of destination(Segal,
Mayadas, & Elliott, 2006). The "push" factors, for example, might
include poverty, political instability, or unemployment, whereas
the "pull" factors might include economic or educational opportuni-
ties(Dorigo & Tobler, 1983; Greenwood & Hunt, 2003).

Despite that the Push and Pull Theory is effective in explaining
some important factors that account for individual's migration.
However, it highlights the importance of economic factors while
neglecting some other factors such as cultural and political factors
(Wei & Yang, 2014).

2.1.1.2.2   The Dual Market Theory

While primarily, this theory focuses on economic development
in less-developed countries, it also describes the causes of rural-to-
urban migration. The dual market theory was first proposed by
Lewis(1954) in "Economic Development with Unlimited Supplies
of Labor." In his paper, Lewis put forward a dual-sector model
which differentiated between two separate economic sectors in less
developed countries: the modern capitalist sector(or the formal,
industrial, or urban sector) and the rural subsistence sector(or the
informal, agricultural, or traditional sector)(Fields, 2004). The
subsistence sector yields zero marginal productivity and has a surplus of labor(Arango, 2000). By contrast, the modern capital sector, which "uses reproducible capital and pays for the capitalist
thereof"(Lewis, 1954, p.407), provides higher wages for labor than the

rural subsistence sector(Jorgenson, 1967). Lewis(1954) noted:

> Earnings in the subsistence sector set a floor to wages
> in the capitalist sector, but in practice wages have to be
> higher than this, and there is usually a gap of 30 per cent
> or more between capitalist wages and subsistence earnings.
> (p.150)

The underlying assumption of the dual economy theory(Lewis, 1954) is that there is an abundance of labor in countries with large populations and the labor supply is unlimited. The wage gap between the sectors draws surplus labor from the subsistence sector to the modern capitalist sector(Kirkpatrick & Barrientos, 2004). At first, the supply of rural labor is unlimited. With the increase of the supply of labor, the accumulation of the capital in the modern sector continues and more employment opportunities are provided to surplus rural labor(Yang, 2018). However, increasing demand for the rural surplus labor will result in a shortage of the rural labor supply. The turning point will occur as rural labor supply becomes more scarce, and wages in the subsistence sector begin to rise (Wang, 2005). Eventually, the rural surplus labor supply will be exhausted and the wages of the subsistence sector and the capital sector will converge(Kirkpatrick & Barrientos, 2004).

The Dual Market Theory views the economic disparity between the modern sector and the rural section is the reason for migration. Nonetheless, it neglects individual motivation or agency in making the migration decision(Wang, 2005).

2.1.1.2.3　The Neo-classical Economics Theory

The dominant theory of migration during the 1970s and the 1980s was the Neo-Classical Economics Theory(Harris & Todaro, 1970; Sjaastad, 1962; Todaro, 1969). The Neo-Classical Economics Theory explains the causes of labor migration in developing countries using macro and micro dimensions(Massey, Arango, Hugo, Kouaouci, Pellegrino, & Taylor, 1993). The macro dimension postulates that the main cause of migration is wage differentials resulting from "the geographic differences in the supply of and demand for labor"(Massey et al., 1993, p.433). Individuals moving from rural areas to urban areas attempt to maximize their expected income, which is determined by the real wage difference and the probability of obtaining an urban job(Todaro, 1969).

The micro theory of neo-classical economics highlights the role of individual choice, positing that migration is determined by the migrants' "rational economic calculations despite the existence of high urban unemployment" (Todaro, 1980, p. 364). As Sjaastad (1962) noted, migration is "an investment increasing the productivity of human resources, an investment which has costs and which also renders returns"(p.83). Despite the potential benefits of migrating to a destination "where they can be most productive, given their skills"(Massey et al., 1993, p.434), migrants must still calculate some costs which include "the material costs of traveling, the costs of maintenance while moving and looking for work, the effort involved in learning a new language and culture, the difficulties experienced in adapting to a new labor market, and the psychological costs of cutting old ties and forging new ones"(Massey et al., 1993, p.434). Migration occurs when potential migrants think that the benefits gained from migration will surpass the costs.

The Neo-classical Economics Theory holds that wage differentials are the reasons of rural to urban migration. However, it is criticized because that it is difficult for individuals to calculate the gains and costs of migration. What's more, like push and pull theory, it is limited only to economic factors(Zhang, 2015).

2.1.1.2.4   The New Economics Theory of Migration

The New Economics Theory of Migration(Stark, 1984; Stark & Bloom, 1985; Stark & Taylor, 1989), developed more recently, offers two alternative perspectives on the causes of migration. First, it is not isolated individuals, but rather families or households, are the actors making migration decisions(Stark, 1984). According to the theory, families or households decide to migrate in order to "control the risks to their economic well-being by diversifying the allocation of household resources, such as family labor"(Massey et al., 1993, p.436). In certain underdeveloped countries, rural families are confronted with risks to their household income because of unpredictable markets(e.g., crops, futures, labor, and capital) (Massey, 1988; Massey et al., 1993). Compared with developed countries, there is no adequate insurance system in underdeveloped countries to protect them against these risks, so migration decisions are made to minimize these risks and diversify the sources of family income(Taylor, 1999).

Second, the theory emphasizes that the determinant of an individual choice to migrate or not is not an increase in their absolute income but rather "to improve a household's income position relative to others in the household's reference group"(Stark & Taylor, 1989, p.1). Stark and Bloom(1985) noted that generally, an individual who has a stronger sense of relative deprivation is more likely to migrate than a person who has a lower sense of deprivation.

The New Economics Theory of Migration explains the origins of migration from the perspective of relative deprivation, and emphasizes the role of family in making migration decisions. But this theory just discusses the causes of migration from the perspective of the migration sending countries. It does not consider the pull factors of migration destinations(Wei & Yang, 2014).

2.1.1.3   Comments on Migration Theories

To summarize, the theories of migration reviewed above provide a starting point for us to understand the reasons behind the massive internal migration flows within China. These theories have three important implications to the present study. First, building on the international migration literature, the author has defined the term of internal migrants in the present study. Second, these theories highlight the economic disparity between the migration origin and the migration destination, which indicates that some migrants may be in a low economic position, especially at the beginning of their move to the new residence. Therefore, they will face some problems such as financial difficulties. Third, these migration theories focus more on explaining migration reasons from a macro perspective rather than an individual perspective, and do not take individual differences into account. Finally, these theories did not explain the obstacles and difficulties migrants will face after their movement. Therefore, more theories should be explored to understand the adaptation of migrants.

2.1.2   Intercultural Adaptation Theories

2.1.2.1   Definition of Culture Under Different Paradigms

There are three paradigms to define culture in intercultural research, which differ in their assumptions of human nature, culture, and the relationship between culture and communication(Martin & Nakayama, 1999). The first paradigm is the social science(or functionalist) paradigm. The basis assumption of the functionalist paradigm is that "the social world is composed of knowable empirical facts that exist separate from the researcher and reflects the attempt to apply models and methods(especially quantitative methods) of the natural sciences to the study of human behaviors"(Martin & Nakayama, 1999, p.3). Under this paradigm, culture is defined as "a pattern of learned, group-related perception—including both verbal and nonverbal language, attitudes, values, belief system, disbelief systems, and behavior"(Singer, 1987, as cited in Martin & Nakayama, 1999, p.87). Culture is developed through interactions among members of the same cultural groups who share similar experience.

The second approach to define culture is the interpretivism. Interpretivists assume that human experience is "subjective and human behavior is not determined or easily predicted"(Martin & Nakayama, 1999, p.59). Under this paradigm, culture is "an historically transmitted pattern of meaning embodied in symbols, a system of inherited conceptions expressed in symbolic forms by means of which men communicate, perpetuate and develop their knowledge about and attitudes toward life"(Geertze,1973, as cited in Martin & Nakayama, 1999, p.89). This paradigm builds itself on the ethnography of communication. Researchers of this paradigm often adopt qualitive approach to describe the communication patterns within specific cultural groups rather than compare the communication patterns across cultures.

The third approach to define culture is the critical approach. The critical approach views culture as dynamic and fluid, and "extends across national and regional borders within contexts of history and power"(Hannerz, 1996, as cited in Martin & Nakayama, 1999, p.96). The critical approach emphasizes that heterogeneity exist within different cultural groups and the boundaries of culture are often difficult to define.

From the above-mentioned approaches, we can see that the concept of culture is not fixed, and can be interpreted from various perspectives. Kim(2012) notes that:

> Following common conceptions of culture in cultural anthropology and cross-cultural psychology, the term culture has been employed primarily as a label or category representing the collective life experiences of recognizable large groups such as a nation or world region. Over the years, the conception of culture has been broadened to include subcultures of smaller groups from domestic ethnic or racial groups and other sociological groups along the lines of gender, sexual orientation, psychical ability or disability, and geographic areas, among others.(p.357)

In the present study, culture is defined as regional variations in terms of communication patterns, attitudes, values, norms, practice etc. Because China is a large country with vast territories, there exist some cultural differences that vary across regions. Even though internal migrants move within China, there may exist some heterogeneity among people from different geographic areas. According to Kim(2012), all communication encounters could be potentially "intercultural" because of the "heterogeneity" in the experiential backgrounds of interactants(p.357). Gudykunst and Kim (2003) argue that, intercultural encounters involve different types of situations, including intergroup, interethnic, and interracial contact. Therefore, the present study reviews some theories and concepts from intercultural adaptation literature, which are helpful to explain the "interculturalness" of the adaptation of internal migrants in China.

2.1.2.2 Definition of Intercultural Adaptation

Intercultural adaptation is "one of the historic, foundational, and most investigated areas"(Kulich & Dai, 2012, p.12) of intercultural communication studies. Generally, it is often conceptualized as the process that individuals go through in a new sociocultural milieu, and also as an outcome of intercultural transitions.

Intercultural adaptation as a process. The concept of adaptation refers to the process whereby individuals adjust themselves to their changing sociocultural environment, with an aim of achieving a natural and beneficial fit in the new living environment to sustain and develop themselves(Haviland, 2006). When individuals move away from their original places of residence, they must deal with challenges in the new environment, including different languages, political systems, cultural values and norms, and more. Intercultural adaptation, as defined by Kim(2001), is "a dynamic process by which individuals, upon relocating to an unfamiliar cultural environment, establish(or 'reestablish') and maintain a relatively stable, reciprocal and functional relationship with the environment" (p.31). From this perspective, intercultural adaptation is a process that individuals go through after they move to a new sociocultural milieu, and during this process they make constant adjustments to fit into their new environment.

In addition to being a self-adjusting process, intercultural adaptation is communication process. For individuals entering a new

culture, a crucial factor in their adaptation process is their communication and interaction with the host nationals. Chen(2012b) notes
that intercultural adaptation is "a continuing process of interaction
between two cultural beings"(p.51). Kim(2001) also holds that intercultural adaptation is a process during which migrants communicate with the host society, perhaps to become familiar with the host
sociocultural environment and to develop positive relationships with
the host nationals.

Intercultural adaptation as an outcome. While Kim(2001) and
Chen(2012) conceptualize adaptation as a process, Searle and Ward
(1990) view it as the adjustive outcomes of intercultural contact and
draw a distinction between psychological and sociocultural adaptation. Psychological adaptation is primarily related to the migrants'
psychological well-being and emotional stability(Ward & Rana-Deuba, 1999). As Berry(1997) notes, good psychological adaptation is
typically marked with "a clear sense of personal and cultural identity, good mental health, and the achievement of personal satisfaction in the new cultural context"(p.14). Sociocultural adaptation focuses more on behavioral competence, based on accurate acquisition
of the cultural knowledge and social skills needed to function well
in the host society, i.e., the ability to "fit in"(Ward & Kennedy,
1999, p.660). Sociocultural adaptation is often assessed based on the
amount, type, and severity of difficulties experienced by migrants
in the new culture, including understanding and accepting the host
culture's values and practice, interaction and identification with the
host nationals, and stress experienced in daily lives(Ward & Kennedy, 1999; Ward & Rana-Deuba, 1999).

To sum up, in the present study, intercultural adaptation is
viewed as both a process and an outcome. As a process, individuals
contact and interact with the new sociocultural environment, re-
flecting on the demands, difficulties or stress brought about by the
changes in the new environment and making adjustments to fit in.
As an outcome, adaptation will be manifested as positive or nega-

tive psychological and behavioral results.

A few terms are frequently used in intercultural adaptation literature, including acculturation, adjustment, assimilation, and integration(Lakely, 2003; Sussman, 2000). Acculturation is commonly used as an alternative term to describe the process whereby an individual adapts to a new culture. The concept of acculturation was first proposed by Powell(1880, as cited in Lakely, 2003), referring to the changes brought to two groups during their intercultural contact. Cultural anthropologists Redfield, Linton, and Herskovits(1936, as cited in Lakely, 2003) further refined the concept, noting that:

> Acculturation comprehends those phenomena which result when groups of individuals having different cultures come into continuous first-hand contact, with subsequent changes in the original culture patterns of either or both groups.(p.105)

Earlier conceptualizations of acculturation hold that both the minority group and the majority group experience changes during cross-cultural interactions. However, it is generally accepted that the acculturating, or the minority group, experiences the greatest changes(Berry, 1997; Lakey, 2003).

Berry(2005) views acculturation as "the dual process of cultural and psychological change that takes place as a result of contact between two or more cultural groups and their individual members" (p.2). Acculturation involves physical, biological, economic, and cultural changes occurring at the group level(Berry, 1997). It is also widely examined as an individual-level phenomenon that encompasses change in both psychological and behavioral changes (Berry, Kim, Minde, & Mok, 1987).

Kim(2001) further argues that intercultural adaptation encompasses both "acculturation" and "deculturation." In adapting to a new culture, an individual acquires some new cultural elements and adopts the host cultural values, while at the same time abandoning certain aspects of his original culture and making behavioral and psychological shifts in accordance with the demands of the new cultural system.

A second term that is related to adaptation is adjustment. Adjustment is "the motivational process of an individual's modifying his cognitions and behaviors to decrease negatively valanced interactions and experiences and increase positive ones"(Sussman, 2000, p.355). As an individual adapts to the new culture, he must make constant changes to achieve an environmental fit. Migrants' adjustments occur in both psychology and behavior. Psychologically, migrants try to accept their new roles and identity in the host cultural environment and accommodate themselves to the environmental demands. Meanwhile, behavioral adjustments, due to the influence of the host cultural environment, are typically manifestations of the changes in clothing, eating habits, life styles and so on (Ward & Kennedy, 1999).

Assimilation and integration are used in intercultural adaptation literature as terms denoting the extent of changes made by migrant groups throughout their long-term contact with the host culture. In Gordon's(1964) point of view, assimilation is "a process of acculturation on the part of the immigrants, of becoming like the dominant population in cultural patterns, such as language, behavior, and values" (p.11). While assimilation denotes the complete adoption of the host cultural values and behavior, integration refers to an individual's adoption of some aspects of the host cultural values and behavior while at the same time retaining some from their original culture (Bourhis, 1997). Assimilation and integration can also be viewed as attitudes the immigrant groups take in their adaptation process. According to Berry(1980), immigrant groups often adopt one of four acculturation attitudes (set along two dimensions)—assimilation, integration, separation, and marginalization—depending on the degree of their willingness to maintain their original culture identity and participate in the host cultural activities.

The present study adopts the term adaptation because it is a broad concept which best captures both the process of migrants' fitting to the environment and the outcome indicating how well they fit into the new environment. Moreover, adaptation highlights migrants' psychological experience in adapting to the new environment and the initiative they take to fit into the new environment, whereas acculturation emphasizes the changes towards adoption of the host cultural identity and host cultural practices after a long-term adaptation. In order to adapt to the new environment, migrants need to make certain adjustments, which means the psychological and behavioral changes.

2.1.2.3   Intercultural Adaptation Models and Frameworks

Studies on intercultural adaptation have attracted much attention since the 1950s, driven by the increasing number of people moving across cultures. Over the past several decades, a number of intercultural adaptation models and frameworks have been developed, providing explanations for a wide range of issues covered in international migrant's adaption process. In this section, two theoretical models and frameworks which serve as the theoretical bases of the present study are reviewed.

2.1.2.3.1   Adaptation as a Process of Individual Adjustments

As early as 1964, Oberg put forward the concept of "culture shock" to describe the unsmooth process of intercultural adaptation. Moving to a new culture brings about many changes in one's life such as different language and cultural values, which are often difficult to handle. Stressful situations can easily disturb an individual's emotional stability and cause depression, anxiety, and other negative mental states. The following theoretical models and conceptualizations of intercultural adaptation focus specifically on the process of psychological adjustment that an individual goes through when he moves to the new environment.

The U-curve hypothesis. The U-curve hypothesis, proposed by

Lysgarrd(1955), is one of the earliest models which has laid a solid theoretical foundation for intercultural adaptation research. According to the U-curve hypothesis, sojourners go through several psychological stages when adapting to a new culture, including the honeymoon stage, crisis stage, adjustment stage, and biculturalism stage. The honeymoon stage refers to sojourner's initial joy and excitement when encountering a new culture for the first time. However, in the crisis stage, the newcomer encounters some difficulties and challenges of the new cultural environment. In stage three, adjustment, sojourners tackle adaptation difficulties by making certain adjustments. Finally, in the biculturalism stage, sojourners adopt elements of both their home culture and the host culture, and are ready to have a bi-cultural identity.

The dynamic model of "Stress-Adaptation-Growth". Kim(2001) proposed a model of "Stress-Adaptation-Growth" to explain the dynamic process of intercultural adaptation(see Figure 2.1). The "Stress-Adaptation-Growth" model posits that intercultural adaptation is not a linear and smooth process, but rather a stressful one that is "characterized by forward and backward movements"(Kim, 2001, p.59). Within this process, an individual is an "open system" that exposes himself to and is influenced by the environment he is in. As an individual steps into a new cultural environment, he communicates with the new environment and makes some behavioral changes in response. For instance, one may lack the necessary social competence to meet the demands of the new environment, especially at the initial stage of his adaptation process. Therefore, he will experience some extensive stress arising from his inability to cope with the demands. The stress will cause psychological disequilibrium, which is manifested "in the emotional 'lows' of uncertainty, confusion, and anxiety"(Kim, 2001, p.55). However, an individual who experiences stress is motivated to reflect on his adaptive experience, and he will hopefully learn how to handle the stress properly and gradually becomes more adaptive to the new environment. These resultant internal changes will then lead to growth. Thus, the "Stress-Adaptation-Growth" process proceeds in a continuous and recursive way, through which an individual gradually achieves better functional fitness with his host culture.

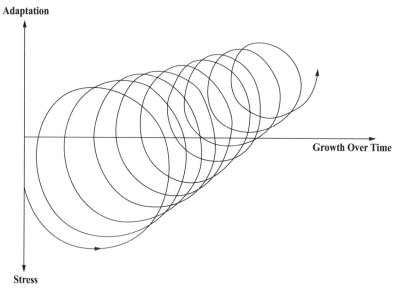

Figure 2.1   The "Stress-Adaptation-Growth" Dynamic
Source: Kim, 2001, p.59.

To summarize, the two models reviewed above show that intercultural adaptation is not a smooth process. As an individual adapts to a new culture, he will encounter difficulties and make necessary adjustment. During this process, some negative psychological states, such as stress, will arise. Finally, some internal changes will occur as the intercultural adaptation process unfolds. The aforementioned models provide a starting point for us to understand migrants' adaptation process. In the next section, other relevant models are reviewed in order to understand the many multi-level factors which affect intercultural adaptation.

2.1.2.3.2   Multi-dimensional Models of Intercultural Adaptation

Intercultural adaptation is a complex process. Many scholars have attempted to provide detailed explanations of the process of intercultural adaptation from multi-dimensional perspectives. In this section, two influential models relevant to the present study are reviewed: Berry's (1997) acculturation framework and Kim's (2001) integrative model of communication and cross-cultural adaptation.

Berry's (1997) acculturation framework. Berry (1997) offered a comprehensive framework for explaining the process of accultura-tion and elaborating on the main factors which influence the accul-turation process (see Figure 2.2). In the framework, he conceptuali-zes acculturation as a process that brings about changes to migrants at both the group and individual level. At the group level, some changes will inevitably take place as a result of long-term exposure to intercultural contact, including physical, biological, economic, social, and cultural changes. At the individual level, migrants will experience certain psychological and behavioral changes (Berry, 2001).

As can be seen from Figure 2.2, Berry's (1997) framework views stress and coping as the core of intercultural adaptation. When individuals are exposed to intercultural contact, they experi-ence a series of life events in their acculturation. They appraise these life events "either as a source of difficulty (i.e. stressors) or as benign, sometimes even as opportunities" (Berry, 1997, p. 18). When the stressors are difficult to cope with, individuals will expe-rience high levels of acculturative stress (Smith & Khawaja, 2011). In each case, they will move towards adaptative outcomes (either well-adapted or poor-adapted).

Beyond that, Berry's (1997) framework lists exhaustively the factors that affect migrants' adaptation. Some of these are at the society level, such as political and economic context, demographic factors of migrants' former society and other factors of the settle-ment society, such as attitudes towards multiculturalism, social sup-port systems, and so on. At the individual level, Berry (1997) dis-tinguishes between some pre-disposing variables and those that arise during the adaptation process. Pre-disposing variables include age,

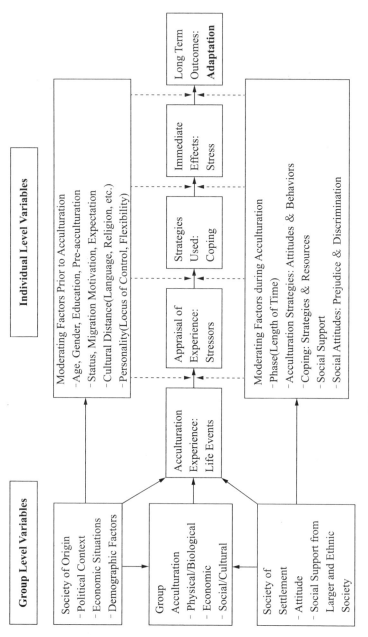

Figure 2.2 Acculturation Framework

Source: Berry, 1997, p.15.

gender, education, pre-acculturation knowledge of the host society, socioeconomic status, migration motivation, expectations, cultural distance, and personality. Those mediating and moderating
variables which appear during the adaptation process include length
of stay, acculturation strategies, coping strategies, social support,
prejudice, and discrimination from the host society. These factors
provide important explanations to understand the individual level
differences in migrants' adaptation process.

In sum, Berry's (1997) model provides a fundamental framework for examining the holistic process of examining migrants' adaptation, expounding on factors affecting adaptation from both
group and individual levels. It provides important insights for the
present study to formulate the framework to study the adaptation of
internal migrants. First, Berry's (1997) framework highlights the
important role of acculturative stress as a mediating variable that
relates intercultural adaptation experience and adaptation outcomes. Acculturative stress is an important indicator that represents
how well individuals adapt to the new environment, and is also a
factor that affects adaptation outcomes. Given that internal migrants face stress in their adaptation process, the present study will
follow Berry's (1997) framework, incorporating a set of variables
including acculturative stress and outcome variables to examine the
overall and dynamic process of internal migrants' adaptation.

Second, Berry's (1997) framework sheds light on some specific
individual factors which affect migrants' adaptation, including
some pre-disposing factors (e.g., sociodemographic factors, personality) and factors arising during the adaptation process (e.g., length
of time, social support, perceived discrimination). It has implications for examining factors affecting internal migrants' adaptation.
Combining Berry's (1997) framework and domestic literature on the
adaptation of internal migrants, the present study will identify
some important factors affecting internal migrants' adaptation and
examine their effects on internal migrants' adaptation.

Despite the implications of Berry's(1997) framework, it does not explain the outcomes of adaptation. What's more, as adaptation is a communication process, Berry(1997) does not incorporate communication as an important factor into the model. Therefore, it is necessary to refer to other models to address questions related to the present study.

The integrative model of communication and cross-cultural adaptation. Kim(2001) presented a multi-dimensional structural model of communication and cross-cultural adaptation with the aim of describing the patterns in individuals' adaptive experience(see Figure 2.3). Kim (2001) argues that as individuals go through the adaptation process, they will interact with the host environment and experience some internal transformations related to functional fitness, psychological health, and the development of an intercultural identity.

Individual level factors that influence the migrants' adaptation are identified in the model, including (1) predispositional distributes(preparedness for change, ethnic proximity, and adaptive personality), (2) host communication competence[1] in cognitive, affective, and operational aspects, and (3) social communication(interpersonal communication and mass communication with both the host and the ethnic environment). The model also postulates that certain environmental factors, including host receptivity, host conformity pressure, and ethnic group strength, influence the extent to which individuals will participate in the host activities and how well they will be treated by the host nationals.

Kim(2001)'s model provides important insights for the present study. First and foremost, it emphasizes the key role of communication in the adaptation process. As Kim(2001) notes, intercultural adaptation is "an interactive and continuous process

---

[1]   Host communication competence is defined as "an individual's overall ability to receive and process information appropriately and effectively (decoding) and to design plans to initiate messages or respond to others(encoding) in accordance with the host communication system"(Kim, 2001, p.73).

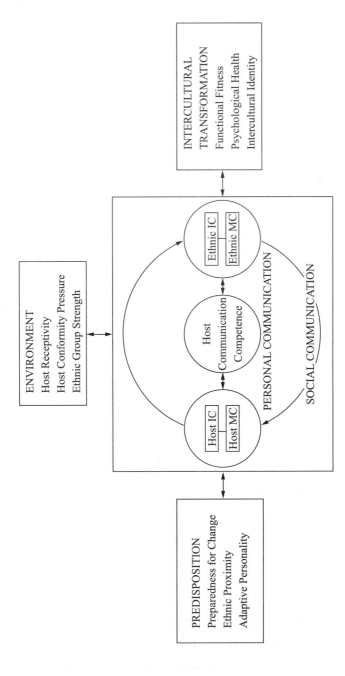

Figure 2.3   An Integrative Model of Cross-cultural Adaptation

Source: Kim, 2001, p.87.

that evolves in and through the communication of an immigrant with the new sociocultural environment" (p.380). She points out that through communication, individuals develop insights into their new environment.

Second, the model discusses the role played by different communication patterns in intercultural adaptation. In examining social communication patterns, Kim(2001) drew a distinction between interpersonal communication and mass communication. Interpersonal communication generally refers to face-to-face communication or other forms of electronically mediated interpersonal communication via telephone, e-mails, letters etc. She argues that interpersonal communication provides opportunities for migrants to first, observe the host nationals directly and learn the host culture's values and practice, and second, acquire the social support of host nationals to handle difficulties in their daily lives. Mass communication, on the other hand, can help improve migrants' host language proficiency and increase migrants' knowledge of the host culture. Apart from host social communication, migrants' ethnic social communication, i.e., their communication with their home culture is also important to their adaptation in that it provides various kinds of social support (material, informational, emotional etc.) which are difficult to get through host communication, and will help relieve migrants' stress.

Finally, Kim's(2001) model specifies three important ideal adaptation outcomes. Kim(2001) argues that individuals will experience personal transformation during their adaptation process. This transformation involves functional fitness, psychological health, and intercultural identity. Functional fitness refers to an individual's ability to handle the daily activities in the new environment. Psychological health is indicated by an individual's positive attitudes towards his life in the new cultural milieu. Intercultural identity refers to their internal endorsement of both the home and the host cultural identity.

In sum, in addition to identifying important factors affecting intercultural adaptation as Berry's(1997) framework, Kim's(2001) model has two important implications for the present study worthy of note. First, Kim's(2001) model notes intercultural identity as an outcome variable of adaptation, enriching Berry's (1997) framework which focuses on the process of migrants' psychological adjustments. Second, it highlights the role of different communication patterns in intercultural adaptation. However, due to the fact that Kim's (2001) model was built when social media had not been widely used as a tool of communication, it only focuses on the impact of face-to-face communication and mass communication during the intercultural adaptation process. As social media has become an important tool of communication nowadays, it is thus necessary to examine the effects of social media on migrants' adaptation, which will supplement Kim's(2001) model and further our understanding of how to make use of social media to facilitate migrants' adaptation.

2.1.2.4 Summary of Intercultural Adaptation Theories

As the concept of "intercultural" has been broadened to include some subcultures and regional differences(Kim, 2012), intercultural adaptation theories and frameworks have important implications on examining within-nation adaptation of internal migrants in China due to its regional differences and cultural diversity. The intercultural adaptation models and frameworks reviewed above shed light on migrants' adaptation process and outcomes. The present study will integrate Berry's (1997) framework and Kim's (2001) model, selecting variables to assess the overall adaptation of internal migrants from perspectives of acculturative stress, sociocultural adaptation, and psychological adaptation, and examining the effects of social media use on these adaptation variables.

2.1.3 Theories Related to Social Media

2.1.3.1 Definition of Social Media

The revolution of Information and Communication Technologies(ICTs) is taking place at an incredible speed and has greatly

changed the patterns of human communication (Chen, 2012a).
Nowadays, social media has become an important tool of human
communication and is enjoying increasing popularity across the
world.

The term of social media was first proposed by American
scholar Anthony Mayfield in 2008. Social media is formally defined
as "a group of internet-based applications that build on the ideolog-
ical and technical foundations of Web 2.0[①], and that allow the cre-
ation and exchange of user generated content"(Kaplan & Haenlein,
2010, p.61). Social media has various forms, including social networking sites(SNSs)(e.g., Facebook and Myspace), online games,
blogs, microblogs, collaborative projects(e.g., online encyclopedia
Wikipedia), and content communities(e.g., Youtube)(Olivas-Lujan &
Bondarouk, 2013).

2.1.3.2   Characteristics of Social Media

Social media has many distinctive features. Mayfield (2008)
concludes that social media boasts characteristics of "participation,
openness, conversation, community, and connectedness"(p.5). According to him, social media is open for everybody to participate in
generating and giving feedback to the contents. It also enables a
two-way conversion between media and the audience. What's more,
social media is effective in forming communities and making connections among various sites, resources, and people. Chen(2012)
summarizes five characteristics of social media: "digitality," "con-
vergency," "interactivity," "hypertextuality," and "virtuality"
(p.2). Compared with traditional types of media such as television,
radio, and newspapers, "interactivity" is viewed as one of the most
notable features of social media. Social media provides platforms
that enable the users to "connect, communicate, and interact with
each other and their mutual friends through instant messaging or

---

① Web 2.0 refers to "a platform on which all users participate and collectorate to
create content and applications"(Kaplan & Haenlein, 2010, p.61).

social networking sites" (Correa, Hinsley, & De Zuniga, 2010, p.248).

Social media has changed the way human beings communicate. It has extended the patterns of interpersonal communication from face-to-face interaction to internet-mediated communication, enabling people to communicate regardless of time and geographical boundaries(Shuter, 2012). In addition, social media allows people to engage in a broad scale of "many-to-many communication"(Pfister & Soliz, 2011, p.249) by enabling its users to participate in the dissemination of dialogue and information in a large scale.

2.1.3.3 Uses and Gratification Theory

Uses and Gratification Theory(U&G)(Katz, Blumler, & Gurevitch, 1974) is a communication theory that explains individuals' gratification of needs from media use(Shao, 2009). The premise of Uses and Gratification Theory is that users of the media are not passively influenced by media, but are "active audience, aware of their needs and the ways that they can be provided for, and select the means perceived as most appropriate to fulfill these needs" (Lev-On, 2012, p.99). Unlike early studies focusing on the effects of media exposure on the audiences, Uses and Gratification Theory (U&G) explains why an individual chooses a certain medium to fulfill his specific needs and what gratification he can get from the media use(Dunne, Lawlor & Rowley, 2010; Ifinedo, 2016; Wang, Tchernev, & Solloway, 2012).

Uses and Gratification Theory(UGT)(Katz et al., 1974) originated from Herzog's(1944) study of the motivations of listeners of daytime radio programs and was later extended to examine the motivation and gratifications of individuals' television viewing(Ogan & Cagiltay, 2006). With the increasing popularity of the Internet, research has made further attempts to investigate individuals' purposes of using the Internet and the gratification that they obtained from the Internet(e.g., Diddi & LaRose, 2006; Ko, Cho, & Roberts, 2005).

As social media has become ubiquitous in our everyday lives, examining individuals' use of social media under the U&G framework has become increasingly popular. Research findings suggest various purposes of individuals' social media use as well as the gratification obtained from social media. For example, Ellison, Steinfield and Lampe(2007) found that university students used Facebook to connect with their existing social networks and to build new social networks. Raacke and Bonds-Raacke(2008) found a variety of purposes for using social networking sites(Myspace and Facebook), including "to keep in touch with old friends," "to keep in touch with current friends," "to post/look at pictures," "to make new friends," and "to locate old friends." Less commonly reported uses and gratifications included "to learn about events," "to post social functions," "to feel connected," "to share information about yourself," "for academic purposes," and "for dating purposes" (p.171). In another study, Park, Kee, and Valenzuela (2009) summed the reasons of using Facebook into socializing, entertaining, self-status seeking, and information seeking. Moreover, Quan-Haase and Young(2010) found that Facebook and Instant Messaging served purposes of expressing affection and sharing problems.

In summary, despite that Uses and Gratification Theory(Katz, et al., 1974) was proposed in the 1970s, it is still used today as a powerful theory to explain individuals' personal needs of media use. Despite individual differences in the motivation for using social media, increasing social interaction is an important motive of individuals' social media use(Valenzuela, Park & Kee, 2009). In the present study, U&G Theory helps explain internal migrants' purposes of using social media and the multi-functionality provided by social media, which deepens our understanding of the role social media plays in their adaptation process.

2.1.3.4 Social Network Theory

Social network theory is not a theory in and of itself, but is a set of theoretical conceptualizations that explains human behaviors through social relations and interactions among individuals (Berkman & Glass, 2000). A social network is fundamentally defined as "a social structure comprising of persons or organizations, which usually are represented as nodes, together with social relations, which correspond to the links among nodes" (Yu & Kak, 2012, p.2). An individual's social network is a reflection of the "the existence and nature of social ties" (Israel & Rounds, 1987, p.314), through which an individual "maintains his social identity and receives emotional support, material aid, services, information and new social contacts" (Walker, MacBride, & Vachon, 1977, p.35).

Generally speaking, there are two fundamental indicators underlying the structure of social networks: social network size and social network density. According to Berkman (1984), social network size refers to the number of the nodes or actors in a social network. Social network density, or in other words, intensity or strength, is characterized by the frequency of the contact among the actors and the relational closeness among them.

Granovetter (1973)'s theoretical conceptualization of "the strength of ties" (SWT) is a fundamental concept in the social network framework. A "tie" refers to the bond or the linkage among the nodes or actors, and the strength of a tie is a "(probably linear) combination of the amount of time, the emotional intensity, the intimacy (mutual confiding) and the reciprocal services which characterize the tie" (Granovetter, 1977, p.348). Social Network Theory postulates that there are two types of ties: strong ties and weak ties. Strong ties are formed among people who are closely knitted, such as family, close friends, or relatives, while weak ties are composed of acquaintances or friends of friends with whom people are not closely or frequently socially involved (Granovetter, 1977; Marsden & Campbell, 1984). Strong ties feature a sense of intimacy and close contact among the network members, as well as voluntary and mutual investment in maintaining the relations (Wellman & Wortley, 1990). Weak ties, by contrast, lack emotional bonding and frequent contact(Virk, 2011). Granovetter(1973) underscored the strength of weak ties. As strong ties typically involve peripheral proximity, there is likely to be an overlap of social relations among people who are strongly connected and will hence provide similar information(Atterton, 2007). Weak ties, which link a large number of diverse and heterogeneous members, have more potential in providing nonredundant information and generating new ideas(Kavanaugh, Reese, Carroll, & Rosson, 2005).

Social Network Theory provides theoretical lenses to explain the relationship between an individual's social media use and his social networks. Social media provides platforms for the users to "construct virtual representations of their social networks"(Spier, 2011, p.72). Social media enables people to communicate and interact and will thus make it easier to foster "weak ties" among contacts, friends, or followers. What's more, social media helps to maintain "strong ties" among family and close friends by extending the offline relationship "through communication, display of affection, and joint activities over social media"(Spier, 2011, p.72).

2.1.3.5 Social Capital Theory

Social capital was defined by Bourdieu(1986) as "the aggregate of the actual or potential resources which are linked to possession of a durable network of more or less institutionalized relationships of mutual acquaintance or recognition"(p.248). Putnam(2001) viewed social capital as "connections among individuals—social networks and the norms of reciprocity and trustworthiness that arise from them"(p.32) and differentiated between two forms of social capital: bonding social capital and bridging social capital. Bonding capital refers to connections within a closely-knit group, such as family members, kinship or intimate friends, and bridging capital is about external connections across a wide range of loosely-tied groups. (Adler & Kwon, 2002; Ellison, Steinfield & Lampe, 2007; Valenzuela et al., 2009; Williams, 2007).

The question whether social media contributes to the acquisition of social capital or not has been examined recently. For example, Yoder and Stutzman(2011) pointed out that directed communication on Facebook such as chat interactions deepens interpersonal bond and contributes to the increase of one's social capital. Also, some activities such as status updating provide content for conversation, allowing people to keep in touch and thus relating to social capital. Ellison et al.(2007) argued that Facebook is beneficial for the acquisition of three types of social capital: bonding, bridging, and maintained social capital(referring to ones' previous social networks which are now physically disconnected from).

2.1.3.6   Summary of Theories Related to Social Media

The theories reviewed above aim to explain that social media fulfills various functions that are beneficial to human communication. These theories provide the theoretical lenses to understand the role social media could play in migrants' adaptation process. By extending the human communication patterns from "face-to-face" communication to mediated forms, social media increases the interaction and connections among its users and can thus enlarge internal migrants' social networks which are beneficial to their social capital accumulation and social support acquisition.

2.1.4   Theories of Social Support

2.1.4.1   Definition and Categories of Social Support

Social support has long been a research interest in sociology and has been explored by a number of scholars since the 1970s. In a general sense, social support is the tangible or intangible resources provided by other people to help individuals when they are in need (Cohen, Mermelstein, Kamarck, & Hoberman, 1985). Cobb(1976) was among the first to conceptualize social support. He underscored the functionality of social support, defining it as "information that lead the individuals to realize that (1) he is be loved and taken care of; (2) he is to be esteemed and valued; and(3) belongs to a community"(p.300). Caplan (1976) emphasized the sources of social support, arguing that social support is rendered by the connections embedded in one's social networks. Thoits(1985) pointed out that social support provides "socioeconomic aid, instrumental aid and informational aid" by "significant others such as family members, friends, coworkers, relatives and neighbors"(p.53). Albrecht and Adelman(1987) argued that social support is obtained through both verbal and nonverbal communication, and could reduce the uncertainties of the support seekers as well as enhance their perceptions of personal control in one's experience. Shumaker and Brownell (1984) defined social support as an exchange of resources between two individuals, which is intended to enhance the well-being of the recipients.

Social support takes on various forms. Bowlby (1969, 1973, 1980, as cited in Sarason, Levine, Basham, & Sarason, 1983) pointed out two basic categories of social support: "one is expressive behavior, such as affect and love; the other is instrumental aid, such as help and money"(p.127). House(1981) categorized four types of social support, which include "emotional (liking, love, empathy), instrumental (goods or services), informational (about the environment) and appraisal support(information relevant to self-evaluation)"(p.39). Cohen and Mckay(1984) divided social support into three broad categories, including tangible support(provision of material resources), appraisal support(assessment of threat or assessment of coping ability), and emotional support (self-esteem and feelings of belonging). Chen and Choi(2011) explained that social support provides important sources in terms of information(such as advice), tangible resources(such as food or money) and emotional needs(such as respect and caring), as well as network and companionship(a sense of belonging).

In addition to the various categories of social support, a distinction is drawn between perceived social support and received social support(Cohen, 2000). Perceived social support is not the actual help an individual receives when he needs it, but rather his cognitive assessment of the availability of the help(Thoits, 1995). By contrast, received social support, also termed as actual social support or enacted social support, is the tangible aid or the emotional help that is actually given to an individual.

2.1.4.2   Models of the Functions of Social Support

Social support is important to an individual's psychological well-being. Social support can buffer stress arising from difficult life events and can help people cope with difficulties such as economic strain(Uchino, 2004). In addition, there is ample research evidence that social support has a positive influence on individuals' psychical health, psychological well-being, and life satisfaction(Barrear, 1986; Trepte, Dienlin, & Reinecke, 2015; Uchino, Uno, & Holt-Lunstad, 1999).

Cohen and Wills (1985) proposed two models regarding the protective functions of social support. One is the direct model of the function of social support on mental health; the other is the buffering model of the protective process of social support on stress. The direct model of social support postulates that social support directly influences an individual's physical and psychological well-being. An individual with larger support networks has "a sense of predictability and stability in one's life situation, and a recognition of self-worth" (Cohen & Wills, 1985, p.311). In addition, a large social support network provides the potential for acquiring the resources an individual needs to cope with difficulties. The direct model of the effect of social support also postulates that social support influences an individual's physical health through "emotionally induced effects on neuroendocrine or immune system functioning" (Cohen & Wills, 1985, p.312). The stress-buffering model of social support explains the effect of social support on reducing stress. According to the stress-buffering model, perceptions of the availability of social support make an individual reappraise the threat of a stressful situation and boost his confidence in his ability to cope with the stress. What's more, social support provides solutions to problems and thus

reduces or alleviates the stress reaction of the individual(Cohen &
Wills, 1985).

2.2   Research on Adaptation of International Migrants

There is a large body of literature examining various issues
related to intercultural adaptation of international migrants. In
this section, the author discusses some empirical research on the
adaptation of international migrants from the following perspectives: outcomes of intercultural adaptation, acculturative stress,
and factors affecting intercultural adaptation.

2.2.1   Outcomes of Intercultural Adaptation

Moving to a new culture brings about many changes in migrants'
living environment, and has important effects on their lives. Previous studies have identified multiple variables as key indicators of
migrants' adaptation outcomes. There is research evidence that the
intercultural adaptation process affects migrants' life satisfaction.
For example, Gokdemir and Dumludag(2012) found that Turkish
immigrants in the Netherlands reported less life satisfaction than
Dutch natives due to their relatively low socioeconomic position.
Some studies found that migrants experience some negative psychological states, such as depression, anxiety, low levels of self-esteem, feelings of alienation, and so on(Baker, Soto, Perez, &
Lee, 2012; Bernstein, Park, Shin, Cho, & Park, 2011; Shen &
Takeuchi, 2001; Wei, Ku, Russell, Mallinckrodt, & Liao,
2008). In addition, some studies examined migrants' cultural identification with the culture of origin and the culture of settlement
(Berry, Phinney, Sam, & Vedder, 2006; De Vroome, Verkuyten,
& Martinovic, 2014). The author will focus on the two most widely
investigated adaptation outcomes: life satisfaction and cultural
identification.

2.2.1.1   Migrants' Life Satisfaction

Life satisfaction is a common indicator of an individual's psychological well-being(Marsiglia,Booth, Baldwin, & Ayers, 2013). In general, life satisfaction is defined as "an appraisal of the overall conditions of one's existence"(Shin & Johnson, 1978, p.491). Life satisfaction is about the cognitive aspects of an individual's subjective feelings of how good one's life is rather than an "objective" assessment of one's life conditions(Lowenstein & Katz, 2005; Malinauskas, 2010).

Life satisfaction is usually employed as an outcome variable of intercultural adaptation. As noted earlier, migration is motivated by some benefits at the place of destination. As noted by Ziegler and Britton(1981, as cited in De Jong, Chamratrithirong, & Tran, 2002), "It is assumed that people view the migration decision as one of utility maximization, i.e., they migrate in order to become better off in some subjective sense"(p.841). On the one hand, migration will bring opportunities for migrants to better their life conditions in terms of employment, residence, and education, and will thus enhance their satisfaction with life. On the other hand, changes of the sociocultural environment are likely to bring about some unexpected difficulties and cause some adjustment problems, thus exerting some negative influences on migrants' life satisfaction. For example, Gokdemir and Dumludag(2012) found that Turkish immigrants reported less life satisfaction than the Dutch natives due to their relatively low socioeconomic position.

Previous studies have identified multiple factors that affect migrants' life satisfaction. Some studies found that immigrants' length of stay in the host country were positively related with their life satisfaction(Nesterko, Braehler, Grande, & Glaesmer, 2013; Ullman & Tatar, 2011). Some studies found that immigrants' perceived discrimination negatively predicted their life satisfaction (Chow, 2007; Vohra & Adair, 2000). Lowenstein and Katz(2005) found that migrants' life satisfaction was related to their employment and social support. Amit(2009) found that a high standard of living and a strong sense of Israeli identity predicted a higher level of life satisfaction among immigrants in Israel.

2.2.1.2   Migrants' Cultural Identification

Cultural identification is defined by Erikson(1968, as cited in Lee, 2006) as "an individual's way of identifying himself or herself with culture(s) in which he or she functions"(p.289). Cultural identification is an important topic of research in intercultural adaptation studies. It generally refers to the degree to which migrants identify themselves as members of either the culture of origin or the culture of settlement. Cultural identification is "an inherently processing activity"(Pembecioğlu, 2012, p.46). When individuals encounter two different cultures, they will "voluntarily or involuntarily and consciously or unconsciously"(Lee, 2006, p.290) get involved in the cultural identification process. Cultural Identification encompasses cognitive(self-perception or self-definition as members of a cultural group), affective(sense of belongings or attachment to a cultural group), and behavioral aspects(adoption of the cultural practices of a group)(Oetting, 1997; Roberts, Phinney, Masse, Chen, Roberts, & Romero, 1999).

Early literature argued that migrants' cultural identification was a linear process, during which their cultural identification with the heritage culture weakened while their cultural identification with the dominant culture strengthened(Oetting & Beauvais, 1991). Recent literature views cultural identification with one's home culture and the host culture as independent dimensions(Ryder, Alden, & Paulhus, 2000). Phinney(1996) argues that cultural identification "includes one's orientation to both one's ethnic culture and the larger society"(p.922). Berry(1980) postulates four orientations that migrants could take towards their original cultural maintenance and host culture participation, namely assimilation, integration, marginalization, and separation. Assimilation refers to that "migrant group members choose to identify solely with the culture of the dominant society, and relinquish all ties to their ethnic culture" (Sam & Berry, 1995, p.11). Integration means strong identification and involvement with both home and host culture. Separation means identifying with the home culture while rejecting participation in the host cultural activities. Marginalization refers to a rejection of both home and host culture. Benet-Martínez, Leu, Lee, and Morris(2002) explain that in adapting to a new culture, some migrants might perceive the host culture and home culture as "compatible" and "complementary", while others might view the two cultural systems as "oppositional" and "contradictory"(p.493). As a result, they might have bicultural identification towards their home culture and the host culture.

Previous studies examined the effect of cultural identification on migrants' adaptation. Some research findings indicated that cultural identification with both host and home culture were related to better psychological adjustment, fewer clinical symptoms, and a higher level of life satisfaction(Chae & Foley, 2010; Phinney, Horenczyk, Liebkind, & Vedder, 2001). In another study, Ngo and Li(2016) found that the mainland Chinese immigrants in Hong Kong who had a local identity orientation had better levels of life satisfaction and sociocultural adjustment, whereas those who had a home identity orientation perceived more discrimination and had lower levels of life satisfaction. Ward and Rana-Deuba(1999) found that home cultural identification predicted higher levels of psychological adjustment while host cultural identification was related to fewer sociocultural adjustment difficulties.

Some factors affecting individuals' cultural identification have been identified. For example, Tartakovsky(2013) found that perceived discrimination from the host society was related to identification with the home culture. Benet-Martínez and Haritatos(2005) found that personality traits and acculturative stress affected migrants' bicultural identification.

2.2.2 Acculturative Stress

2.2.2.1 Definition of Acculturative Stress

Acculturative stress is one of the most widely researched topics in intercultural adaptation literature. Berry et al.(1987) noted that acculturative stress "refers to one kind of stress, that in which the stressors① are identified as having their source in the process of acculturation"(p.492). Moving to a new culture is a major event in one's life that brings about many changes and challenges due to the new sociocultural environment and will in turn cause various adjustment issues(Tonsing, Tse, & Tonsing, 2016). For example, individuals moving to a new culture may find it difficult to communicate with the host nationals due to a lack of ability to speak the host language. Besides, they may find it difficult to adopt the host cultural values and practices which are incompatible with those of their culture of origin. Furthermore, they may experience some negative life events due to their immigration status. Acculturative stress arises when individuals find these adjustment issues problematic and difficult to cope with(Berry,1997). Acculturative stress is often associated with "lowered mental health status(specifically confusion, anxiety, and depression), feelings of marginality and alienation, heightened psychosomatic symptom level, and identity confusion" (Berry et al., 1987, p.491).

2.2.2.2 Dimensions of Acculturative Stress

Acculturative stress is a multidimensional construct. Despite the fact that acculturative stress was first proposed as one kind of stress that is caused by intercultural contact, it is believed that acculturative stress is not only limited to cultural aspects. Caplan(2007) classified acculturative stress into three broad dimensions, namely instrumental/environmental, social/interpersonal, and societal as-

---

① Stressor refers to some environmental or internal demand that may cause physical or psychological reaction.(Pan, Yue, & Chan, 2010). It is the source of stress.

pects. "Instrumental and/or Environmental Stressors" include financial stressors and poverty, language barriers, and lack of access to health care, employment, safe working conditions, housing, and neighborhoods. "Social and/or Interpersonal Stressors" include loss of social networks, loss of social status, loss of family cohesiveness or family support, gender role conflict, and intergenerational conflict.

Previous literature has found that migrants experienced multiple stressors in their adaptation process (Nailevna, 2017). Some studies suggested that a primary stressor in the intercultural adaptation process was related to language and communication barriers (Duru & Poyrazli, 2007; Pan, Yue, & Chan, 2010). For example, Kuo and Roysircar(2004) found that English reading ability was a stressor for Chinese immigrants in Canada. Zheng and Berry(1991) found that a sample of Chinese sojourners faced language and communication problems in Canada.

Some studies found that migrants experienced acculturative stress related to cultural difference which involved incongruent cultural values and practices (Crockett, Iturbide, Torres Stone, McGinley, Raffaelli, & Carlo, 2007; Nailevna, 2017; Pan, Yue, & Chan, 2010). In addition, migrants who had more difficulties in accepting and handling cultural differences, such as eating habits and value conflicts had more psychological distress(Bhugra, 2004).

Homesickness has also been identified as a stressor that individuals encounter in the migration process (Kiline & Granello, 2003). Homesickness is "the distress or impairment caused by an actual or anticipated separation from home" (Thurber & Walton, 2012, p.415). Migrants may have left their family, relatives, or friends behind. A loss of previous social networks, especially strong ties, may present emotional deficiencies for individuals and will cause loneliness, anxiety, or depression.

Perceived discrimination is a common stressor in the adaptation process(Lewthwaite, 1996; Wei, Wang, Heppner, & Du, 2012).

Perceived discrimination is an individual's subjective sense of feeling that he is being unfairly treated due to his membership in a disadvantaged or minority group(Samuel, Morton, Violet, Feng, & Joanna, 1999). In the case of the migrant groups and the host majorities, group memberships become salient because of cultural heterogeneity. Operario and Fiske(2001) argued that "group salience increases perceived in-group homogeneity and favorability and increases outgroup entitativity and negativity" (p.552). Therefore, members of the dominant cultural group will exhibit some differential or negative attitudes and actions towards the migrating group. Members of the migrant group are likely to attribute this rejection and exclusion from the mainstream society to discrimination.

In addition to the aforementioned stressors, some migrants experience economic and occupational stress. Improvement in one's economic conditions is one of the major reasons that drives individuals to move away from their home, which, nonetheless, may turn out be difficult and stressful due to their migration status. Some studies found that some immigrants experienced unemployment due to inadequate job qualifications, a lack of host language proficiency, or sociocultural skills(Aycan & Berry, 1996; Finch, Hummer, Kol, & Vega, 2001).

2.2.2.3   Effects of Acculturative Stress on Adaptation Outcomes

Previous research has found that acculturative stress is negatively related to adaptation outcomes. There is empirical evidence that acculturative stress leads to poor physical health(Finch et al., 2001; Salgado, Castañeda, Talavera, & Lindsay, 2012) and some mental problems such as anxiety, depression, and psychological distress(Lee, Koeske, & Sales, 2004; Mui & Kang, 2006; Oh, Koeske, & Sales, 2002 ; Wei et al., 2008; Wang et al., 2012). Some other studies found that acculturative stress negatively affected migrant's self-esteem (Claudat, White, & Warren, 2016; Kim, Hogge, & Salvisberg, 2014) and life satisfaction(Pan, Wong, Joubert, & Chan, 2008).

2.2.3 Factors Affecting Intercultural Adaptation

Intercultural adaptation is a complex process during which multiple factors affect migrants' perceptions of the host culture and how well they fit in. At the individual level, some demographic factors have been found to be important predictors of intercultural adaptation. For example, Virta, Sam, and Westin(2004) found that age was negatively related to life satisfaction and positively related to mental health problems. Gender yielded inconsistent results on its effect on intercultural adaptation. Romero, Martinez, and Carvajal(2007) found that male immigrant youth had higher levels of acculturative stress. On the contrary, Furnham and Shiekh(1993) found that female immigrants had more mental health problems than the male immigrants. Yako and Biswas(2014) found that female Iraqi immigrants reported more stress than male immigrants in the United States. Some other studies found that migrants' educational level, household income, and marital status were related to migrants' psychological well-being(Bernstein et al., 2011; Park & Rubin, 2012).

In addition, some studies found that factors including host language proficiency, migration motivation, and perceived cultural distance affected migrants' adaptation. For example, host language proficiency was found to be related to better levels of sociocultural and psychological adaptation(Jasinskaja-Lahti, 2008) and lower levels of depression(Beiser & Hou, 2001). Migrants with a voluntary migration motivation were more willing to participate in the host's cultural practices(Verkuyten, 2011) and had a lower level of depression(Gong et al., 2011). Perceived cultural distance, which refers to the extent to which the migrants view the two cultures as similar or different(Berry, 1997), was found to be positively associated with social difficulties(Ward & Searle, 1991), acculturative stress, and psychological disfunction(Galchenko & van de Vijver, 2007).

Personality has significant effects on migrants' adaptation. In a survey conducted among 139 Chinese international students in America, Zhang, Mandl and Wang(2010) found that neuroticism and consciousness had negative influences on their psychological adjustment, while extroversion and openness led to higher levels of self-esteem and life satisfaction. Swagler and Jome (2005) found that psychological adjustment was positively related to agreeableness and conscientiousness, but negatively related to neuroticism. Their findings also showed that extroversion was positively related to sociocultural adaptation.

The effects of social support on intercultural adaptation has been well documented. Studies found that the perceived availability of social support could buffer the acculturative stress that an individual experienced in adapting to the new cultural environment. For example, Crockett et al.(2007) found that Mexican American college students who perceived high availability of social support reported lower levels of acculturative stress than students who perceived low availability of social support. In addition, there is consistent empirical evidence that social support has a positive influence on the mental health of migrants(Brisset, Safdar, Lewis, & Sabatier 2010; Han, Kim, Lee, Pistulka, & Kim, 2007; Min, Moon, & Lubben, 2005). Jasinskaja-Lahti, Liebkind, Jaakkola, and Reuter(2006) found that social support mediated the effects of perceived discrimination on immigrants' depression. Chou (2009) found that perceived social support was negatively related to depressive symptoms of mainland Chinese immigrants in Hong Kong and moderated the harmful effects of poor migration planning on their depressive symptomatology.

2.2.4   Communication and Intercultural Adaptation

Communication is an integral part of intercultural adaptation. Kim's(2001) integrative theory of communication and cross-cultural adaptation postulates that migrants' interpersonal communication and media-mediated communication with both home and host cultures are of vital importance to their adaptation process. Through various patterns of communication, migrants "come to better understand social practices and cultural patterns of the host society" (Hsu, Grant, & Huang, 1993, p.25).

Some early literature focused on interpersonal communication of migrants in the host society. As Baxter and Braithwaite(2008) stated, interpersonal communication "has become the way that humans negotiate meanings, identity and relationship through person-to-person communication"(p.4). Interpersonal communication, especially face-to-face communication, helps migrants observe the host nationals and is conductive to their cultural learning process (Kim, 1976). Ward and Kennedy(1992) found that the quantity of migrants' contact with host members was conducive to their psychological well-being. In a similar study, Ward and Rana-Deuba(2000) found that satisfaction with the quality of both host and co-national relations was negatively related to mood disturbance of migrants.

The role of mass media communication in migrants' intercultural adaptation was examined in the previous literature. Kim (1988) argued that consumption of mass media in the host culture increased migrants' exposure to the host language, values, norms and practice. Johnson(1996) pointed out that viewing television of the host country fulfilled immigrants' learning needs and facilitated their acculturation to the host society. Miglietta and Tartaglia (2009) found that the immigrants' emotional attachment to the host culture was positively related to their consumption of the host culture's mass media, but negatively related to homeland mass media consumption. Moon and Park (2007) found that Korean immigrants' consumption of American mass media contributed significantly to their acceptance of American cultural values. In another study, Dalisay(2012) found that the use of host mass media increased migrants' host language proficiency.

In response to the increasing importance of social media as an effective tool of communication, more and more attention has been given to examining the role of social media in intercultural adaptation. Studies have found that social media play important roles in migrants' daily lives. For example, Sin and Kim(2013) found that social networking sites were effective in international students' daily searches for information. Cao and Zhang(2010) found that Chinese international students in New Zealand used social networking sites(SNSs) such as QQ to keep in touch with their family and friends. Lim and Pham(2016) found that international students used social media to maintain contact with their family or friends left behind. Their studies also found that social media helped increase migrant students' interactions with the locals.

Social media has some positive effects on migrants' intercultural adaptation process. Use of online social networks is related to less acculturative stress and depression(Park, Song, & Lee, 2014). Ye (2006a) found that use of ethnic online social networking reduced migrant students' acculturative stress and provided them with emotional and informational support. Croucher(2011) argued that the use of social networking sites affects migrants' interaction with the host nationals and affects their in-group identity. Li and Tsai(2014) found that Hispanic immigrants' use of social media affected their cultural identification with both home and host culture. Some other studies found that social media helped migrants maintain their pre-existing social networks as well as establish new ones(Dekker & Engbersen, 2014; Komito, 2011).

2.3 Studies on Adaptation of Internal Migrants in China

Internal migration in China has received a great deal of attention since the late 1980s with the appearance of large-scale rural to urban migration(Ren & Wu, 2006). Internal migrants' adaptation is of great importance to their physical and psychological well-being, and has been widely discussed in internal migration studies. This section first introduces the definition of internal migrants in China, and then discusses internal migrants' adaptation status, adaptation obstacles and stress, social support and adaptation, and their social media use.

2.3.1   Definition of Internal Migrants in China

So far, there is not a uniform definition of internal migrant in China. A few different terms are used to describe the large number of people moving within China. One of the most commonly used terms is "migrant workers"(*nong min gong*), who are also called "rural migrant workers," "rural-to-urban migrants," or "rural labor migrants." Migrant workers are people "who leave their farmland and move to urban areas and/or for non-agricultural activities" (Huang & Zhan, 2005, p.67). The term "migrant workers" is a product of the distinction between rural and urban household regis- tration and is indicative of China's urban-rural dualistic structure (Tong & Ma, 2008).

A second term commonly used is the "floating population." The "floating population," or *liu dong ren kou*, is defined in the 2000 census as "individuals who have resided at the place of destination for at least six months without local household registration status" (Liang & Ma, 2004, p.470). The term "floating population" high- lights the differences between a temporary migrant(a person who has a temporary permit in the current residence) and a permanent migrant(a person who has permanently transferred his place of household registration to a new residence)(Roberts, 1997).

More recently, some scholars proposed a new term "new-gen- eration migrants"(or "new urban migrants") to define people who move within China, because of the increasing tendency that some of them settle down and become regular residents in the new loca- tion. The term "new-generation migrants" or "new urban migrants" covers a broader concept than the term "floating population." Tong

and Ma(2008) define new-generation migrants as people who experience residential transition with family members or by themselves
after China's reform and opening up, who have stable jobs and
dwellings in their migration destination, and who intend to stay in
their current residences for a long period of time. Zhang and Lei
(2008) view migrants as people who move to and live in a new environment from their original residence.

Despite different terms used in the literature, the present study
uses the term "internal migrants" to describe people moving within
the country. Internal migrants are defined as people who "move
from one area (a province, district or municipality) to another
within one country"(Castle, 2000, p.269). In the present study, internal migrants refer to people who have moved to a new residence
from their birthplace or the original place of household registration
within China, who have already taken up their new residence for
more than 6 months, and who have stable jobs and dwellings. It includes permanent migrants and long-term temporary migrants.

The author uses the term "internal migrant" for the following
reasons. First, the term "internal migrants" breaks the rural and urban dualism, covering a broad range of migrants moving from different origins and including the migrants from "rural-rural, rural-
urban, urban-urban and urban-rural"(Sun, 2019, p.1). Second, the
concept of internal migrants encompasses different migrant groups.
Zhou(2014) divided internal migrants into three main types, namely
labor migrants(undereducated people who are engaged in manual
work), intellectual migrants(well-educated people who are engaged
in highly-skilled and professional work), economic migrants(pri-
vate business owners or people who are self-employed). Tong and
Ma(2008) identified three categories: (1) rural to urban migrants
(or migrant workers), (2) urban-to-urban migrants (individuals
who have the urban Hukou and who move to a new residence), and
(3) university graduates who move to a city outside their hometowns. Zhang and Lei(2008) distinguished white-collar migrants

from blue-collar migrants.

Despite various types of internal migrants, as internal migrants relocate themselves in the new residence, they need to make some psychological and behavioral adjustments to fit in(Zheng, 2011). In the next section, domestic studies on the adaptation of internal migrants are reviewed.

2.3.2   Adaptation Status of Internal Migrants

Migrants experience a series of changes in their new residence in terms of living environment, lifestyles, socioeconomic status, and so on. How well internal migrants adapt to the local society is an important issue in internal migration studies. Generally, the adaptation status of internal migrants is examined from four dimensions: economic adaptation, social adaptation, cultural adaptation, and psychological adaptation(Zhu, Zhao, & Wu, 2010). This section presents three perspectives to examine the adaptation status of internal migrants, namely social integration, life satisfaction, and cultural identification.

2.3.2.1   Social Integration

Most domestic studies examined internal migrants' adaptation from the perspective of social integration. According to Ren and Wu(2006), social integration is "a mutual process during which different individuals, groups, or cultures develop mutual acceptance of each other, with an aim to build a harmonious society"(p.87). While Ren and Wu(2006) underscore the bi-directional acceptance of both internal migrants and the local society, Tong and Ma (2008) emphasize the initiatives that internal migrants take to integrate into the local society, pointing out that the social integration of internal migrants is a process during which "the migrants make changes in terms of residence, employment, values and way of life, so as to adapt to the life in the cities and be more similar to the local citizens"(p.79).

Zhang and Lei(2008) described four dimensions of the social

integration of white-collar migrants in Shanghai, including cultural integration, psychological integration, identity integration, and economic integration. According to them, cultural integration is indicated by migrants' local language ability, acceptance of local cultural values, and conformity to local customs. Psychological integration includes satisfaction with occupation, residence, and the local society as a whole. Identity integration includes job stability, identification with the local society, and Hukou status. Economic integration is indicated by the intention to purchase houses and have more relatives move to Shanghai. Zhang and Lei(2008) found that the overall level of social integration was low among the white-collar migrants in Shanghai, with a comparatively higher level of psychological and identity integration and a lower level of cultural and economic integration.

Yang(2009) underscored the willingness of the rural migrants' "assimilation" into the local society and proposed a framework which incorporated four dimensions: economic integration or incorporation(indicated by job opportunities, occupation status, earnings, social security, housing and educational opportunities, etc.), cultural acceptance(indicated by understanding and acceptance of the local language, local cultural values, norms and customs, etc.), behavioral adaptation or adjustment(indicated by conformity to the local rules, social relations, social networks, marriage, and everyday life activities such as eating and entertainment), and identity integration(indicated by the migrants' psychological distance from people from their hometown and with the locals, sense of belonging to the local society, and perceptions of who they are).

Ren and Qiao(2010) investigated social integration of temporary internal migrants in Shaoxing from four dimensions: self-definition(whether migrants identify themselves with the local people), attitudes towards the city(whether migrants would like to obtain the local Hukou), social interactions with locals, and their perceived discrimination from local residents. Their studies found that most internal migrants did not fully integrate into the local society.

The previous studies provide different dimensions and a set of indicators to examine the overall level of internal migrants' adaptation. Generally, internal migrants' adaptation status is indicated by both subjective factors(e.g., cultural identification) and objective factors(e.g., Hukou status). Despite the various dimensions, some scholars argue that internal migrants' adaptation proceeds step by step, and psychological adaptation is the outcome indicator(Yang, 2009; Zhu, Zhao, & Wu, 2010).

2.3.2.2 Life Satisfaction of Internal Migrants

Life satisfaction is an important psychological indicator of internal migrants' adaptation(Liu, Zhu, Ma & Zhang, 2014). Domestic studies examined the level of life satisfaction of internal migrants and some factors affecting their life satisfaction. Guo, Xu, and Gu(2018) found that social insurance, housing conditions, and living environment were associated with life satisfaction among the internal migrants in 129 cities. Chen and Zhu (2008) investigated the life satisfaction of 248 knowledge migrants in several cities, including Nanjing, Shanghai, Beijing, and Suzhou. Their studies found that most knowledge migrants were satisfied with their life in terms of income, working conditions, working time, housing conditions and social interaction. Liu, Liu, and Li(2014) examined the relationship between life satisfaction and settlement intention among three types of migrants(business migrants, knowledge migrants, and labor migrants) in six cities(Guangdong, Dongguan, Shenyang, Chengdu, Hangzhou and Zhengzhou). Their study revealed that life satisfaction was positively related to migrants' settlement intention. Wen and Wang(2009) found that job stability and living environment were positively related to life satisfaction among the rural migrants in Shanghai.

2.3.2.3 Cultural Identification of Internal Migrants

During the process of internal migrants' adaptation to their new residence, they are faced with changes not only in their living environment and lifestyles, but also in their cultural identification (Ma & Li, 2010; Tan, 2005). Previous studies found that internal migrants experienced confusion about their cultural identification (Xu, 2007; Zhai, 2009). On one hand, they were willing to identify with the local culture. On the other hand, they perceived that they were treated as outsiders by the locals. Kou(2004) found that migrant workers in Shanghai perceived a large difference between them and the local Shanghainese and had a low level of local cultural identification. Lei (2008) found the white-collar migrants in Shanghai had a low level of local cultural identification. Most of them identified them as " *waidiren* "(47.7%). 21.3% of the samples identified them as "the new Shanghainese." 21% of the samples had bi-cultural identification while only a few(2.5%) identified themselves as "the *Shanghainese*." Some other studies found that rural migrants had a low cultural identification with the urban residence (Cai & Cao, 2009; Guo & Li, 2009).

Internal migrants' local cultural identification is viewed as the most important indicator of their adaptation outcomes(Lu & Wei, 2011; Yang, 2009). Wang, Liu, and Lou(2011) pointed out that migrants' local cultural identification mainly involved their willingness to stay, their self-definition as local citizens, and their acceptance of local cultural practices. Zhang and Lei(2009) measured the local cultural identification of white-collar migrants in Shanghai from the following perspectives: cultural knowledge of the social norms of the local society, acceptance of the cultural values of the local society, willingness to learn the Shanghai dialect, and willingness to celebrate local festivals.

Local cultural identification of internal migrants is affected by some objective factors as well as some individual factors. Some scholars point out that the Hukou system was the most important factor affecting the local cultural identification of internal migrants (Chen, 2005; Peng, 2007). Zhai(2009) argued that some factors, including the Hukou status, the employment opportunities, the social security system, and the educational opportunities affected cultural identification of rural migrants. Zhao and Li(2013) conducted a survey among internal migrants in 6 cities(Guangzhou, Hangzhou, Chengdu, Shenyang, Dongguan and Zhengzhou) and found that their local cultural identification was influenced by factors such as age, income level, housing conditions, and Hukou status. Xu (2007) conducted a detailed study on the cultural identification of migrant workers in Chengdu and found that migrants' income, life satisfaction, social interactions with the locals, and participation in the local community had positive effects on their local cultural identification.

2.3.3   Adaptation Stress

As has been noted earlier, adaptation is not a smooth process. While migration brings some opportunities to change migrants' lives, changes in the sociocultural environment bring about some difficulties and obstacles which may be stressful to migrants.

Recently, more and more scholars have begun to examine the difficulties faced by internal migrants and the stress they experienced in their adaptation process and have identified multiple stressors at different levels, including cultural levels, institutional levels, economic levels, and interpersonal levels. In a study conducted among 475 migrant workers in Shanghai, Wong and Song(2008) found that migrants experienced migration stress in the following aspects: financial and employment difficulties, cultural differences, lack of social life, and interpersonal tensions and conflicts. They further found that financial and employment difficulties accounted for the greatest stress among others. In addition, their studies found that migration stress was negatively related to their mental health status. Zhong et al.(2016) found that the rural to urban migrants in Shenzhen experienced stress in the following aspects: difficulties in adapting to the city environment, work-related stress, financial hardship, and a lack of sense of belonging to cities.

Chen, Yu, Gong, Zeng, and MacDonell (2015) identified four types of domestic migration stress: separation of the place of origin, perceived discrimination, lack of self-confidence, and maladaptation. Guo et al.(2016) found that the female rural-to-urban migrants in Wuhan experienced stress from separation from their spouses and children. Guo and Zhang(2010) found that ethnic migrants in Shenzhen experienced homesickness. In addition, they encountered cultural differences and were faced with difficulties in learning Mandarin.

2.3.4   Factors Affecting Internal Migrants' Adaptation

Studies have found that the adaptation of internal migrants is affected by multiple factors, including some personal factors and institutional factors (Yu & Li, 2012). In a study of migrants in Shanghai, Wang et al. (2008) examined adaptation of migrant workers in Shanghai from five dimensions, including residential conditions, economic situation, social relations, political participation, and cultural identification. Their studies showed that some sociodemographic factors, including age, gender, marriage, educational level, and length of stay affected internal migrants' adaptation to the local surroundings. Besides this, they found that factors such as previous employment and job training, as well as their residential status(whether they have a residence permit or not) predicted their adaptation in Shanghai.

Yu, Gao, and Guo(2012) found that compared with male migrants, female migrants were more willing to assimilate to the local society. In addition, migrants who were unmarried had a higher level of social integration than those who were married. Their studies also showed that migrants' monthly economic income was positively related to their adaptation. Some other factors such as migrants' housing conditions, whether they had a residence permit, employment contract, and social welfare also affected their adaptation.

Zhang(2011) identified five dimensions of the adaptation of white-collar migrants in Shanghai, including self-identification, ability to speak the Shanghai dialect, affection towards Shanghai, social interaction with the local Shanghainese, and a sense of belonging to Shanghai. This study also revealed that white-collar migrants' adaptation was positively related to their ability to learn the Shanghai dialect, circle of local friends, frequency of visiting Shanghai prior to migration, frequency of contact with the local Shanghainese, and the duration of their stay in Shanghai.

Ren and Wu(2006) found that factors of human capitals, such as education, job training and work experience, are important in affecting internal migrants' adaptation. Increased human capital was also conducive to social integration of the migrants. From the communication perspective, Song and Tao(2012) found that local residents' attitudes towards migrants significantly affected migrants' adaptation. Moreover, institutional factors were found related to internal migrants' adaptation. For example, Ren and Qiao(2010) found that some institutional factors, such as whether the residents had residence permits, insurance, or employment contracts affected their adaptation.

2.3.5 Social Support and Adaptation

Internal migrants' social support is of vital importance to their adaptation. Domestic studies focused on three aspects: the characteristics and changes of internal migrants' social support networks in migration, internal migrants' social support types and factors affecting their social support acquisition, and the effect of social support on internal migrants' adaptation.

Migration is a process during which migrants expand their social networks and seek social support(Li, 2003). Some studies examined the characteristics of internal migrants' social networks and the changes of their social networks after they moved to the new residences. Studies found that the strong ties in migrants' social net-

works which were based on geographic bondage and kinship were
still important to migrants in their new location(Li, 1996; Wang,
2005; Zhu & Liu, 2007). However, during the migration process,
internal migrants' social support networks change as they leave
their original residence and reside in the new place. Li, Yang,
Yue, and Jin(2007) found that the size of social support networks
decreased among migrants who moved to Shenzhen. More specifically, their emotional support networks became less intense due to
separation from their family and relatives. Wang and Tong(2004)
pointed out that the size of migrants' social support networks was
smaller compared with that of local citizens, and their social support networks were more intense than local citizens. Besides, their
social support networks were characterized by a higher level of
strong homophily (referring to the similarity of the sociodemographic features between the migrants and their social relations)
and a lower level of heterogeneity(referring to the dissimilarity of
the sociodemographic features between the migrants and their social relations). In a recent study conducted among new-generation
rural migrants in Guangzhou, Liu and Breitung(2012) found that
new-generation migrants in Guangzhou tended to seek social support from diverse networks(e.g., colleagues and neighbors). However, their home-based networks and migrant networks were still
important.

Some studies focused on the types of internal migrants' social
support and factors affecting their social support acquisition. Lei
(2008) distinguished three types of social support of white-collar
migrants in Shanghai: emotional support, instrumental support,
and social companionship. Research results indicated that gender,
length of residence, Hukou status, and social contact with the local Shanghainese were strong predictors of white-collar migrants'
perceived social support. Yang(2014) found that social support of
rural migrants in Zhengzhou was negatively related with their
age but positively related with their educational status. What's

more, female migrants perceived more social support than male migrants.

The role of internal migrants' social support and support networks on their adaptation has been well-documented. Yue, Li, and Jin(2011) examined social networks among rural-to-urban migrants in Fujian, and found that the non-kin residential ties positively affected their psychological integration although their effects on socioeconomic integration were not significant. Li and Wu(2010) found that the social support networks of low-skilled migrants in Beijing were helpful in providing some financial assistance and emotional help. Some studies found that social support provided the resources that migrants needed to deal with some difficulties(e. g. financial difficulties) in their lives and was positively related to migrants' mental health(Zhen, Zhang, & Zhu, 2015). Dong and Liu(2014) found that social support from family, friends, and neighbors facilitated the adaptation of the rural migrants in Hebei Province. Li, Ren, and Jin(2008) distinguished three types of social support of rural migrants in Shenzhen: emotional support, instrumental support, and companion support. Their studies found that companionship support was positively related to the rural migrants' life satisfaction, and emotional support was negatively related to the rural migrants' perceived discrimination. In addition, social support has positive relationship with the subjective well-being of rural migrants (Jing, 2013; Shao & Fu, 2014) and the white-collar migrants (Yuan, 2015).

In sum, previous studies have widely discussed the effects of social support on internal migrants' adaptation. However, most researchers used the Social Support Rating Scales (SSRS) (Xiao, 1993), which is a measurement of general support. Internal migrants may need to seek social support to deal with some problems or difficulties(e.g., learning about the cultural norms of the local society) they are facing in their new residence. It is therefore necessary to develop social support scales to address the special needs of internal migrants.

2.3.6   Social Media Use of Internal Migrants

Media plays an important role in internal migrants' adaptation. Previous studies indicated that internal migrants' use of media affected their perception of their living environment and their interpersonal communication(Wei & Chen, 2015). Domestic studies mainly discussed the purposes of internal migrants' social media use and the role of social media in internal migrants' adaptation process.

Using the users and gratifications(U&G) approach, some studies examined internal migrants' purposes of using social media. Studies indicated that social media served a variety of purposes related to their adaptation. Hu(2018) found that rural migrants in Pearl River Delta cities used social media to learn the development of the city they were residing in, and to obtain some information related with migration issues(e.g., polices about household registration and social welfare). Besides, they used social media to communicate and interact with the local citizens, and sought social support. Chen(2011) investigated QQ use of rural migrants in Guangzhou and found that a primary purpose of their use of QQ was to maintain contact with their family and friends and thus they could obtain emotional support and tangible support from their previous social networks. In addition, they used QQ to meet some new friends in the virtual world. Zhou and Lu(2011) found that new-generation rural migrants in Shanghai used some forms of social media(e.g., QQ) to maintain social contact with their offline friends and to make new friends. Besides, they used QQ to learn about the news about Shanghai and their hometowns. Kong and Zhang(2013) examined Weibo use among migrant workers in cities around Zhujiang Delta. Their investigation indicated that information seeking and socialization were the two main purposes of Weibo use among internal migrants.

Wei and Chen(2015) investigated the social media use of migrants in Hangzhou and found that internal migrants used some types of social media(Sina Weibo, Renren, Douban, Tencent Weibo, and Sohu Weibo) for social interaction, and for seeking and exchanging information. Their studies showed that migrants' social media use could increase their identification with the local society. Besides, social media use increased their contact with the locals, which was conducive to the expansion of their weak ties. Guo (2017) found that internal migrants' social media use (e.g., WeChat, Weibo, and QQ) increased their knowledge of the local society. However, he found that social media use limited their social participation.

To sum up, domestic studies focused on describing the purposes of social media use among internal migrants. However, there is a lack of examination of how social media use affects their adaptation. Therefore, the present study seeks to address this issue in a quantitative study.

2.4 Chapter Summary

This chapter reviewed some theories and existing empirical research relevant to the topic of the present study at home and abroad. To summarize, a few main limitations of the existing research were found. First, there was a limited number of studies examining how internal migrants' use of social media affects their adaptation process and outcomes. Second, when examining factors affecting internal migrants' adaptation, personality traits were not considered. Third, the existing social support scales used in domestic studies measure the general social support of the individuals but could not capture some specific support needed by internal migrants.

Based on the review of theories and empirical studies relevant to the present study, the author proposed a conceptual framework on the effect of social media use on the adaptation of internal migrants in China (See Figure 2.4). In the conceptual framework,

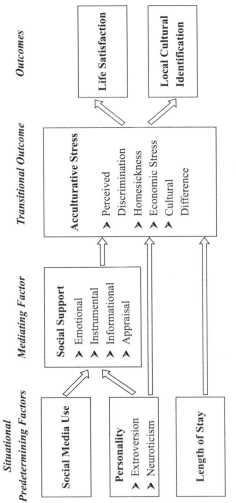

Figure 2.4 Conceptual Framework

social media use is the starting point of the path of the effect. Two personality variables (extroversion and neuroticism) and internal migrants' length of stay in the current residence are also identified as the pre-determining factors as these factors will cause some individual differences on adaptation process and outcomes. Social media use will increase internal migrants' social networks and in turn increase their social capital. Accumulated social capital provides more sources for internal migrants to obtain social support. In addition, based on the literature review, social support has been identified as an important factor that positively affects adaptation. Therefore, social support is the mediating factor of the relationship between social media use and adaptation variables. Finally, based on the literature review, three variables are identified as important indicators of internal migrants' adaptation: acculturative stress, life satisfaction, and local cultural identification. Following Berry's (1997) model, the adaptation variables are divided into two categories: the transitional outcome (acculturative stress) and the final outcomes (life satisfaction and local cultural identification). In doing so, it deepens our understanding of the overall adaptation of internal migrants, and meanwhile helps examine the dependence relationships among the adaptation variables. In the next chapter, a structural model will be proposed to illustrate the relationships among these variables.

Chapter Three
A Hypothesized Structural Model

In the previous chapter, a conceptual framework was proposed to examine the adaptation of international migrants and the effect of social media use on their adaptation. Based on the existing theoretical and empirical research evidence, this chapter first presents the research hypotheses on the direct and indirect relationships among the main variables. Then, it presents the hypothesized structural model illustrating the dependence relationships among the main variables.

3.1   Research Hypotheses

Drawing upon the conceptual framework proposed in Chapter Two, the author identified three variables as important indicators of the overall adaptation of internal migrants: acculturative stress, life satisfaction, and local cultural identification. Moreover, the present study extended beyond the simple direct relationship among the variables by identifying social support as an important mediating factor through which social media use affects internal migrants' adaptation. In addition, in order to make sure the relationships among the main variables were robust, two personality variables (extroversion, and neuroticism) and length of stay were added to the model as covariates because they have been identified as factors causing individual differences on adaptation. In this section, the existing theoretical and empirical bases to explain the relationships among these variables are presented. As there was limited quantitative research evidence from the domestic literature, some empirical

research evidence from intercultural adaptation literature abroad
was provided. Despite the differences among the subjects of the research, some commonalities exist in their adaptation process(e.g.,
personal factors affecting their adaptation, psychological changes
in the adaptation process, and adaptation outcomes) (DeWind &
Holdaway, 2005).

3.1.1   The Direct Effects

3.1.1.1   Social Media Use and Social Support

Emergence of social media has extended communication patterns among individuals, enabling its users to connect with each
other through various platforms (Haythornthwaite, 2002). Facebook, for instance, provides the function of "friending" to connect
individuals and allows for online interactions among its users
through the 'wall' on which messages can be posted and responded
to(Kim, Jeong, & Lee, 2010).

With these platforms, social media plays an important role in
the maintenance of in individual's pre-existing social networks as
well as the establishment of new ones(Dekker & Engbersen, 2014;
Ellison, Steinfield & Lampe, 2007). A study by Reich, Subrahmanyam and Espinoza(2012) illustrated how social media maintained
pre-existing social networks. They found that adolescent high school
students from various ethnic minority groups in South California
used Facebook for socialization, in particular with those they knew
offline. Thus, their intimacy with their offline friends increased by
using this social media platform. Social media also provides the potential to foster the development of new ties among its users, which
would otherwise be difficult in traditional face-to-face context(Liu
et al., 2017; Reich et al., 2012). Dekker and Engbersen (2014)
points out that use of social media fosters some "latent ties" at the
beginning, which will develop into "weak ties" when activated
through some form of social interaction.

Social support is defined as important resources embedded in an individual's social networks(Lin, 2008). Given that the use of social media could help maintain an individual's pre-existing social networks and expand new ones, the use of social media could enlarge people's perceived social support. Previous research has found empirical evidence on the positive effects of social media use on perceived social support. For example, Liu and Yu(2013) found that Facebook use was positively associated with perceived online social support among a sample of 355 Taiwan college students, which in turn led to more perceived general social support. Olson and Shultz (2012) found that Facebook users spending more time on Facebook perceived more social support from both their face-to-face and Facebook friends. Oh, Ozkaya, and LaRose(2014) found that the number of Social Networking Sites(SNSs) friends had a positive effect on the perceived social support among its users. In addition, Ellison, Steinfield, and Lampe(2007) found that Facebook use intensity was predictive of college students' perceived social support from both their high school classmates and their new acquaintances at their university. Oh(2016) found that Missy USA(an online community of immigrant Korean women in the US) was effective in providing informational support(e.g., information for obtaining legal status and Korean-style cuisine) and emotional support(e.g., encouragement and companionship).

Within the adaptation literature, research evidence has also demonstrated that social media use is positively associated with migrant groups' social networks and their social support. For example, Forbush and Foucault-Welles(2016) found that Chinese international students in America who used more Social Networking Sites (SNS) had larger and more diverse social networks than those who did not use Social Networking Sites(SNS), especially at the first stage of their relocation. Through qualitative studies, Chen and Yang(2015) found that Living in Singapore group(LSg)[1] was very

---

[1]   LSg is an online forum used by the Chinese international students in Singapore.

effective in helping Chinese international students in Singapore seek informational, emotional and instrumental support. Also, LSg provided network support. For example, through the messages posted on the forum, Chinese international students could join virtual groups of hometown association or find travel companions. Kim, Yun, and Yoon (2009) discovered that Cyworld① and WeChat helped Asian international students in South Korea obtain informational support. Chen(2010) found that the use of QQ by internal migrants in Guangzhou facilitated their acquisition of both emotional support and informational support. Therefore, it is predicted that the use of social media will be positively associated with the perceived availability of the social support of internal migrants in Shanghai. The hypothesis is made as follows:

H1: The more that internal migrants use social media, the higher the level of social support they will perceive.

3.1.1.2   Social Media Use and Acculturative Stress

Previous studies yielded inconsistent findings on the relationship between social media use and individuals' psychological outcomes. On one hand, given the unique features of social media in facilitating communication among people regardless of the boundaries of time and space, the use of social media could increase the social connectedness among people. There is research evidence that use of social media produces some positive psychological outcomes. For example, Grieve, Indian, Witteveen, Tolan, and Marrington (2013) found that people's use of social networking sites was associated with lower rates of depression and anxiety, as well as greater subjective well-being.

On the other hand, use of social media has some negative effects on individuals' well-being. Chou and Edge(2012) argued that social media users tended to have comparisons with others, and exposing to positive self-presentation of others cause low appraisals on

---

① Cyworld is a social networking site in Korea.

their own lives and thus making them feel stressful. Other studies found that too much use of social media(e.g., Facebook) was associated with loneliness, depression, and stress(Kontos, Emmons, Puleo, & Viswanath, 2010; O'Dell, 2011). In addition, according to Hampton, Lu, and Shin(2016), there were circumstances under which the social media use increased awareness of stressful events in the lives of others, and would lead to higher levels of stress of social media users.

Acculturative stress is the stress caused by encountering difficulties in the new cultural environment, such as unfamiliarity with the host cultural system, undesirable social interactions, or loss of previous social networks. For migrants who relocate to a new sociocultural environment, social media helps them connect with their pre-existing social networks. Therefore, use of social media helps relieve their homesickness or negative feelings brought about by separation from family members. In addition, the use of social media provides opportunities for migrants to enlarge their social connectedness with the host people beyond face-to-face contact. Increased contact with host nationals will be likely to have positive effects on the relationships between migrants and host nationals, and will thus reduce the perceived discrimination experienced by migrants. It is therefore reasonable to believe that social media use will help alleviate the acculturative stress that migrants experienced in their adaptation process. One study conducted by Park, Song, and Lee (2014) found that Chinese and Korean international students in the US who used Facebook more experienced less acculturative stress and had a higher level of psychological well-being. However, as previously discussed, there are possibilities that use of social media also contributes to stress, anxiety, and distress among their users. In the same study conducted by Park et al.(2014), they found that when migrant students used social media of their home countries, they strengthened their home cultural identity and practices and thus experienced more acculturative stress in adapting to the home culture. Therefore, it is thus hypothesized that there will be both positive and negative association between social media use and acculturative stress. The hypothesis is presented as follows:

H2a: The more that internal migrants use social media, the less acculturative stress they will experience.

H2b: The more that internal migrants use social media, the more acculturative stress they will experience.

3.1.1.3   Personality Variables, Social Support and Acculturative Stress

Personality is a descriptive term that indicates individual differences in psychological features or dispositions (Hofstede & McCrae, 2004). Personality variables have been identified as one of the key individual factors that affect the dynamics of the adaptation process(Arends-Tóth & van de Vijver, 2006; Berry, 1997; Shen & Takeuchi, 2001).

Extroversion and neuroticism are two general personality traits that are the most widely researched in adaptation literature. Extroversion is associated with positive affect and the general tendency to be assertive, active, cheerful, enthusiastic and happy(Carver & Connor-Smith, 2010; Roesch, Wee, & Vaughn, 2006). Extroversion is also associated with sociability(Ashton, Lee, & Paunonen, 2002). Extroversion has been found to be associated with some positive adaptation outcomes, such as lower levels of depression and higher levels of cultural fit and life satisfaction(Ward, Leong, & Low, 2004; Zhang, Mandl, & Wang, 2010).

Extroversion and neuroticism have some influences on social support. Extroverted individuals are more positioned to be active in social support seeking (Amlrkhan, Risinger, & Swickert, 1995; Connor-Smith & Flachsbart, 2007; Watson & Hubbard, 1996), while neuroticism is linked to avoidance of coping(Roesch, Wee, & Vaughn, 2006). Moreover, since extroverted individuals tend to be more active in social interactions, they have larger social support networks and more frequent contact with their network members.

This will be beneficial in social support seeking and will enhance the perceived availability of the social support they could acquire (Russell, Booth, Reed, & Laughlin, 1997; Zhu, Woo, Porter, & Brzezinski, 2013). Neurotic individuals, however, are more socially reserved and tend to have less closeness with their social network members(Kalish & Robins, 2005). Studies have provided empirical evidence that individuals high in extroversion and low in neuroticism reported higher levels of perceived social support or enacted social support(Lincoln, Larsen, Phillips, & Bove, 2003; Swickert, Hittner, & Foster, 2010; Swickert, Hittner, Harris, & Herring, 2002).

Extroversion and neuroticism are found to be related to social support of migrants in their adaptation process. Migrants who are more extroverted tend to be less anxious in social interactions with host nationals and have better intergroup contact quality, which will facilitate their social support seeking(Searle & Ward, 1990). It is thus hypothesized that extroversion will be positively related with perceived social support while neuroticism will be negatively associated with perceived social support. The hypotheses are presented as follows:

H3: Internal migrants high in extroversion will have higher levels of perceived social support.

H4: Internal migrants high in neuroticism will have lower levels of perceived social support.

With respect to the relationship between extroversion and acculturative stress, extroverted migrants may have more positive appraisals towards stressors they encounter in their adaptation and will be more adaptive to acculturative stressors. In addition, studies found that extroversion was positively related to support-seeking and active coping(Roesch, Wee, & Vaughn, 2006; Watson & Hubbard, 1996). This will help migrants acquire more resources and will be conducive to alleviating the stress migrants experience. Thus, it is hypothesized that extroversion will be positively associated with acculturative stress. The following hypothesis is presented:

H5: The more extroverted internal migrants are, the less acculturative stress they will experience.

Neuroticism, on the contrary, is correlated with a predisposition to experiencing negative affect. Neurotic people are more apt to experience feelings such as stress, alienation, worry, anxiety, anger, hostility, impulsivity, and depression (Costa & McCrae, 1990; Larsen & Ketelaar, 1989). When exposed to stress in their lives, individuals with higher levels of neuroticism tend to be more upset or remain distressed for a longer time (Bolger & Schilling, 1991). Also, neurotic individuals may "have intense emotional and physiological reactivity to stress" (Connor-Smith & Flachsbart, 2007, p.1081).

Individuals experience multiple stressors when they move to a new culture. Studies found that neuroticism was positively related to the acculturative stress migrants experience. For example, Mangold, Veraza, Kinkler, and Kinney (2007) found that neuroticism predicted acculturative stress of the Mexican college students in the USA. Poyrazli, Thukral and Duru (2007) found that neuroticism was positively related to stressors of migrant students' acculturative stress, including perceived discrimination, homesickness, fear, and perceived hate/rejection. Based on the previous findings, it is predicted that neuroticism will be positively associated with acculturative stress experienced by migrants. The following hypothesis is made:

H6: The more neurotic internal migrants are, the more acculturative stress they will experience.

3.1.1.4 Social Support and Acculturative Stress

Social support could provide resources individuals need to cope with the difficulties in their lives, including information (such as advice), tangible resources (such as food or money) and meeting emotional needs (such as esteem, caring and a sense of belonging)

(Chen & Choi, 2011). As noted earlier, it is generally believed that social support could serve as a stress buffer(Cohen & Wills, 1985). Consistent findings have demonstrated that perceived availability of social support alleviates the acculturative stress an individual experienced during his adaptation process. For example, Thomas and Choi(2006) found that social support reduced the level of acculturative stress of Korean and Indian immigrant adolescents in America. Crockett et al.(2007) found that Mexican American college students who perceived high availability of social support reported low levels of acculturative stress than students who perceived low availability of social support. Lee, Koeske, and Sales(2004) found that social support buffered the acculturative stress of the Korean international students living in the Pittsburgh area. It is thus predicted that a higher level of perceived availability of social support will be associated with a lower level of acculturative stress. The following hypothesis is made:

H7: The more that internal migrants perceive the availability of social support, the less acculturative stress they will experience.

3.1.1.5   Length of Stay and Acculturative Stress

Adapting to a new culture, according to Kim (2001), is a stress-adaptation-growth process. With the increase of individuals' length of stay in the new society, they are more likely to acquire the social skills needed to cope with adjustment difficulties(Ward & Kennedy, 1999). Besides this, they have the advantages in expanding their social networks in the host society, compared with those who have stayed in the host culture for a shorter period of time. Moreover, length of residence is positively associated with migrants' level of host language ability(Sodowsky & Plake, 1992). Therefore, migrants will experience less acculturative stress because they are more adaptive to the new sociocultural environment.

There is empirical evidence that migrants' length of stay affects their acculturative stress level. For instance, Ayoob, Singh, and Jan(2011) found that length of stay was negatively associated with acculturative stress and positively related to the health status of the Kashmiri migrant students in Bhopal. Similarly, Vergara, Smith, and Keele(2010) found that among a sample of 216 international students in Thailand, those who stayed longer reported a lower level of acculturative stress, compared with those who stayed for a shorter period of time. Some other studies demonstrated positive links between migrants' length of stay and some dimensions of acculturative stress. Wilton and Constantine(2003) found that longer stay in the host culture was associated with less distress in adjusting to cultural norms. Miglietta and Tartaglia (2009) found that migrants' length of stay was positively associate with their host language proficiency. Nasirudeen, Josephine, Adeline, Seng, and Ling(2014) found that length of stay was negatively associated with homesickness. It is thus predicted that migrants who stay longer in the new residence will experience less stress than those who stay there for a short period of time. The following hypothesis is presented:

H8: The longer that internal migrants stay in the new residence, the less acculturative stress they will experience.

3.1.1.6   Acculturative Stress and Local Cultural Identification

Individuals migrating to a new culture are faced with two cultural systems that are to some extents different in terms of language, values, or cultural practices. An important issue in the intercultural adaptation process is cultural identification. Some studies have demonstrated evidence that migrants' acculturative stress affected their cultural identification. Benet-Martínez and Haritato (2005) found that acculturative stress was negatively related to migrants' identification with the host culture. In addition, a study conducted by Vroome, Verkuyten, and Martinovic (2014) found that some stressors affected migrants' cultural identification. More specifically, host language proficiency and contact with host nationals were positively associated with migrants' identification with the host culture, while perceived discrimination was negatively associated with identification with the host culture. Therefore, it is predicted that the acculturative stress experienced by internal migrants will be negatively associated with their local cultural identification. The hypothesis is presented as follows:

H9: Internal migrants who experience higher levels of acculturative stress will have lower levels of local cultural identification.

3.1.1.7   Social Support and Local Cultural Identification

A few studies have investigated the relationship between migrants' social support and their identification with the host culture. In one study on the adaptation of Vietnamese students in France, Brisset et al.(2010) attempted to test the relationship between international students' perceived social support and their cultural identification. Their studies demonstrated evidence that in-group social support was positively associated with international students' co-national identification. Chirkov, Safdar, De Guzman, and Playford(2008) found that perceived social support of international students in Canada from their family, home culture and host culture were positively associated with their psychological well-being and negatively associated with the social difficulties they experienced. They further pointed out that fewer social difficulties would decrease the discrepancies that migrants perceived between the host culture and the home culture, and would in turn increase their identification with the host culture. Thus, it is predicted that internal migrants' perceived social support will be positively associated with their identification with the local culture. The following hypothesis is presented:

H10: The more that internal migrants perceive social support, the higher level of local cultural identification they will have.

3.1.1.8   Social Support and Life Satisfaction

Life satisfaction is an individual's subjective appraisal of his living conditions. Social support provides the resources an individual needs in the forms of tangible support, emotional support, companionship, or belonging support. Social support has some positive effects on life satisfaction among different kinds of people(Yalçin, 2011; Adriaansen, van Leeuwen, Visser-Meily, van den Bos, & Post, 2010; Newman, Nielsen, Smyth, & Hooke, 2015). The positive role of social support on migrant's life satisfaction has been well-documented in adaptation literature. For example, Wong, Chou, and Chow(2012) found that perceived social support of new immigrants from mainland China to Hong Kong was positively related with their concept of quality of life. Young(2001) found that social support alleviated the stressors of life events and increased their life satisfaction. In addition, He and Wang(2016) found that social support of internal migrants in cities of Beijing, Shanghai, and Shenzhen was positively associated with their life satisfaction. It is hence hypothesized that migrants' social support will be positively associated with their life satisfaction. The following hypothesis is made:

H11: The more that internal migrants perceive social support, the higher levels of life satisfaction they will have.

3.1.1.9 Acculturative Stress and Life Satisfaction

Previous research has demonstrated that migrants' acculturative stress is a significant predictor of their life satisfaction. For example, Pan, Wong, Joubert,and Chan(2008) found that acculturative stress of Chinese international students in Australia was negatively associated with their life satisfaction. They also found that the mainland Chinese students in Hong Kong who reported higher levels of acculturative stress had lower levels of life satisfaction. In another study, Chow(2007) found that lack of perceived discrimination was related to a higher level of life satisfaction among the adolescent immigrants who came from Chinese Hong Kong to Canada. It is thus predicted that acculturative stress will be negatively associated with life satisfaction. The following hypothesis is made:

H12: Internal migrants who experience higher levels of acculturative stress will have lower levels of life satisfaction.

3.1.2   The Mediation Effects

Based on the hypothesized direct relationships among the variables, some mediation effects among the variables are proposed:

h1: Social support will mediate the relationship between social media use and acculturative stress.

h2: Acculturative stress will mediate the relationship between social support and life satisfaction.

h3: Acculturative stress will mediate the relationship between social support and locational cultural identification.

h4: Acculturative stress will mediate the relationship between social media use and life satisfaction.

h5: Social support will mediate the relationship between social media use and life satisfaction.

h6: Social support and acculturative stress will mediate the relationship between social media use and life satisfaction.

h7: Acculturative stress will mediate the relationship between social media use and local cultural identification.

h8: Social support will mediate the relationship between social media use and local cultural identification.

h9: Acculturative stress and social support will mediate the relationship between social media use and local cultural identification.

3.2   The Hypothesized Model

Based on the research hypotheses presented above, the hypothesized structural model illustrating the effects of social media use on internal migrants' adaptation is presented as follows (See Figure 3.1).

In the hypothesized structural model, the latent variables were drawn as ellipses, including social media use, social support, acculturative stress, life satisfaction, and local cultural identification. The observed variables were drawn as squares, including extroversion,

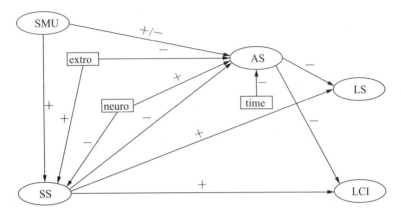

Figure 3.1   A Hypothesized Structural Model

Notes: SMU: Social Media Use, SS: Social Support, AS: Acculturative Stress, LS: Life Satisfaction, LCI: Local Cultural Identification, extro: extroversion, neuro: neuroticism, time: Length of Stay.

neuroticism, and the length of stay. The relationships among the variables in the study were indicated on the hypothesized model. " + " indicated a positive relationship between two variables while " − " suggested a negative relationship between two variables.

The latent variables in the hypothesized structural model will be measured with observed variables. Based on the literature, the author identified four sub-dimensions of acculturative stress: perceived discrimination, cultural discomfort, economic strain, and homesickness. Moreover, given a lack of perceived social support scale for internal migrants, the author will develop a social support scale based on some established scales to measure internal migrants' perceived social support and performed exploratory factor analysis (EFA) to derive the factorial structure of the perceived social support scales. In the following analysis, the hypothesized direct and mediation effects among the variables will be tested.

3.3 Chapter Summary

Drawing on the existing theoretical and empirical research bases, a hypothesized structural model was proposed to describe the factors affecting the adaptation of internal migrants in China and the effects of social media use on their adaptation. The research hypotheses on both the direct and mediation effects among the variables were presented. The following chapter will discuss the research methodologies adopted to test the hypothesized structural model.

Chapter Four
Research Methodology

This study adopts a quantitative approach to test the hypothesized model proposed in Chapter Three. This chapter provides a detailed description of the research methodology. It includes five sections. The first section introduces the target sample. The second section introduces the measurement of the variables. The third section introduces the process of questionnaire design, including the questionnaire, the panel validity, translation and backtranslation of the questionnaire, and the pilot study. The fourth section introduces the data collection, including the sample size estimation and data collection procedures. The fifth section introduces the data analysis methods.

4.1 Target Sample

Based on the literature, internal migrants in China are defined as people who have moved from their birthplace or the original Hukou registration place to a new location, who have jobs and lodging in the new place of residence, and who have been living there for more than six months.

The present study selected internal migrants in Shanghai as the target sample. First, Shanghai is widely acknowledged as "a city of migration," and internal migrants in Shanghai come from various places in China(Zhu, Liu, & Chen, 2008). The diverse origins of the migrants may help us understand a more general picture of their adaptation process. Second, compared with other cities, Shanghai has some distinctive local cultural characteristics, such as the *ben-bangcai* (the local Shanghai food) and the local Shanghai dialect. Therefore, adaptation in Shanghai might be more representative of "local adaptation" than other locations. Third, as previous studies suggest, internal migrants in Shanghai may experience stressors such as financial difficulties and discrimination (Wong & Song, 2008). Therefore, examination of the social media use of internal migrants in Shanghai will better our understanding of the role social media plays in the adaptation process of internal migrants as a whole.

Respondents of the survey were selected based on the following three criteria: (1) individuals who moved to Shanghai from their birthplace or the place where their original Hukou was registered, (2) who have been living in Shanghai for more than 6 months, and (3) who have stable jobs and dwellings in Shanghai. According to the definition of internal migrants, migrant students and short-term visitors are not included in the present study.

4.2   Measurement of the Variables

4.2.1   Social Media Use

The measurement of social media use was adapted from the Facebook Intensity Scale (Ellison et al., 2007). Respondents were asked to indicate the types of social media they usually used in their daily lives from the given choices, including WeChat, QQ, Sina Weibo, and so on. Then they were asked to indicate the approximate time of their social media use in their daily lives by answering, "On average, approximately how much time per day have you spent on Social Media in the past week?" The scores ranged from 0 (less than 10 minutes) to 5 (more than 3 hours). Respondents were also asked to rate the intensity of their social media use by indicating to what extent they agreed or disagreed on six items. Sample items were "Using social media is part of my everyday activity," and "I feel out of touch when I do not use social media." Scores were put on a 9-point Likert scale ranging from 1(Strongly disagree) to 9(Strongly agree). Higher scores indicated more intense use of social media.

4.2.2   Social Support

As has been noted earlier, perceived social support(individuals' perception of the availability of the support they could obtain) and enacted social support(the actual support provided to them when they were in need) are two constructs measured separately. The present study measured perceived social support of internal migrants in Shanghai. To the best of the author's knowledge, there were no established scales of perceived social support for internal migrants. As internal migrants may need some special kinds of social support to facilitate their adaptation, the author developed a perceived social support scale for internal migrants on her own.

The self-developed scale consisted of fifteen items. Eight items were selected and adapted from the Medical Outcome Study-Social Support Survey (MOS-SSS) (Sherboume & Stewart, 1991) which measures individuals' perceptions of the availability of informational/emotional support, social companion support, affectionate support, and tangible support. Among the eight items, four items were selected and adapted from the subscale of informational/emotional support. Sample items were "There is someone I can count on to listen to when I need to talk," and "There is someone to give me good advice about a crisis." One item was selected from the social companion support: "There is someone to get together with for relaxation." Four items were selected and adapted from the Index of Sojourner Social Support (ISSS) Scale (Ong & Ward, 2005) which measures sojourners' perceived socioemotional support and instrumental support. Among the four items, one item was selected and adapted from the subscale of perceived socioemotional support:

"There is someone to share my good times." Three items were selected from the subscale of perceived instrumental support. Sample
items were "There is someone to provide necessary information to
help orient me to the surroundings of Shanghai," and "There is
someone to help me understand the local culture." In addition,
three items on job-related support were added to the author's self-
developed scale. This is because migrants may need special help on
job-related issues due to their change of residence. Sample items
were "There is someone to recommend me for some positions when
I seek jobs," and "There is someone to give me suggestions to help
me with my career development." The scores of the items were put
on a 9-point Likert Scale ranging from 1(strongly disagree) to 9
(strongly agree). Higher scores indicated a higher level of perceived
social support. These items were rearranged randomly on the questionnaire. Exploratory Factor Analysis(EFA) was done to extract
the factors of the self-developed perceived social support scale for
internal migrants in Shanghai.

4.2.3   Acculturative Stress

Acculturative stress is a multi-dimensional construct. Based on
the previous literature, the author identified four important dimensions of acculturative stress experienced by internal migrants in
Shanghai: perceived discrimination, cultural discomfort, economic
strain, and homesickness.

Perceived discrimination consisted of respondents' perceptions
of the discrimination they experienced in Shanghai because they-
were "*waidiren*." Measures of perceived discrimination were adapted from the subscale of perceived discrimination of the Acculturative Stress Scale for International Students(ASSIS) developed by
Sandhu and Asrabadi(1994). There were six items in the perceived
discrimination subscale. Sample items were "I am treated differently in social situations because I am from outside Shanghai," and
"Many opportunities are denied to me because I am from outside

Shanghai." Scores were put on a 9-point Likert scale ranging from 1 (strongly disagree) to 9(strongly agree), with higher scores indicating higher levels of perceived discrimination.

Measures of homesickness were adapted from the subscale of homesickness of the Acculturative Stress Scale for International Students(ASSIS) developed by Sandhu and Asrabadi(1994). There were four items in the subscale of homesickness. Sample items were "Homesickness bothers me," and "I feel sad leaving my relatives behind." Scores were put on a 9-point Likert scale ranging from 1 (strongly disagree) to 9(strongly agree), with higher scores indicating higher levels of homesickness.

Cultural discomfort measured respondents' psychological discomfort caused by cultural differences in terms of language, food, values, and so on. Measures of cultural discomfort were adapted from the subscale of culture shock/stress due to change of the ASSIS(Sandhu & Asrabadi, 1994). There were four items in the subscale of cultural discomfort. Sample items were "I feel uncomfortable adjusting to Shanghai food," and "I feel uncomfortable adjusting to the values of the local Shanghai culture." Scores were put on a 9-point Likert scale ranging from 1(strongly disagree) to 9 (strongly agree), with higher scores indicating higher levels of cultural discomfort.

Measurement of economic strain was adapted from the Family Economic Strain Scale developed by Wadsworth and Compas (2002). There were four items. Sample items were "I worry about the bills I have to pay each month," and "I have to save my salary for several months if I want to buy a car." Scores were put on a 9-point Likert scale ranging from 1(strongly disagree) to 9(strongly agree), with higher scores indicating higher levels of economic strain.

4.2.4   Local Cultural Identification

The Multidimensional Acculturation Scale(AAMAS) developed by

Chung, Kim, and Abreu(2004) was used to measure respondents' local cultural identification. The AAMAS measures two fundamental dimensions of migrants' cultural identification: identification with the home culture and identification with the host culture. Items measuring identification with the local culture of internal migrants in Shanghai were adapted from the subscale of host cultural identification. Respondents were asked to rate their attitudinal or behavioral identification with Shanghai culture on specific aspects including language, food consumption, social customs, social relations, and so on. There were five items in the local cultural identification scale. Sample items were "I identify with the Shanghainese people," and "I would like to follow the customs of Shanghai." The scores were put on a 9-point scale ranging from 1(strongly disagree) to 9(strongly agree). Higher scores indicated a higher level of identification with the Shanghai culture.

4.2.5 Life Satisfaction

Measures of internal migrants' life satisfaction were adapted from the Satisfaction with Life Scales(SWLS) developed by Diener, Emmons, Larsen, and Griffin(1985). Respondents were asked to rate their overall assessment of their life in Shanghai on a 9-point Likert scale(from 1 = strongly disagree to 9 = strongly agree). There were five items on this scale. Sample items were "In most ways my life in Shanghai is close to my ideal," and "The conditions of my life in Shanghai are excellent." Higher scores indicated a higher level of satisfaction with life in Shanghai.

4.2.6 Extroversion and Neuroticism

Extroversion was measured with the subscale of extroversion of the Eysenck Personality Questionnaire Revised-Short-Scale (EPQ-RSS) developed by Eysenck, Eysenck, and Barrett(1985). The subscale of extroversion contained 12 yes/no questions. Sample items were "Are you a talkative person?" and "Are you rather lively?"

The scores of the scale are 1 = "yes" and 0 = "no". In this subscale, the score of item 14("Do you tend to keep in the background on social occasions?") was reversed. Higher summed scores indicated a higher level of extroversion.

Neuroticism was measured with the subscale of neuroticism of the Eysenck Personality Questionnaire Revised-Short-Scale (EPQ-RSS) developed by Eysenck, Eysenck, and Barrett(1985). The subscale of neuroticism contained 12 yes/no questions. Sample items were "Does your mood often go up and down?" and "Do you ever feel 'just miserable' for no reason?" The scores of the scale were 1 = "yes" and 0 = "no". Higher summed scores indicated a higher level of neuroticism.

4.3   Questionnaire Design

4.3.1   Composition of the Questionnaire

A questionnaire was designed to collect data. The questionnaire included seven sections. The first section asked respondents' background information. Some demographic information were asked, including respondents' gender, age, hometown, marital status, educational level, average monthly income, occupation, migration reasons, length of stay in Shanghai, current residential status in Shanghai, housing conditions in Shanghai, ability to understand and speak the Shanghai dialect, and their intention to stay in Shanghai for a long period of time(more than 5 years). The following sections were composed of the scales of the study variables in the hypothesized model, including social media use, personality variables(extroversion and neuroticism), social support, acculturative stress, life satisfaction, and local cultural identification. The scales of personality variables(extroversion and neuroticism) were yes/no questions. Other variables were measured with 9-point Likert scales(1 = strongly disagree; 9 = strongly agree).

4.3.2   Panel Validity

After developing the English questionnaire, the author invited two American scholars in intercultural communication studies to review the items. Each professor provided their comments on the relevance, clarity, and appropriateness of the items. Some items were revised according to their comments. For example, the original item "Many opportunities are denied to me because I am not a local person" was changed to "Many opportunities are denied to me because I am from outside Shanghai."

4.3.3   Translation and Backtranslation of the Questionnaire

As the original questionnaire was developed in English, the English questionnaire was translated into Chinese by a university English teacher in Shanghai who has a doctoral degree in English Linguistics and Literature. After that, another university English teacher in Shanghai with a doctoral degree in English Linguistics and Literature translated the Chinese version of the questionnaire back to English. Then the original English version of the questionnaire was compared with the back-translated version to see whether the two versions were conceptually equivalent. Based on the comparison, the author talked with the translator of the original English questionnaires and reworded a few items in the Chinese questionnaire so as to guarantee the correctness of the translation and the consistency with the original scales. As there is an established Chinese version of the Eysenck Personality Questionnaire Revised-Short-Scale(EPQ-RSS), which has been translated by Qian, Wu, Zhu, and Zhang(2000) and has been validated in domestic literature, the present study used the Chinese versions of the two subscales of extroversion and neuroticism directly.

4.3.4   Pilot Study

After the development of the Chinese questionnaire, a pilot

study was carried out in April and May, 2018 before the main study. Respondents of the pilot study included twelve post-graduate students majoring in intercultural communication at a university in Shanghai, two university teachers teaching intercultural communication in Shanghai, four university English teachers in Shanghai, and a university teacher in Shanghai who specialized in sociology. Respondents of the pilot study completed the questionnaires and made comments on the understandability, clarity, and appropriateness of the questionnaire. Based on their comments, several items were reworded again in order to make the items more understandable and appropriate, which led to a final version of the Chinese questionnaire(See Appendix 1).

In addition, the completion time of the questionnaire was recorded by the author in the pilot study. It was estimated that a minimum of 10 minutes was needed to complete the questionnaire. The minimum completion time was used as one of the screening criteria in the data collection procedure.

4.4   Data Collection

4.4.1   Sample Size Estimation

The present study adopted structural equation modelling(SEM) to do the data analysis. It is important to determine the sample size in SEM in order to guarantee the stability of the parameter estimates and standard errors(Schumacker & Lomax, 2010). Scholars have different criteria when determining the sample size in SEM. Bentler and Chou(1987) suggest that at least 5 cases be needed for one indicator in SEM. As there were 52 indicators in the structural model, a minimum number of 210 samples was needed for the present study.

As the perceived social support scale was developed by the author herself, an exploratory factor analysis(EFA) was conducted to

derive the factorial structure of perceived social support. Hair,
Black, Babin, and Anderson(2010) suggest that the minimum number of the samples for EFA should be 5 times the number of the
items on the scales. As there were 15 items on the social support
scale, a minimum number of 75 samples was required. Therefore,
the total number of the samples of the present study should be at
least 285.

4.4.2 Data Collection Procedures

The data of the present study was collected through the administration of an online survey from July, 2018 to October, 2018. Respondents were recruited on *wenjuanxing*, a large and well-known
online survey website in China. The author contacted the online
survey company and submitted the requirements for the sample
collection. The author was charged 20 yuan for each usable questionnaire.

Wenjuanxing has an inventory of a large number of people registered on its website. *Wenjuanxing* checked the IP addresses of its
registers, and recruited people whose IP addresses were in Shanghai
by sending an invitation to do the survey via cell phone or e-mail. A
URL link to the website with the self-administered questionnaire
was posted in the invitation. The IP address of each participant was
monitored by *wenjuanxing* so that each IP address has access to the
questionnaire only once.

A set of automatic screening requirements were set in the questionnaire to make sure the correct group of respondents was recruited. A primary requirement was the hometown of the respondents.
In the demographic information section, respondents were asked to
choose their hometowns from the choices provided. Those whose
hometown was Shanghai were excluded automatically. A second requirement was the completion time. Based on the pilot study, a
minimum of 10 minutes was needed to complete the questionnaire.
Therefore, respondents whose completion time was less than 10 mi-

nutes were excluded automatically.

4.5   Data Analysis Methods

Structural equation modeling(SEM) was used to test the relationships among the variables in the hypothesized structural model. SEM is a statistical method that combines factor analysis and multiple regression analysis, which has advantages over multiple regression analysis as it is able to test a set of interrelations among multiple variables simultaneously(Weston & Gore Jr, 2006). In SEM, a construct is a latent variable and is measured by some observed variables, which are also called the manifest variables, measured variables, or indicators(Kline, 2011). SEM comprises two models: the measurement model and the structural model. The measurement model examines the factorial validity of the measuring instrument, i.e., whether the observed variables best represent the latent constructs or not(Byrne, 2010; Hair et. al., 2010). The structural model is also called the path model, and it examines the dependence relationships among the latent constructs (Nachtigall, Kroehne, Funke, & Steyer, 2003).

The present study took two steps to conduct the SEM analysis, as suggested by Anderson and Gerbing (1988). First, the author specified five measurement models of the latent constructs of social media use, social support, acculturative stress, life satisfaction, and local cultural identification. As the social support scale was self-developed, exploratory factor analysis(EFA) was performed to extract the factors of the social support variables. Second, using the remaining set of samples, confirmatory factor analysis(CFA) was conducted to develop the measurement models of the latent variables, so as to derive the most valid factorial structure of the latent constructs that fit the current data. Third, the factor scores of each latent variable were calculated, and the Independent Samples t Test on the factor score was used to test the effects of the demographic variables on the adaptation variables. Fourth, the direct effects among the latent variables in the structural model were tested. Fifth, item parceling was conducted to simplify the model and the simplified structural model was tested to examine whether the research results were robust. Last, the Bootstrap method was used to test the hypothesized mediation effects among the latent constructs.

The SEM analysis was conducted using Mplus 7.4 and AMOS 24. Mplus provides methods of parameter estimation under the circumstance that the multivariate normality of the data was violated, which was often the case in practice(Geiser, 2013). AMOS 24 was used to draw the diagrams and calculate the factor score of the latent variables.

4.6 Chapter Summary

This chapter introduced the research methodology used to conduct the empirical research. The target samples of the present study were the individuals who moved to Shanghai from their original household registration place, and who had been living and working in Shanghai for more than 6 months. The process of questionnaire development was presented. The data used for the quantitative study was collected though an online survey. SEM was used to test the hypothesized model. In the next chapter, the preliminary analysis of the data will be carried out.

Chapter Five
Preliminary Analysis

This chapter describes the preliminary analysis of the data using SPSS 24.0. It includes four sections. The first section provides an overview of the survey questionnaires, including the response rate and the missing values. The second section describes the characteristics of the respondents. The third section describes respondents' social media use types and use frequency. The fourth section describes the data screening, including the examination of multivariate outliers, the correlation analysis among the variables, the test of multicollinearity, and the reliability of the scales.

5.1   An Overview of the Questionnaires

5.1.1   Response Rate

An online survey was conducted to collect data from July 2018 to October 2018.The response rate of the questionnaires is presented in Table 5.1. The online survey company (*wenjuanxing*) invited 1506 people to participate in the online survey, among whom 1103 completed the questionnaires, accounting for a returned response rate of 73.2%. After the collection of the questionnaires was completed, the author checked each questionnaire carefully. Among the 1103 completed questionnaires, 400 questionnaires were eliminated.

Some responses were eliminated automatically because they were completed in less than 10 minutes. Some responses were eliminated

Table 5.1   Response Rate of the Questionnaires

		N	%
People invited		1506	100
Returned responses	Problematic responses	400	36.3
	Usable responses	703	63.7

because the respondents' length of stay was shorter than 6 months. Some responses were eliminated because of a lack of engagement with the questions. Others were eliminated because of some problematic responses in the respondents' background information. For example, some survey respondents' length of stay in Shanghai exceeded their age. In the end, a total number of 703 responses was retained for further statistical analysis, which accounted for 63.7% of the returned responses.

5.1.2   Missing Values

There were no missing values in respondents' questionnaires because the web-based survey required them to finish all the questions before they were able to submit. When respondents missed some items on the questionnaire before they submitted it, the items would appear on the screen to remind respondents to finish them. Respondents could terminate the survey at any time, and in this case, their questionnaires were not collected. Therefore, all the questionnaires collected via the online survey were complete.

5.2   Respondents' Characteristics

Gender. The gender distribution of the respondents is shown in Table 5.2. Among the 703 respondents, there were 273 males, accounting for 38.8%. The number of female respondents was 430, which accounted for 61.2%.

Table 5.2   Respondents' Gender Distribution

Gender	Frequency	Percentage
Male	273	38.83
Female	430	61.17
Total	703	100.00

Age. The characteristics of respondents' age are shown in Figure 5.1. Those aged between 18 and 25 accounted for 22.05%. Respondents aged between 26 and 30 accounted for 34%. Respondents aged between 31 and 40 accounted for 36.56%. Respondents aged between 41 and 50 accounted for 6.26% and respondents aged between 51 and 60 accounted for 1.14%.

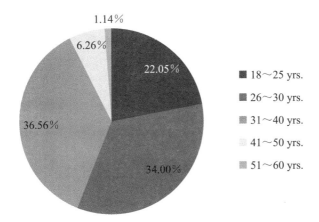

Figure 5.1   Respondents' Age Distribution

Overall, respondents aged below 40 accounted for 92.61%, showing that the majority of the respondents were young and middle-aged adults. This might be due to the reason that young and middle-aged people are more adept at using internet technology. Respondents' age distribution was appropriate for the present study. The present study is more interested in young and middle-aged migrants, as they constitute the majority of internal migrants in China. Besides, they are the primary users of social media.

Hometown(place of origin). The characteristics of respondents' hometowns(places of origin) are presented in Figure 5.2. It can be observed that respondents' hometowns (places of origin) covered nearly all the administrative regions of China except Tibet, Qinghai, Hong Kong, and Taiwan. The diversified composition of survey respondents' hometown is a manifestation of the widely-acknowledged fact that Shanghai is a migration city that embraces internal migrants from all over the country.

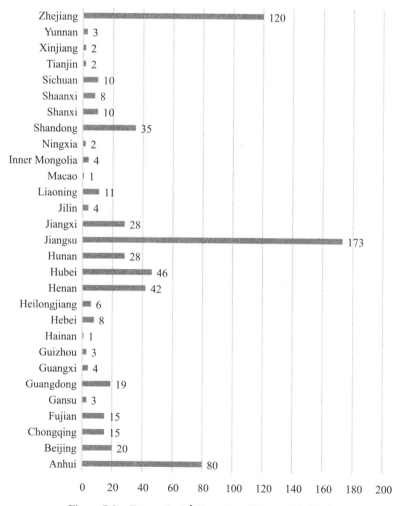

Figure 5.2   Respondents' Hometown (Place of Origin)

It can also be observed from Figure 5.2 that the majority of respondents came from provinces near Shanghai, such as Jiangsu

(24.6%), Zhejiang(17%), and Anhui(11.4%). People from these nearby provinces represent the majority of internal migrants in Shanghai. The reason can be explained by the geographical closeness and cultural similarity between these provinces and Shanghai, as well as the long tradition of people migrating from these provinces to Shanghai.

Marital status. Respondents' marital status is presented in Table 5.3. Most respondents were married, accounting for 63.2% (N = 444) of the total number. 36.8% of the respondents were unmarried (N = 259).

Table 5.3   **Respondents' Marital Status**

Marital Status	Frequency	Percentage
Married	444	63.16
Unmarried	259	36.84
Total	703	100.00

Educational level. Respondents' educational levels are shown in Table 5.4. Overall, the number of the respondents whose educational level was higher than a college diploma amounted to 95.59%. This shows that most respondents were well-educated, which could explain their high monthly incomes. It also shows that it is easier for migrants with a high educational level to find well-paid jobs and settle in the city.

Table 5.4   **Respondents' Educational Level**

Educational Level	Frequency	Percentage
Junior High School or Lower	3	0.43
Senior High School or Junior College	28	3.98
College Diploma	98	13.94
Bachelor Degree	462	65.72
Master Degree	104	14.79
Ph. D./Post-Doc.	8	1.14
Total	703	100.0

Length of stay in Shanghai. Table 5.5 shows respondents' length of stay in Shanghai. Their average length of stay in Shanghai was 90.93 months(about 7 years and 6 months), ranging from 6 months to 560 months(nearly 46 years and 7 months) with a standard deviation of 80.383 months(See Table 5.5). The median of length of stay was 66 months. A normal distribution curve based on the mean and the standard deviation was added into the histogram of respondents' length of stay in Shanghai(See Figure 5.3). As the skewness and kurtosis were far above zero, it showed that the data did not fit the normal distribution. Because the data was positively skewed, it indicated that most of the respondents' length of stay in Shanghai was below the mean(See Figure 5.3).

Table 5.5   Descriptive Statistics of Respondents' Length of Stay in Shanghai

	Min	Max	Mean	SD	Median	Skewness	Kurtosis
Length of Stay	6	560	90.935	80.383	66	1.996	5.168

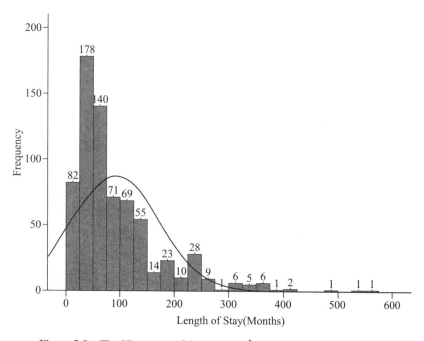

Figure 5.3   The Histogram of Respondents' Length of Stay in Shanghai

Migration reasons. Figure 5.4 shows the reasons why respondents migrated to Shanghai. The main reason that respondent moved to Shanghai was employment(62.45%), followed by the pursuit of study(22.05%). Some other reasons included movement with family members(10.10%) and investment(10.10%). 3.56% of the respondents did not indicate their specific reasons of migration to Shanghai.

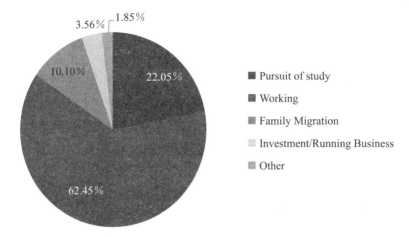

Figure 5.4   Respondents' Migration Reasons

Occupation. Respondents' occupational status was divided into eleven categories(See Table 5.6). It can be observed that respondents' occupation categories were wide-ranging. Most respondents were company employees(35.3%) and professionals(20.3%). This may be because these types of professions provide more opportunities for employment which could attract a large number of internal migrants.

Table 5.6   Respondents' Occupational Status

Categories of Occupation	Frequency	Percentage
Leaders of all levels of the government, enterprise and public institutions, Party and government offices, and public organizations	67	9.53
Professionals(e.g., teachers, doctors, engineering and technical personnel, lawyers and accountants)	143	20.34
Public servants, staff at enterprise and public institutions or the government	78	11.10
Company employees	248	35.28

continued

Categories of Occupation	Frequency	Percentage
Workers(e.g., factory workers, construction workers, and urban sanitary workers)	13	1.85
Personnel in the business and service industry (e. g., salesclerks, waiters/waitresses, and hotel clerks)	65	9.25
Laborers in farming, forestry, animal husbandry, side-line production and fishery	3	0.43
Private business owners/individual operators	75	10.67
Self-employed	9	1.28
Housewives	1	0.14
Other(e.g., volunteers)	1	0.14
Total	703	100.00

Current household registration status in Shanghai. As is shown in Table 5.7, the number of respondents who had the permanent Shanghai Hukou amounted to 327, accounting for 46.5%. 42.1% of the respondents(N = 296) had the Shanghai residence permits. 6.0% (N = 42) had the collective registered Shanghai Hukou, and 5.4% of the respondents(N = 38) had other types of household registration status.

Table 5.7　Respondents' Current Household Registration Status

Household Registration Status	Frequency	Percentage
Permanent Shanghai Hukou	327	46.5
Collective Registered Shanghai Hukou	42	6.0
Shanghai Residence Permit	296	42.1
Other	38	5.4
Total	703	100.0

According to the data of the National Bureau of Statistics and the Ministry of the Public Security of the People's Republic of China, the number of regular residents in Shanghai amounted to 24.2378 million by the end of 2018. 14.4757 million people had the Shanghai Hukou, accounting for 59.72% of the regular residents in

Shanghai. The regular residents who did not have the Shanghai Hukou has amounted to 9.7621 million, accounting for 40.28%.

As is shown in Table 5.7, the number of respondents having the Shanghai Hukou accounted for 52.49%, indicating that respondents' household registration status was close to the actual situation and these respondents represented the real population well. This is because in mega cities like Shanghai, there are some restrictions on the household registration, such as the migrants' educational levels and their length of stay in Shanghai. Therefore, it might not be easy for internal migrants to obtain the permanent Shanghai Hukou.

Current housing conditions. Table 5.8 presents respondents' current housing conditions in Shanghai. 45.80% of the respondents (N = 322) have purchased their own houses in Shanghai. 45.95% of the respondents(N = 323) were renting houses in Shanghai. 1.99% of the respondents(N = 14) were living in their relatives' or friends' houses, and 5.83% of the respondents(N = 41) were living in dormitories provided by their employers.

Table 5.8   Housing Conditions of Respondents

Housing Conditions	Frequency	Percentage
Self-owned housing	322	45.80
Renting	323	45.95
Lodging with relatives or friends	14	1.99
Dormitory provided by the employer	41	5.83
Other	3	0.43
Total	703	100.0

Income level. Respondents' average income of the past year is presented in Figure 5.5. Most respondents earned a monthly income of over 5000 yuan. 38.12% of the respondents earned a monthly income of between 5001 yuan and 10000 yuan. 26.74% of the respondents earned a monthly income of between 10001 yuan and 15000 yuan. 14.79% of the respondents earned a monthly income of between 15001 and 20000 yuan. The rest of the respondents earned more than 20000 yuan a month(9.96% of the respondents earned a monthly income of between 20001 and 30000, and 5.12% of the respondents earned more than 30000 yuan a month).

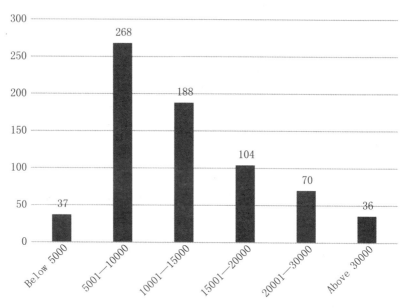

Figure 5.5   Respondents' Average Monthly Income(Unit: yuan)

The author estimated the mean of respondents' average monthly income. For respondents who were in the class interval of "below 5000", their monthly income was estimated as 5000 yuan per month. For respondents who fell into the class intervals of "5001—10000 yuan," "10001—15000 yuan," "15001—20000 yuan," and "20001—30000 yuan," their monthly income was estimated as the midpoint value. For respondents who were in the class interval of "above 30000," their monthly income was estimated as the value of the lower limit. As a result, it was estimated that the mean of respondents' average monthly income was 13079.66 yuan, which was far above the average monthly income of the employees in Shanghai and its suburbs in 2018(8764.67 yuan)[1]. The results indi-

①   It is based on "the average income of the employees in the city and townships in Shanghai" released on the website of the Shanghai Statistics Bureau. Retrieved from http://www. stats-sh. gov. cn/html/xwdt/201906/1003597.html(Available on September 4th, 2019).

cated that respondents were good at earning money. This might be related to their high level of education, which made it easier for them to find jobs with high wages.

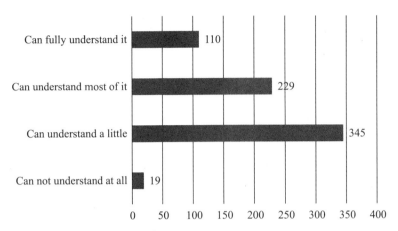

Figure 5.6 Respondents' Ability to Understand the Shanghai Dialect

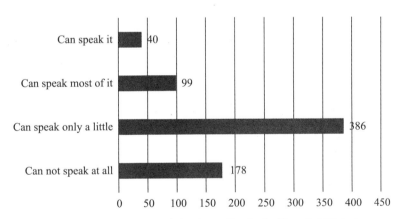

Figure 5.7 Respondents' Ability to Speak the Shanghai Dialect

Ability to understand and speak the Shanghai dialect. Respondents' ability to understand and speak the Shanghai dialect are shown in Figure 5.6 and Figure 5.7. The statistics showed that most respondents had the ability to understand the Shanghai dialect well. 25.65% (N = 110) of the respondents reported being able to totally understand the Shanghai dialect. 32.57% (N = 229) of the respondents reported being able to understand most of the Shanghai dialect.

49.08% (N = 345) of the respondents reported being able to understand only a little of the Shanghai dialect, while a small portion of
the respondents(2.7%, N = 19) reported being unable to understand
the Shanghai dialect.

However, respondents' ability to speak the Shanghai dialect
was not as good as their ability to understand the Shanghai dialect.
Only 5.69% of the respondents(N = 40) reported being able to speak the
Shanghai dialect. 14.08% (N = 99) of the respondents reported being
able to speak most of the Shanghai dialect. 54.91% (N = 386) of the
respondents reported being able to speak some Shanghai dialect,
while 25.32% (N = 178) of the respondents reported the inability to
speak the Shanghai dialect at all.

Intention for long-term residence (more than 5 years). Respondents'
intention for long-term residence is shown in Table 5.9. An over-
whelming majority of the survey respondents(93.31%) would like
to stay in Shanghai for a long period of time(more than 5 years),
while only a small portion of the respondents (6.69%) indicated
that they would not like to stay in Shanghai for a long period of
time(more than 5 years).

Table 5.9   Respondents' Intention for Long-Term Residence

Intention for long-term residence	Frequency	Percentage
Yes	656	93.31
No	47	6.69
Total	703	100

5.3   Respondents' Social Media Use Types and Use Frequency

In the questionnaire, respondents were asked to indicate the
types of social media they used most often in their daily lives from a
list of choices, including WeChat, QQ, Sina Weibo, Douban, and
so on. Table 5.10 presents the summary of the types of social media
they used most often.

Table 5.10   Summary of Types of Social Media Used Often by Respondents

Types of social media	Responses		Percent of Cases
	N	Percent	
WeChat	692	23.7%	98.4%
Tencent QQ	572	19.6%	81.4%
Sina Weibo	460	15.7%	65.4%
Douban	154	5.3%	21.9%
Renren	89	3.0%	12.7%
Zhihu	339	11.6%	48.2%
Baidu Tieba	298	10.2%	42.4%
Tianya BBS	119	4.1%	16.9%
LinkedIn	77	2.6%	11.0%
Kaixin	36	1.2%	5.1%
Skype	58	2.0%	8.3%
Others	28	1.0%	4.0%
Total	2922	100.0%	415.6%

It can be observed that the types of social media the respondents used most often included WeChat, Tencent QQ, Sina Weibo, Zhihu, and Baidu Tieba. Nearly all the respondents used WeChat, which accounted for 98.4% of the total sample. Tencent QQ and Sina Weibo also enjoyed popular use among respondents, which accounted for 81.4% and 65.4% respectively. The other two types of social media used widely by the respondents were Zhihu(48.2%) and Baidu Tieba(42.4%). Some types of social media(including Douban, Tianya BBS, Renren, and LinkedIn) enjoyed a comparatively low percentage of use among respondents, ranging from 11.0% to 21.9%. Renren enjoyed the second lowest use among respondents(8.3%), and Kaixin enjoyed the lowest percentage of use among respondents(5.1%). The characteristics of respondents' use of social media were in consistent with the statistics on social media use of Chinese netizens presented in Chapter One(See Figure 1.2), which shows that the data was representative.

In order to learn the frequency of respondents' social media use, they were asked the following question: "On average, approximately how much time per day have you spent on Social Media in

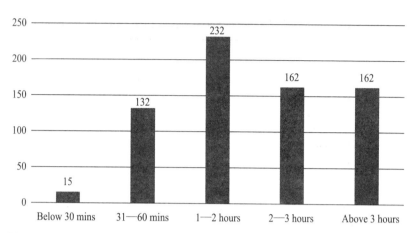

Figure 5.8   Time Spent in Social Media Per Day by Respondents in the Past Week

the past week?" Five choices were given: "below 30 mins," "31—
60 mins," "1—2 hours," "2—3 hours," and "above 3 hours." Figure
5.8 presents the histogram of the frequency of respondents' social
media use. Overall, a vast majority of the respondents had used social media for more than one hour per day in the past week, accounting for a percentage of 79.09% of the total sample. More specifically, respondents who had used social media one to two hours
per day in the past week accounted for 33% of the total sample.
Respondents who had used social media two to three hours per day
in the past week accounted for 23.04%. And those who had used social media more than three hours per day in the past week accounted for 23.04% as well. Results indicated that most of the respondents used social media very frequently in their daily lives. It suffices
to say that social media has become an important tool of communication in respondents' daily lives.

5.4 Data Screening

Before the main analysis, data screening was conducted using
SPSS 24.0. This section presents the results of multivariate outliers,
correlations, multicollinearity, and reliability of the scales.

5.4.1 Multivariate Outliers

An outlier refers to an observation "whose scores are substantially different from all the others in a particular set of data" (Byrne, 2010, p.105). A Multivariate outlier, according to(Kline, 2011), is the observation of two or more variables whose scores are extremely distinct from the rest. The present study detected some multivariate outliers by calculating and examining the squared Mahalanobis distance for each case. Mahalanobis distance indicates "the distance in standard deviation units between a set of scores (vector) for an individual case and the sample means for all variables (centroid), correcting for intercorrelations" (Kline, 2011, p.54). A rule of thumb is that observations with a significance level lower than 0.001 are considered to be multivariate outliers(Gallagher, Ting, & Palmer, 2008). In the present study, 73 multivariate outliers having a significance level less than 0.001 were identified (See Table 5.11). Hair et al.(2010) claim that removing the multivariate outliers limits the generalizability of analysis to the entire population unless there is evidence that these multivariate outliers "are truly aberrant and not representative of any observations in the population"(p.65). Therefore, the 73 multivariate outliers were retained for further analysis.

Table 5.11 Detection of Outliers Using Mahalanobis Distance(n=73)

Observation No.	Mahalanobis d-squared	Sig.
380	179.6136	0.000000
631	168.7141	0.000000
1001	167.2346	0.000000
102	149.3593	0.000000
270	148.7062	0.000000
192	147.4718	0.000000
938	141.8950	0.000000
476	141.3411	0.000000
1063	139.9265	0.000000

continued

Observation No.	Mahalanobis d-squared	Sig.
828	138.1855	0.000000
669	137.2163	0.000000
560	137.1024	0.000000
834	133.0941	0.000000
82	130.4149	0.000000
350	129.8521	0.000000
1038	126.5245	0.000000
809	122.6399	0.000000
474	122.2094	0.000000
796	121.7145	0.000000
1026	119.7534	0.000000
170	115.1985	0.000001
830	115.1370	0.000001
213	114.7049	0.000001
379	114.3678	0.000001
975	112.4370	0.000002
1009	110.5470	0.000003
1078	110.1903	0.000003
728	109.1636	0.000004
1064	108.2707	0.000005
1030	107.8662	0.000006
373	107.5929	0.000006
66	107.3058	0.000007
393	105.4870	0.000011
76	105.4473	0.000012
84	103.6993	0.000019
996	103.3562	0.000020
224	103.1110	0.000022
592	102.0407	0.000029
795	101.9567	0.000030
912	100.5528	0.000043
400	100.1135	0.000049
1043	99.4740	0.000057

continued

Observation No.	Mahalanobis d-squared	Sig.
787	99.2437	0.000061
1056	99.0467	0.000064
739	98.8321	0.000068
434	98.2311	0.000079
127	97.9590	0.000085
489	97.8373	0.000088
570	96.8284	0.000114
754	96.6029	0.000121
584	96.5135	0.000124
1042	96.1054	0.000137
784	95.6229	0.000155
161	95.1804	0.000173
988	94.8636	0.000188
987	93.8300	0.000243
1076	93.7073	0.000251
917	93.5453	0.000261
633	93.4828	0.000265
1098	93.0987	0.000291
1035	92.8877	0.000307
1007	92.7365	0.000319
954	92.3955	0.000346
98	92.0216	0.000380
347	91.4914	0.000432
825	91.3446	0.000448
679	91.1319	0.000471
660	91.0552	0.000480
298	90.9942	0.000487
597	90.7933	0.000511
931	89.8859	0.000636
235	89.2288	0.000743
841	88.4397	0.000895

Note: Sig. = 1-The cumulative distribution probability of the Chi-square distributed Mahalanobis d-squared with degrees of freedom(df), here $df = 51$.

5.4.2   Correlation Analysis

Pearson's correlation analysis was performed to examine the bivariate linear relationships among the variables in the hypothesized model(See Appendix 3). It should be noted that as there were five latent variables in the present study(social media use, social support, acculturative stress, life satisfaction, and local cultural identification), the mean of the observed variables of each latent variable was calculated. After that, Pearson's correlation analysis among these constructs was conducted to test the significance of the correlations.

It can be observed from Appendix 3 that respondents' length of stay was negatively correlated with acculturative stress but positively correlated with their life satisfaction and local cultural identification. Length of stay had no significant correlations with social media use, extroversion, and neuroticism. Social media use was positively correlated with extroversion, social support, life satisfaction, and local cultural identification, but negatively correlated with neuroticism. Social media use had no significant correlation with acculturative stress. Social support was negatively correlated with acculturative stress but positively correlated with life satisfaction and local cultural identification. Acculturative stress was negatively correlated with life satisfaction and local cultural identification. Life satisfaction was positively correlated with local cultural identification. These correlations suggested that most of the hypotheses on direct effects in the hypothesized model were supported as predicted, except for the direct relationship between social media use and acculturative stress.

Additionally, in order to derive a higher-order latent variable of acculturative stress, the four sub-dimensions of acculturative stress(PD, HS, CD, and ES) should have significant correlations with each other. As is seen from Appendix 3, the four sub-dimensions of acculturative stress(PD, HS, CD, and ES) had significant-

ly positive correlations with each other, which suggested the probability of deriving a higher-order latent variable of acculturative
stress.

5.4.3 Multicollinearity

Multicollinearity can be defined as "the high correlations
among the exogenous constructs" (Grewal, Cote, & Baumgartner,
2004, p.519). When multicollinearity exists between two independent variables, the predicting effect of any of them will be con-
founded because they may represent the same underlying construct
(Hair et al., 2010). Generally, the correlation coefficient between
two variables greater than 0.7 indicates multicollinearity (Hair et
al., 2010). As can be seen from Appendix 3, the correlation coefficients among the variables in the current research were all below
0.7 except the correlation between extroversion and neuroticism
(-0.706). It indicated that there was concern for multicollinearity
between these two variables.

5.4.4 Reliability of the Scales

Reliability refers to the internal consistency of the scales, i.e.,
the extent to which the items are consistent in measuring the same
variable (Hair et al., 2010). Reliability of the scales in the present
study was assessed through Cronbach's α. As is shown in Table 5.12,
Cronbach's α of the variables in the present study ranged from a
low value of 0.624 to a high value of 0.907, all above the lowest acceptable value of 0.6 (Hair et al., 2010). It indicated that the variables in the structural model were internally consistent. Besides, despite that the subscales of cultural discomfort and economic strain
were less than 0.7, the Cronbach's α of the overall scale of acculturative stress was 0.868. It indicated that the reliability of the overall
scale of acculturative stress was good (Wu, 2008).

Table 5.12   Scale Reliability Analysis

Construct	Item	Cronbach's α if item deleted	Cronbach's α
Social Media Use(SMU)	smu1. Using social media is part of my everyday activity.	0.661	0.717
	smu2. I feel out of touch when I do not use social media.	0.692	
	smu3. I am willing to share some information on social media.	0.670	
	smu4. I use social media to seek help.	0.699	
	smu5. I communicate with my family frequently via social media.	0.683	
	smu6. I maintain close contact with my friends via social media.	0.668	
Social Support (SS)	ss1. There is someone to recommend me for some positions when I seek jobs.	0.905	0.907
	ss2. There is someone I can count on to listen to me when I need to talk.	0.900	
	ss3. There is someone to share my good times.	0.902	
	ss4. There is someone to get together with for relaxation.	0.901	
	ss5. There is someone to provide necessary information to help orient me to the surroundings of Shanghai.	0.900	
	ss6. There is someone to help me understand the local culture.	0.903	
	ss7. There is someone to confide in or talk to about myself or my problems.	0.902	
	ss8. There is someone to give me information to help me understand a situation.	0.901	
	ss9. There is someone to help me learn about some local institutions' official rules and regulations.	0.903	
	ss10. There is someone to take me to the doctor if I need it.	0.902	
	ss11. There is someone to do things with to help me get my mind off things.	0.899	

continued

Construct		Item	Cronbach's α if item deleted	Cronbach's α
Social Support (SS)		ss12. There is someone to give me good advice about a crisis.	0.900	
		ss13. There is someone to share my most private worries and fears with.	0.901	
		ss14. There is someone to give me necessary information to help me find jobs.	0.901	
		ss15. There is someone to give me suggestions to help me with my career development.	0.901	
Acculturative Stress(AS)	Perceived Discrimination (PD)	as1. I am treated differently in social situations because I am from outside Shanghai.	0.889	0.907
		as2. Many opportunities are denied to me because I am from outside Shanghai.	0.892	
		as3. Others are biased toward me because I am from outside Shanghai.	0.884	
		as4. I feel that I receive unequal treatment because I am from outside Shanghai.	0.887	
		as5. I am denied what I deserve because I am from outside Shanghai.	0.895	
		as6. I feel that people from outside Shanghai are discriminated against.	0.894	
	Homesickness (HS)	as7. Homesickness bothers me.	0.745	0.819
		as8. I feel sad living in unfamiliar surroundings.	0.775	
		as9. I miss my hometown and the people at my hometown.	0.814	
		as10. I feel sad leaving my relatives behind.	0.748	
	Cultural Discomfort (CD)	as11. I feel uncomfortable adjusting to Shanghai foods.	0.630	0.697
		as12. I feel uncomfortable adjusting to the values of the local Shanghai culture.	0.570	
		as13. I feel nervous when people speak Shanghai dialect around me.	0.635	
		as14. It hurts when people don't understand my cultural values.	0.689	

continued

Construct		Item	Cronbach's α if item deleted	Cronbach's α
Acculturative Stress(AS)	Economic Strain (ES)	as15. I worry about having money to pay the bills each month.	0.461	0.624
		as16. I have to save salaries of several months if my family want to buy a car.	0.531	
		as17. I have extra money that my family and I can use to travel abroad once every year.(R)	0.641	
		as18. The mortgage (house rent) accounts for a large percentage of my household income.	0.563	
Life Satisfaction(LS)		ls1.In most ways my life in Shanghai is close to my ideal.	0.820	0.869
		ls2. The conditions of my life in Shanghai are excellent.	0.826	
		ls3. I am satisfied with life here in Shanghai.	0.822	
		ls4. So far I have gotten the important things I want in life here.	0.850	
		ls5. I do not want to change anything about my life in Shanghai.	0.886	
Local Cultural Identification(LCI)		lci1. I like to associate with the Shanghainese.	0.733	0.750
		lci2. I feel I have much in common with the Shanghainese.	0.666	
		lci3. I identify with the Shanghainese.	0.736	
		lci4. I would like to learn Shanghai dialect.	0.678	
		lci5. I would like to follow the customs of Shanghai.	0.714	

Notes: 1. Item as 18 is the composite of two original items. The two original items were "The mortgage accounts for a large percentage of my household income." for the respondents who have purchased their own houses and "The house rent accounts for a large percentage of my household income." for the respondents who are renting or lodging with their relatives or friends.

2. "R" represents a reversed item. The above table reports the reversed score of this item.

3. Acculturative Stress is a second-order variable, which comprises four first-order variables: Perceived Discrimination(PD), Homesickness(HS), Cultural Discomfort(CD), and Economic Strain(ES).

5.5   Chapter Summary

This chapter described the preliminary analysis of the study. After the data collection via an online survey, the author scrutinized the data and retained 703 questionnaires for data analysis. Respondents of the questionnaires came from nearly all administrative regions of China except Tibet, Qinghai, Hong Kong, and Taiwan. The characteristics of the respondents such as their hometowns, household registration status, and income level indicated that they were representative. Moreover, results indicated that social media enjoyed a high frequency of use among the respondents. WeChat, Tencent QQ, and Sina Weibo were the three types of social media used most frequently by the respondents. Then, the data was examined for its multivariate outliers, correlations and multicollinearity. In addition, the reliabilities of the scales were examined. The Cronbach's coefficients indicated that the scales of the variables were reliable. The next chapter will present the development of the measurement models of the latent variables.

Chapter Six

Data Analysis: Measurement Models

The present study employs the technique of structural equation modeling(SEM) to test the hypothesized structural model proposed in Chapter Three. This chapter expounds on the development of the measurement models of the latent constructs in the hypothesized model. First, it introduces the methods of factor analysis used to develop the measurement models. Then, it describes the process of establishing the measurement models of the latent constructs, including social support, social media use, acculturative stress, life satisfaction, and local cultural identification. Next, it examines the construct validity and reliability of the overall CFA model. Then, it tests the Common Method Variance (CMV) of the overall CFA model. Last, it introduces the Independent Samples t Test which examines the effects of the demographic variables on the adaptation of internal migrants.

6.1 Introduction of the Methods of Factor Analysis

The measurement model in a SEM represents the relationships between the latent variables (i.e., latent constructs or latent factor) and their indicator variables (i.e., observed variables, measured variables, indicators, or manifest variables). There are two basic methods of factor analysis that can be used to develop the measurement models: exploratory factor analysis(EFA) and confirmatory factor analysis(CFA) (Yong & Pearce, 2013). In this section, the basic concepts of these two methods were introduced.

6.1.1   Exploratory Factor Analysis(EFA)

Exploratory factor analysis(EFA)is a technique used to identi-fy the underlying structure of a set of variables(Williams, Onsman, & Brown, 2010). It is used when the researcher does not know how many factors can explain the interrelationships among these varia-bles(Yong & Pearce, 2013). Through exploratory factor analysis (EFA), the researcher will be able to extract a minimum number of factors that best explain the relationships between the latent factor and the observed variables.

The following steps are taken when conducting EFA. The first step is to test some basic assumptions of performing EFA to see whether the data was suitable to do EFA. Kaiser-Meyer-Olkin (KMO) Measure of Sampling Adequacy, and Bartlett's Test of Sphericity are two commonly used methods. The second step is to examine the communalities of the variables to see whether there is need to delete variables or adding variables to extract additional factors. The third step is to decide the extraction method. The fourth step is to determine the factors to be retained and name the factors. The fifth step is to examine the correlation matrix to see whether the correlations among the variables are significant or not.

As the perceived social support scale for internal migrants was self-developed, EFA was conducted using SPSS 24.0 to derive the factorial structure of the social support variables using a number of 300 questionnaires randomly drawn from the total questionnaires.

6.1.2   Confirmatory Factor Analysis(CFA)

In the present study, confirmatory factor analysis(CFA) was conducted using the remaining 403 questionnaires to establish the measurement models of the latent constructs in the hypothesized model with Mplus 7.4. CFA aims to determine and confirm the rela-tionships between the latent variables(i.e., latent constructs or la-tent factor) and their observed variables(i.e., indicator variables, indicators, measured variables, or manifest variables). This section introduces some basic concepts involved in conducting CFA.

6.1.2.1   Normality Test

A basic assumption of CFA is the normality of the data. Skewness and kurtosis are two measures to examine the shape and symmetry of the distribution of the variables(Hair et al., 2010). The absolute value of skewness and kurtosis should be zero if the data are symmetrically distributed(Hair et al., 2010). However, in practical analysis, more liberal standards are adopted. West, Finch, and Curran(1995) propose that the univariate normality of the variables is severely violated when the absolute skew values are above 2 and/or the absolute kurtosis values are higher than 7. Kline(2011) claims that variables with absolute values of skewness greater than 3.0 and/or with absolute values of Kurtosis greater than 8.0 are indicative of non-normal distribution, and Kurtosis over 20.0 is considered as "extremely" non-normally distributed(p.63).

The multivariate kurtosis is used to assess whether the data are departing substantially from multivariate normality. According to the common rule of thumb, the critical ratio(C. R.)[1] of the multivariate kurtosis greater than 5 indicates a violation of multivariate normality(Hair et al., 2010).

6.1.2.2   Estimation Methods

When conducting CFA, it is important to determine the method used for parameter estimation. Maximum Likelihood(ML) Estimation is the most commonly used estimation method in CFA(Curran & West, 1996). ML estimation method provides parameter estimates based on the assumption of multivariate normality of the observed variables(Bollen, 1989). When the observed variables depart from multivariate normality, the results using ML estimation are erroneous. When multivariate normality is violated, some alterna-

---

[1]   Critical ratio is "the ratio of a sample statistic over its standard error"(Kline, 2011, p.33).

tive methods should be considered.

Arbitrary Distribution Function(ADF) is an estimation method usually used when multivariate normality is violated (Browne, 1984). However, ADF estimation method typically requires a large sample size to produce stable results, usually 1000 to 5000 samples (West, Finch, & Curran, 1995). As the sample size of the present study was less than 1000, ADF method was not appropriate for the current data.

Another option of parameter estimation in the case of multivariate non-normality is to use a corrected normal theory method (Klein, 2011). A commonly used one is the Satorra-Bentler statistic (Satorra & Bentler, 1994). In Mplus 7.4, the MLM estimation method "provides robust standard errors and mean-adjusted χ^2 test statistic that are equivalent to Satorra & Bentler(SB) χ^2"(Wang & Wang, 2012, p.60).

6.1.2.3   Parameter Estimation

A primary issue when conducting CFA is to test the significance of the parameters. The critical ratio(C. R.), which "represents the parameter estimate divided by its standard error"(Kline, 2011, p.33), is used to check the statistical significance of the parameters. According to the rule of thumb, the C. R. needs to be greater than 1.96 to suggest that the null hypothesis that the estimate equals to 0 should be rejected(Byrne, 2010, p.68).

6.1.2.4   Model Evaluation

After an CFA model is established, it is necessary to evaluate the model fit, i.e., how well the specified model fits the data(Anderson & Gerbing, 1988; Hair et al., 2010). Some fit indices are commonly reported to evaluate the model fit, such as the Chi-square(χ^2), χ^2/df, The Satorra-Bentler χ^2, The Tucker-Lewis Index(TLI), The Comparative Fit Index (CFI), The Root Mean Square Error of Approximation(RMSEA), and the Standardized Root Mean Square Residual(SRMR)(For details, see Hair et al., 2010; Kline, 2011). According to some authors (Hu & Bentler,

1999; Hair et al., 2010), the criteria for evaluating the model fit indices reported by Mplus 7.4 are summarized in Table 6.1.

Table 6.1   Summary of Model Fit Criteria

Model Fit Index	Criterion
Satorra-Bentler χ^2	smaller is better
df(Degree of Freedom)	bigger is better
Normed Chi-squared(χ^2/df)	$1<\chi^2/df<3$
RMSEA(90% confidence interval)	<0.08
Pr(RMSEA$\leqslant$0.05)	bigger is better
SRMR	<0.08
TLI(NNFI)	>0.9
CFI	>0.9

6.1.2.5   Reliability and Validity Test

The reliability of the CFA model is tested by its Composite Reliability(CR), which measures the overall reliability of a set of items loaded on a latent construct(Hair et al., 2010). Higher composite reliability indicates higher levels of internal consistency of the measurement models. Fornell and Larcker (1981) recommend that composite reliability should be 0.7 or higher to indicate adequate internal consistency. Bagozzi and Yi(1988) suggest that CR value $\geqslant$ 0.6 is indicative of internal consistency.

Construct validity is used to test the validity of the CFA model. Construct validity refers to "the extent to which a set of measured items actually reflects the theoretical latent construct those items are designed to measure"(Hair et al., 2011, p.618). Construct validity includes convergent validity and discriminant validity. Convergent validity demonstrates the convergence or the agreement of the indicators in measuring a specific construct while divergent validity shows the difference or discrimination between the measures of two conceptually different constructs(Kline, 2011).

A commonly used criterion to assess convergent validity is the Average Variance Extracted(AVE)(Fornell & Larcker, 1981). Average Variance Extracted(AVE) is "the average percentage of vari-

ation explained (variance extracted) among the items of a construct" (Hair et al., p.601). An AVE of 0.5 or higher is indicative of
adequate convergence, and an AVE between 0.36 to 0.5 is considered the lowest acceptable level(Fornell & Larcker, 1981).

Discriminant validity is examined by comparing the square root of
AVE with inter-construct correlations. The square root of AVE for a
specific construct should be greater than correlation between it and any
other construct to indicate discriminant validity(Hair et al., p.601).

In the following sections, CFA was conducted for each latent
construct. As the perceived social support scale was developed by
the author herself, an EFA was conducted to derive the factorial
structure of social support. Rrespondents were divided into two
groups. Group one is a number of 300 randomly drawn from the total sample used to do the EFA. Group Two is the remaining 403 respondents that was used to do the CFA. The next section introduces
the process of measuring social support.

6.2   Measuring Social Support

Social support is a multi-dimensional construct, and can be divided into some subcategories, such as informational support, emotional support, instrumental support, esteem support, appraisal
support, tangible support, belonging support (Cohen & Mckay,
1984; Cohen et al., 1985; House, 1981). However, to the author's
knowledge, there were no established scales measuring perceived
social support of internal migrants. Therefore, the author adapted
some existing scales measuring general social support and the sojourner's
social support, and developed a scale specifically aimed at measuring the
perceived social support of internal migrants in Shanghai.

There were 15 items in the self-developed social support scales.
First, the exploratory factor analysis(EFA) was performed to cate-
gorize the social support items into groups and to determine their
underlying factors. Then, confirmatory factor analysis(CFA) was

conducted to validate the factorial structural of social support.

6.2.1   Exploratory Factor Analysis(EFA) of Social Support

A number of 300 respondents were drawn randomly from the total number of 703 respondents to conduct exploratory factor analysis(EFA). These respondents were chosen through the "Rand( )" function in Excel. First, the "Rand" command applied a number between 0 and 1 to individual cases. Then, the random numbers were sorted in an ascending order. The first 300 cases were chosen as the data to conduct exploratory factor analysis(EFA) on the perceived social support scale and the rest 403 cases were retained to conduct the CFA of social support further.

6.2.1.1   Test of Assumptions

Prior to performing the EFA, some assumptions were tested to see whether the data was adequate and suitable for the EFA. Kaiser-Meyer-Olkin(KMO). Measure of Sampling Adequacy and Bartlett's Test of Sphericity were two commonly adopted measures. The purpose of the KMO Measure of Sampling Adequacy is to see whether the data are adequate to be grouped into a small set of underlying variables(Williams, Onsman, & Brown, 2010). The KMO value ranges from 0 to 1. According to Kaiser(1960), the KMO value should be greater than 0.5 to proceed with the exploratory factor analysis, and the KMO value greater than 0.90 indicates a marvelous adequacy of the data. As can be seen in Figure 6.1, the KMO value for the current data was 0.921, indicating the data was satisfactory to conduct the EFA.

The Bartlett's Test of Sphericity examines whether there are correlations among the variables (Yong & Pearce, 2013). The Bartlett's Test of Sphericity should be significant($p < 0.05$) to suggest that the correlations among the variables were sufficiently large for conducting the EFA(Yong & Pearce, 2013). As is shown in Figure 6.1, the significance of the Bartlett's Test of Sphericity for the current data was 0.000, indicating that the observed variables of social support had patterned relationships and were suitable for the EFA.

Kaiser-Meyer-Olkin Measure of Sampling Adequacy.		.921
Bartlett's Test of Sphericity	Approx. Chi-Square	1919.288
	Df	105
	Sig.	.000

Figure 6.1   SPSS Output for KMO and Bartlett's Test

6.2.1.2   Communalities of the Variables

Communalities are the proportion of variance of each variable that can be explained by the factors (Costello & Osborne, 2005). Communalities between 0.4 and 0.7 are considered as appropriate for conducting the EFA, and communalities below 0.40 indicate that the variables are not loading properly on their associated factors. As is shown in Table 6.2, the extracted communalities for the

Table 6.2   Communalities for the Indicators of Social Support

Items	Initial	Extraction
ss1. There is someone to recommend me for some positions when I seek jobs.	0.384	0.439
ss2. There is someone I can count on to listen to me when I need to talk.	0.448	0.436
ss3. There is someone to share my good times.	0.425	0.408
ss4. There is someone to get together with for relaxation.	0.405	0.437
ss5. There is someone to provide necessary information to help orient me to the surroundings of Shanghai.	0.444	0.470
ss6. There is someone to help me understand the local culture.	0.426	0.508
ss7. There is someone to confide in or talk to about myself or my problems.	0.479	0.523
ss8. There is someone to give me information to help me understand a situation.	0.489	0.487
ss9. There is someone to help me learn about some local institutions' official rules and regulations.	0.421	0.547
ss10. There is someone to take me to the doctor if I need it.	0.469	0.470
ss11. There is someone to do things with to help me get my mind off things.	0.563	0.609
ss12. There is someone to give me good advice about a crisis.	0.546	0.516
ss13. There is someone to share my most private worries and fears with.	0.424	0.455
ss14. There is someone to give me necessary information to help me find jobs.	0.467	0.590
ss15. There is someone to give me suggestions to help me with my career development.	0.463	0.526

Extraction Method: Principal Component Analysis.

social support items ranged from 0.408 to 0.609, all above the lowest acceptable limit of 0.40, and thereby indicating the extracted factors represented the indicator variables well. As a result, there was no need to consider deleting any items nor add similar items to extract additional factors.

6.2.1.3   Factor Extraction Methods

There are two commonly used extraction methods to conduct EFA: Maximum Likelihood (ML) and Principal Axis Factoring (PAF). ML "allows for the computation of a wide range of indexes of the goodness of fit of the model[and] permits statistical significance testing of factor loadings and correlations among factors and the computation of confidence intervals"(Fabrigar, 2011, as cited in Costello & Osborne, 2005, p.2). However, the prerequisite of Maximum Likelihood(ML) is the multivariate normality of the data. Principal Axis Factor is recommended when the data violates the assumption of multivariate normality(Costello & Osborne, 2005). As the multivariate normality of the current data was violated, the author adopted the Principal Axis Factoring(PAF) method for factor extraction.

There are two common rotation techniques in conducting EFA: Orthogonal Rotation and Oblique Rotation. Orthogonal Rotation method produces clearly differentiated but uncorrelated factor structure, while Oblique Rotation method allows for correlation among the factors(Costello & Osborne, 2005). As in social science studies, some correlations are generally expected to exist among the factors, Oblique Rotation methods were more appropriate(Wang, 2014). Therefore, Principal Axis Factoring(PAF) with Oblique Rotation(Promax with Kaiser Normalization) was used in the present study to conduct the EFA on the perceived social support scale.

6.2.1.4   Number of Factors Extracted

The eigenvalues and the scree plot were used to determine the number of factors to be retained. A general rule of thumb is to use Kaiser's(1960) criterion, which suggests that all factors whose eigenvalues are above 1 be retailed. As can be seen from Figure 6.2, there were three factors with eigenvalues greater than 1. Therefore, three factors were retained, and they explained 49.464% of the cumulative variance.

The scree plot can also be used to identify the number of the factors to be retained. It is suggested that the appropriate number of factors to be extracted should be the "elbow" point of the change of the eigenvalues(Hair et al., 2010, p.132). As is shown in Figure 6.3, the elbow of the eigenvalues changes appeared at the third factor, thereby indicating a three factor-solution for the perceived social support items.

Total Variance Explained

Factor	Initial Eigenvalues			Extraction Sums of Squared Loadings			Rotation Sums of Squared Loadings[a]
	Total	% of Variance	Cumulative %	Total	% of Variance	Cumulative %	Total
1	6.635	44.233	44.233	6.132	40.883	40.883	5.602
2	1.249	8.330	52.563	.762	5.081	45.964	4.341
3	1.018	6.788	59.351	.525	3.500	49.464	4.512
4	.804	5.358	64.709				
5	.699	4.659	69.368				
6	.664	4.427	73.795				
7	.593	3.954	77.749				
8	.573	3.822	81.571				
9	.496	3.308	84.879				
10	.479	3.193	88.072				
11	.413	2.753	90.825				
12	.406	2.708	93.534				
13	.345	2.298	95.832				
14	.328	2.183	98.015				
15	.298	1.985	100.000				

Extraction Method: Principal Axis Factoring.
a. When factors are correlated, sums of squared loadings cannot be added to obtain a total variance.

Figure 6.2   SPSS Output for the Total Variance Explained for Extracted Factors

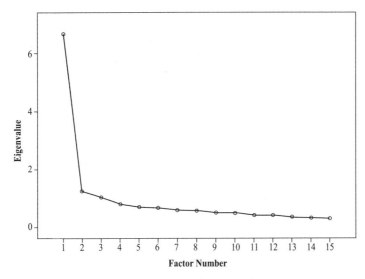

Figure 6.3   Scree Plot for Social Support

6.2.1.5   Pattern Matrix

EFA on the perceived social support scale was conducted using Principle Axis Factoring(PAF) with Oblique Rotation(Promax with Kaiser Normalization). The Pattern Matrix after the rotation is shown in Table 6.3.

As can be seen from the Pattern Matrix(See Table 6.3), three factors were extracted. Eight variables had clear loadings on Factor 1, including ss11, ss7, ss13, ss10, ss3, ss2, ss4, and ss12. Three variables had clear loadings on Factor 2, including ss14, ss1, and ss15. Three factors clearly loaded on Factor 3, including ss9, ss6, and ss15. However, ss8 had cross-loadings as the differences between its loadings on each pair of the factors were all smaller than 0.2. As a result, there was need to consider removing ss8 to find a clean factor structure.

6.2.1.6   Exploratory Factor Analysis(EFA) after Deleting ss8

Exploratory factor analysis(EFA) was rerun after deleting ss8. Kaiser-Meyer-Olkin (KMO) Measure of Sampling Adequacy and Bartlett's Test of Sphericity were performed again. As is shown in

Table 6.3   Pattern Matrix for Social Support

	Component		
	1	2	3
ss11. There is someone to do things with to help me get my mind off things.	0.813	−0.111	0.050
ss7. There is someone to confide in or talk to about myself or my problems.	0.797	0.063	−0.176
ss13. There is someone to share my most private worries and fears with.	0.717	0.025	−0.085
ss10. There is someone to take me to the doctor if I need it.	0.600	−0.182	0.250
ss3. There is someone to share my good times.	0.568	0.077	0.024
ss2. There is someone I can count on to listen to me when I need to talk.	0.563	0.224	−0.097
ss4. There is someone to get together with for relaxation.	0.559	−0.112	0.220
ss12. There is someone to give me good advice about a crisis.	0.469	0.211	0.117
ss8. There is someone to give me information to help me understand a situation.	0.338	0.295	0.156
ss14. There is someone to give me necessary information to help me find jobs.	−0.070	0.779	0.053
ss1. There is someone to recommend me for some positions when I seek jobs.	−0.022	0.710	−0.058
ss15. There is someone to give me suggestions to help me with my career development.	0.047	0.639	0.081
ss9. There is someone to help me learn about some local institutions' official rules and regulations.	−0.099	0.048	0.777
ss6. There is someone to help me understand the local culture.	0.012	−0.006	0.708
ss5. There is someone to provide necessary information to help orient me to the surroundings of Shanghai.	0.187	0.123	0.449

Figure 6.4 SPSS Output for KMO and Bartlett's Test(After Deleting ss8), the KMO value was 0.912. Based on the Kaiser(1974) criteria, the current data was good to conduct the EFA. Also, the significance of Bartlett's Test of Sphericity(p = 0.000) suggested that the data had patterned correlations and was suitable for the EFA.

KMO and Bartlett's Test

Kaiser-Meyer-Olkin Measure of Sampling Adequacy.		.912
Bartlett's Test of Sphericity	Approx. Chi-Square	1724.164
	Df	91
	Sig.	.000

Figure 6.4 SPSS Output for KMO and Bartlett's Test(After Deleting ss8)

Table 6.4 Communalities for the Indicators of Social Support(After Deleting ss8)

Items	Initial	Extraction
ss1. There is someone to recommend me for some positions when I seek jobs.	0.378	0.453
ss2. There is someone I can count on to listen to me when I need to talk.	0.444	0.438
ss3. There is someone to share my good times.	0.422	0.418
ss4. There is someone to get together with for relaxation.	0.404	0.438
ss5. There is someone to provide necessary information to help orient me to the surroundings of Shanghai.	0.444	0.473
ss6. There is someone to help me understand the local culture.	0.426	0.520
ss7. There is someone to confide in or talk to about myself or my problems.	0.479	0.527
ss9. There is someone to help me learn about some local institutions' official rules and regulations.	0.412	0.533
ss10. There is someone to take me to the doctor if I need it.	0.468	0.472
ss11. There is someone to do things with to help me get my mind off things.	0.556	0.605
ss12. There is someone to give me good advice about a crisis.	0.503	0.492
ss13. There is someone to share my most private worries and fears with.	0.421	0.453
ss14. There is someone to give me necessary information to help me find jobs.	0.465	0.599
ss15. There is someone to give me suggestions to help me with my career development.	0.457	0.515

Extraction Method: Principal Component Analysis.

Communalities of the variables after deleting ss8 are shown in Table 6.4. According to the rule of thumb, Communalities between 0.40 and 0.70 are considered as appropriate for the EFA(Costello & Osborne, 2005). As can be seen form Table 6.4, the extracted communalities for the indicator variables of perceived social support

ranged from 0.418 to 0.605, all above the cutoff value of 0.40. It indicated that the extracted factors represented the variables well. As
a result, there was no need to consider deleting any variables nor
add similar variables to extract additional factors.

Principle Axis Factoring(PAF) with Oblique Rotation(Promax
with Kaiser Normalization) was conducted again after deleting ss8.
Three factors with Eigenvalues greater than 1 were extracted and
they explained 49.549 percent of the cumulative variance(See Figure 6.5). The scree plot also suggested a three-factor structure for
the indicator variables of social support.

Total Variance Explained

Factor	Initial Eigenvalues			Extraction Sums of Squared Loadings			Rotation Sums of Squared Loadings[a]
	Total	% of Variance	Cumulative %	Total	% of Variance	Cumulative %	Total
1	6.155	43.963	43.963	5.652	40.373	40.373	5.158
2	1.242	8.874	52.837	0.760	5.429	45.802	3.808
3	1.018	7.273	60.110	0.525	3.747	49.549	4.134
4	0.763	5.453	65.563				
5	0.691	4.936	70.499				
6	0.663	4.737	75.236				
7	0.583	4.165	79.402				
8	0.556	3.973	83.375				
9	0.482	3.443	86.818				
10	0.415	2.962	89.780				
11	0.408	2.917	92.698				
12	0.383	2.738	95.436				
13	0.341	2.437	97.873				
14	0.298	2.127	100.000				

Extraction Method: Principal Axis Factoring.
When factors are correlated, sums of squared loadings cannot be added to obtain a total variance.

**Figure 6.5 SPSS Output for the Total Variance Explained for
Extracted Factors(After Deleting ss8)**

The Pattern Matrix after the deletion of variable ss8 is presented in Table 6.5. The 14 variables cleanly loaded on three factors and did not have cross-loadings. The three-factor structure was desirable with at least 3 variables loading on per factor, and the factor loadings were all above 0.45. Thus, there was no need to delete more variables. The exploratory factor analysis(EFA) was completed.

Table 6.5   Pattern Matrix for Social Support(After Deleting ss8)

	Component		
	1	2	3
ss11. There is someone to do things with to help me get my mind off things.	0.797	−0.102	0.058
ss7. There is someone to confide in or talk to about myself or my problems.	0.790	0.068	−0.166
ss13. There is someone to share my most private worries and fears with.	0.707	0.027	−0.075
ss10. There is someone to take me to the doctor if I need it.	0.588	−0.161	0.248
ss3. There is someone to share my good times.	0.567	0.092	0.026
ss2. There is someone I can count on to listen to me when I need to talk.	0.561	0.226	−0.088
ss4. There is someone to get together with for relaxation.	0.551	−0.103	0.223
ss12. There is someone to give me good advice about a crisis.	0.470	0.184	0.130
ss14. There is someone to give me necessary information to help me find jobs.	−0.049	0.762	0.069
ss1. There is someone to recommend me for some positions when I seek jobs.	−0.006	0.704	−0.049
ss15. There is someone to give me suggestions to help me with my career development.	0.071	0.607	0.098
ss9. There is someone to help me learn about some local institutions' official rules and regulations.	−0.081	0.051	0.754
ss6. There is someone to help me understand the local culture.	0.009	0.006	0.711
ss5. There is someone to provide necessary information to help orient me to the surroundings of Shanghai.	0.190	0.122	0.455

As is shown in the Pattern Matrix(see Table 6.5), three factors were extracted through the Oblique Rotation(Promax). Eight variables including ss11, ss7, ss13, ss10, ss3, ss2, ss4, and ss12 loaded on Factor 1. Three variables including ss14, ss1, and ss15 loaded on

Factor 2. Three variables including ss9, ss6, and ss5 loaded on Factor 3. Factor 1 was named "emotional support," because variables included in Factor 1 were all related with the survey respondents' perceptions of the emotional help and support they could obtain. Examples were "There is someone to do things with to help me get my mind off things," and "There is someone to confide in or talk to about myself or my problems." Factor 2 included variables of the respondents' perceived support on their occupation-related issues, and was thus labeled "occupational support." Examples were "There is someone to give me necessary information to help me find jobs," and "There is someone to recommend me for some positions when I seek jobs." Variables of Factor 3 were concerned with information-related support that facilitate their adaptation in Shanghai. Therefore, Factor 3 was labeled "informational support." Examples were "There is someone to help me learn about some local institutions' official rules and regulations," and "There is someone to help me understand the local culture."

6.2.1.7 The Factor Correlation Matrix

The factor correlation matrix is presented in Table 6.6. It shows the intercorrelations among the factors. According to Tabachnick and Fidell(2007), the correlations among the factors should exceed 0.30 to suggest the factorability of the variables. Hair et al., (2010, p.115) suggest that correlations above 0.5 was practically significant. The correlations among the three factors were all above 0.5, indicating the three-factor structure of the social support scale was desirable.

Table 6.6   Component Correlation Matrix for Social Support

Component	1	2	3
1	1.000	0.619	0.697
2	0.619	1.000	0.591
3	0.697	0.591	1.000

Extraction Method: Principal Axis Factoring.
Rotation Method: Promax with Kaiser Normalization.

6.2.2　Confirmatory Factor Analysis(CFA) of Social Support

6.2.2.1　Normality Test

Normality of the social support indicators are presented in Table 6.7. It can be observed that the absolute values of the skewness were lower than 2 and the absolute values of the kurtosis were lower than 7, thus indicating univariate normality. As noted earlier, the C.R. value of the multivariate kurtosis greater than 5 is regarded as indicative of departure from multivariate normality. It can be observed in Table 6.7 that the C.R. value of the multivariate kurtosis of the social support indicators was 49.433, indicating a significant departure from multivariate normality. Therefore, we used MLM method provided in Mplus 7.4 to estimate the confirmatory factor analysis(CFA) model of social support.

Table 6.7　Assessment of Normality of the Indicators of Social Support

Variable	Min	Max	Skewness	C.R.	Kurtosis	C.R.
ss14	1.000	9.000	− .851	− 6.971	.708	2.899
ss1	1.000	9.000	− .875	− 7.175	.759	3.109
ss15	1.000	9.000	− .823	− 6.747	.597	2.447
ss11	1.000	9.000	− .812	− 6.659	.274	1.121
ss7	1.000	9.000	− .768	− 6.292	.094	.384
ss13	1.000	9.000	− .570	− 4.672	.049	.202
ss10	1.000	9.000	− .751	− 6.157	− .041	− .168
ss3	1.000	9.000	− 1.254	− 10.275	1.478	6.059
ss2	1.000	9.000	− .961	− 7.879	.580	2.378
ss4	1.000	9.000	− .943	− 7.732	.678	2.779
ss12	2.000	9.000	− .676	− 5.538	.115	.472
ss9	1.000	9.000	− .698	− 5.719	.025	.102
ss6	1.000	9.000	− .786	− 6.443	.326	1.337
ss5	1.000	9.000	− .786	− 6.444	.579	2.371
Multivariate					104.240	49.433

6.2.2.2　First-order CFA of Social Support

In the previous section, an exploratory factor analysis(EFA) of social support was performed with a number of 300 samples randomly drawn from the total samples. Through EFA, three factors were extracted: emotional support, informational support and occupational support. 14 items were retained and were loaded on their corresponding factors. In this section, confirmatory factor analysis

(CFA) of social support was conducted using the second group of the samples (N = 403) to validate the factorial structure derived from EFA. The items of each factor were considered as the observed variables. A first-order CFA was constructed to examine whether these observed variables were well represented by their underlying sub-constructs, and whether the three sub-constructs were correlated(See Figure 6.6). Model fit of the first-order CFA model, construct reliability, convergent validity, and discriminant validity were examined. Then, a second-order CFA model of social support was constructed.

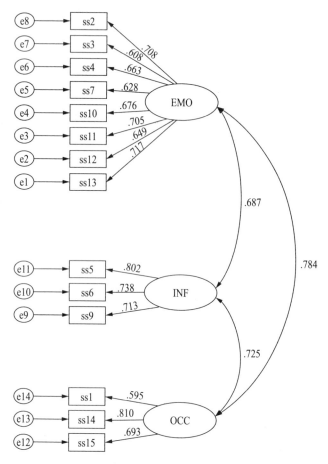

Figure 6.6   The First-order CFA Model of Social Support(Initial Model)

Parameter estimation. The parameter estimates of the social support indicators are reported in Table 6.8. The critical ratio(C. R.) of the

Table 6.8   Estimate Results of the Initial CFA Model of Social Support(First-order)

	Sig. test of parameters				Std.
	Unstd.	S.E.	C.R.	P	
Regression weights					
ss2 ← EMO	1				0.708
ss3 ← EMO	0.819	0.076	10.830	***	0.608
ss4 ← EMO	0.887	0.080	11.140	***	0.663
ss7 ← EMO	0.825	0.074	11.204	***	0.628
ss10 ← EMO	1.063	0.090	11.796	***	0.676
ss11 ← EMO	0.934	0.073	12.871	***	0.705
ss12 ← EMO	0.799	0.069	11.588	***	0.649
ss13 ← EMO	0.937	0.069	13.654	***	0.717
ss5 ← INF	1				0.802
ss6 ← INF	1.013	0.073	13.969	***	0.738
ss9 ← INF	1.048	0.076	13.745	***	0.713
ss1 ← OCC	1				0.595
ss14 ← OCC	1.339	0.125	10.743	***	0.810
ss15 ← OCC	1.204	0.132	9.112	***	0.693
Covariances					
INF ↔ EMO	1.224	0.167	7.343	***	0.687
OCC ↔ EMO	1.033	0.156	6.617	***	0.784
OCC ↔ INF	0.992	0.150	6.619	***	0.725
Variances					
EMO	1.713	0.239	7.158	***	1
OCC	1.850	0.245	7.545	***	1
INF	1.011	0.184	5.506	***	1
Residual Variances					
ss1	1.844	0.151	12.179	***	0.646
ss2	1.707	0.163	10.477	***	0.499
ss3	1.961	0.176	11.145	***	0.630
ss4	1.720	0.139	12.372	***	0.560
ss5	1.028	0.143	7.208	***	0.357
ss6	1.590	0.152	10.433	***	0.456
ss7	1.794	0.175	10.273	***	0.606
ss9	1.959	0.183	10.701	***	0.491
ss10	2.300	0.212	10.869	***	0.543
ss11	1.515	0.136	11.126	***	0.503
ss12	1.502	0.122	12.323	***	0.578
ss13	1.424	0.137	10.377	***	0.486
ss14	0.951	0.163	5.844	***	0.344
ss15	1.585	0.128	12.412	***	0.519

Note: *** p<0.001.

parameter estimates were all above 1.96, thereby indicating that parameter estimates were statistically significant($p < 0.001$). It confirmed that the observed variables could be explained by their associated factors. The standardized factor loadings of the indicators were all greater than 0.6, except ss1 who had a relatively lower loading(0.595) on its associated factor. Nine of the social support indicators had standardized factor loadings greater than 0.7, which was desirable.

Assessment of model fit. The three-factor first-order CFA model of social support was assessed to see whether it fitted the current data or not. The model fit indices reported by Mplus 7.4 are shown in Table 6.9. The Satorra-Bentler $\chi^2 = 100.992$, with $df = 74$. The Normed Chi-squared(χ^2/df) = 1.365, which was within the recommended range between 1 and 3(Hair et al., 2010). The RMSEA = 0.030, below the cutoff value of 0.06(Hu & Bentler, 1999). The SRMR = 0.036, which was below the cutoff value of 0.08(ibid). The TLI(NNFI) = 0.977, greater than the minimum level of 0.9(Hu & Bentler, 1999). The CFI = 0.982, which was above the lowest acceptable level of 0.09(Hu & Bentler, 1999). Based on the criteria of the recommended model fit indices, the initial first-order CFA model of social support yielded a good fit to the data.

Table 6.9   Model Fit of the Initial First-order CFA Model of Social Support

Model Fit Index	Criterion	Initial Model
Satorra-Bentler χ^2	smaller is better	100.992
df(Degree of Freedom)	bigger is better	74
Normed Chi-squared(χ^2/df)	$1 < \chi^2/df < 3$	1.365
RMSEA(90% confidence interval)	< 0.08	0.030[0.012, 0.044]
Pr(RMSEA $\leqslant$ 0.05)	bigger is better	0.993
SRMR	< 0.08	0.036
TLI(NNFI)	> 0.9	0.977
CFI	> 0.9	0.982

Note: Scaling correction factor for the initial modelis 1.555.

Reliability and validity test. The composite reliability and construct validity of the CFA model were tested to examine its internal structure. The Composite Reliability(CR) of the three factors were reported in Table 6.10. The CR values for the three factors ranged from 0.745 to 0.867. According to the common rule of thumb, CR values higher than 0.7 indicate that the CFA model is internally consistent(Hair et al., 2010). Therefore, the internal consistency of the three-factor model was confirmed.

Table 6.10 Reliability and Validity Test of the Initial CFA Model
of Social Support(First-order)

	CR	AVE	1	2	3
1. EMO	0.867	0.449	**0.670**		
2. INF	0.796	0.565	0.687	**0.752**	
3. OCC	0.745	0.497	0.784***	0.725***	**0.705**

Notes: 1. Square root of AVE in bold on diagonals.

2. Off diagonals are Pearson's correlation of constructs.

3. Significance of correlations: † $p < 0.100$, * $p < 0.050$, ** $p < 0.010$, *** $p < 0.001$.

The convergent validity of the CFA model was tested by examining the AVE(Average Variance Extract). As is shown in Table 6.10, the AVE values for the three factors were for 0.449, 0.565, and 0.497 respectively. Fornell and Larcker(1981) suggest that the lowest acceptable level of AVE is between 0.36 and 0.5. So, the convergent validity of the first-order CFA model of social support was confirmed.

The discriminant validity of the CFA model was tested by comparing the squared root of the AVE for the factor and its correlations with the other two factors. The factor correlation matrix is presented in Table 6.10. The diagonal items in the table represent the square roots of the AVE of the latent constructs, and the off diagonal items represent correlations among the three latent constructs. Fornell and Larcker(1981) suggest that the square root of the AVE for each construct should be greater than the correlation coefficients between it and any other construct. As is shown in Table 6.10, the square root of the AVE for emotional support did not exceed the correlation coefficients between emotional support and the other two constructs. Likewise, the square root of the AVE for occupational support did not exceed its correlation with each of the other two constructs. Therefore, the discriminant validity of the first-order CFA model of social support was not confirmed.

Given the lack of discriminant validity of the initial first-order CFA model of social support, there was need to consider deleting the indicators with low factor loadings, so as to improve the AVE for emotional and occupational support.

6.2.2.3　Model Modification of the First-order CFA Model of Social Support

As the initial first-order CFA model of social support violated discriminant validity, modifications were conducted to increase the internal consistency of the model. The author considered removing some indicators with low factor loadings, including ss1, ss3, ss4, ss7, and ss12. Test of multivariate normality, parameter estimation, and model evaluation were performed again after deleting the afore-mentioned variables.

Table 6.11　Assessment of Normality of the Remaining Indicators of Social Support

Variable	Min	Max	Skewness	CR	Kurtosis	C.R.
ss2	1	9	− 0.961	− 7.879	0.58	2.378
ss5	1	9	− 0.786	− 6.444	0.579	2.371
ss6	1	9	− 0.786	− 6.443	0.326	1.337
ss9	1	9	− 0.698	− 5.719	0.025	0.102
ss10	1	9	− 0.751	− 6.157	− 0.041	− 0.168
ss11	1	9	− 0.812	− 6.659	0.274	1.121
ss13	1	9	− 0.57	− 4.672	0.049	0.202
ss14	1	9	− 0.851	− 6.971	0.708	2.899
ss15	1	9	− 0.823	− 6.747	0.597	2.447
Multivariate					43.088	30.736

As is shown in Table 6.11, the C.R. value of the multivariate kurtosis of the variables was higher than 5, indicating that the social support indicators violated assumptions of multivariate normality. Therefore, MLM estimation in Mplus 7.4 was used to conduct parameter estimation.

Parameter estimation. Table 6.12 presents the parameter estimates of the modified CFA model of social support. The C.R. values of the parameter estimates were all greater than 1.96, suggesting a statistically significance of the parameter estimates. The standardized factor loadings of the indicators were all above 0.6, suggesting that the extracted factors well explained the indicators.

Table 6.12   Estimate Results of the Modified CFA Model
of Social Support(First-order)

	Unstd.	S.E.	C.R.	P	Std.
			Sig. test of parameters		
		Regression weights			
ss2 ← EMO	1				0.702
ss10 ← EMO	1.084	0.097	11.177	***	0.684
ss11 ← EMO	0.984	0.081	12.179	***	0.736
ss13 ← EMO	0.957	0.081	11.800	***	0.726
ss5 ← INF	1				0.796
ss6 ← INF	1.023	0.076	13.409	***	0.740
ss9 ← INF	1.062	0.081	13.142	***	0.718
ss14 ← OCC	1				0.787
ss15 ← OCC	0.979	0.082	11.904	***	0.733
		Covariances			
INF ↔ EMO	1.144	0.170	6.714	***	0.653
OCC ↔ EMO	1.206	0.163	7.381	***	0.709
OCC ↔ INF	1.286	0.164	7.853	***	0.728
		Variances			
EMO	1.686	0.255	6.607	***	1
OCC	1.824	0.249	7.315	***	1
INF	1.713	0.245	6.994	***	1
		Residual Variances			
ss2	1.734	0.169	10.238	***	0.507
ss5	1.054	0.148	7.131	***	0.366
ss6	1.579	0.169	9.371	***	0.453
ss9	1.933	0.188	10.256	***	0.484
ss10	2.255	0.225	10.026	***	0.533
ss11	1.379	0.139	9.937	***	0.458
ss13	1.384	0.169	8.185	***	0.473
ss14	1.053	0.185	5.690	***	0.381
ss15	1.411	0.140	10.107	***	0.462

Note: *** p<0.001.

Assessment of model fit. The fit indices of the modified model are reported in Table 6.13. The Satorra-Bentler χ^2 was 21.664. The df was 24. The Normed Chi-squared (χ^2/df) was 0.903, which was within the acceptable range between 1 and 3 (Hair et al., 2010). The RMSEA value and the SRMR value were 0.000 and 0.024 respectively, both of which were below the cutoff level of 0.08 (Hu & Bentler, 1999). The TLI(NNFI) value was 1.004 and the CFI value was 1.000, all above the lower limit of 0.9 (Hu & Bentler, 1999). According to the criteria, the modified model revealed a good fit as evidenced by its fit indices.

Table 6.13   Model Fit of the Modified First-order CFA Model of Social Support

Model Fit Index	Criterion	Initial Model	Modified Model
Satorra-Bentler χ^2	smaller is better	100.992	21.664
df (Degree of Freedom)	bigger is better	74	24
Normed Chi-squared (χ^2/df)	$1<\chi^2/df<3$	1.365	0.903
RMSEA (90% confidence interval)	<0.08	0.030 [0.012, 0.044]	0.000 [0.000, 0.036]
Pr(RMSEA $\leqslant$ 0.05)	bigger is better	0.993	0.996
SRMR	<0.08	0.036	0.024
TLI(NNFI)	>0.9	0.977	1.004
CFI	>0.9	0.982	1.000

Note: Scaling correction factor for the modified model is 1.5743.

Reliability and validity test. The reliability and validity of the modified first-order CFA model of social support were tested. The Composite Reliability (CR) values of the latent constructs are shown in Table 6.14. The CR values of the three factors were all above the cutoff value of 0.7 (Hair et al., 2010), suggesting that the first-order CFA model of social support had a good composite reliability.

The Average Variance Extracted (AVE) values of the three sub-constructs of social support are presented in Table 6.14. The AVE values of the three sub-constructs were all above 0.5, demonstrating the convergent validity of the first-order CFA model of social support. Besides, the square root of the AVE for each latent

Table 6.14   Reliability and Validity Test of the Modified CFA Model of
Social Support(First-order)

	CR	AVE	1	2	3
1. EMO	0.805	0.507	**0.712**		
2. INF	0.796	0.566	0.709 ***	**0.752**	
3. OCC	0.733	0.579	0.653 ***	0.728 ***	**0.761**

Notes: 1. Square root of AVE in bold on diagonals.
2. Off diagonals are Pearson's correlation of constructs.
3. Significance of correlations: † p<0.100, * p<0.050, ** p<0.010, *** p<0.001.

construct was higher than its correlation coefficient with any of the other two constructs. As a result, the discriminant validity of the first-order CFA model of social support was confirmed. After the modification of the first-order CFA model of social support, the final model is presented in Figure 6.7.

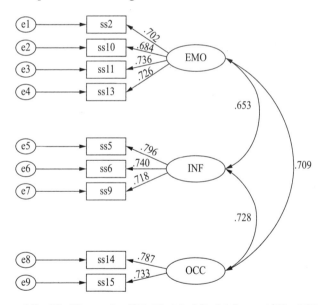

Figure 6.7   The First-order CFA Model of Social Support(Final Model)

6.2.2.4   The Second-order CFA of Social Support

A second-order CFA is to uncover whether the interrelated first-order constructs could be explained by a higher order construct. In order to have a more parsimonious structure of social support indicators, a second-order CFA was conducted using Mplus 7.4

to derive a second-order factor of general social support among the
three interrelated factors: emotional support, informational support, and occupational support. The second-order CFA model of social support is presented in Figure 6.8.

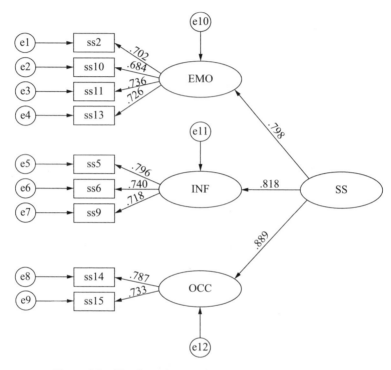

Figure 6.8   The Second-order CFA Model of Social Support

Parameter estimation. The parameter estimates of the second-
order CFA model are reported in Table 6.15. As the critical ratio
(C.R.) values of the parameter estimates were greater than 5, it indicated that the parameter estimates were statistically significant
(p<.001). The standardized factor loadings of the three sub-constructs were all above 0.7, indicating adequate construct reliability.
The SMC(squared multiple correlations)[1] values of the three sub-
constructs of social support(emotional support, informational sup-

---

    [1]   SMC(squared multiple correlations) refers to the "values representing the extent
to which a measured variable's variance is explained by a latent factor"(Hair et al., 2010,
p.602).

port, and occupational support) were all above 0.5, indicating that the variance-extracted of the sub-constructs explained by the second-order factor was more than 50 percent.

Table 6.15   Estimate Results of the Second-order CFA Model of Social Support

| Construct | Sub-construct | Sig. test of parameters | | | | Std. | Item reliability |
		Unstd.	S.E.	C.R.	P		SMC
SS	EMO	1				0.798	0.636
	INF	1.067	0.114	9.354	***	0.818	0.791
	OCC	1.124	0.133	8.480	***	0.889	0.669

Model fit. The model fit indices of the second-order CFA model of social support are presented in Table 6.16. The Satorra-Bentler χ^2 was 21.664, with $df = 24$. The Normed Chi-squared(χ^2/df) = 0.903, which was within the recommended range between 1 and 3 (Hair et al., 2010). The RMSEA was 0.000, which was well below the cutoff value of 0.08(Hu & Bentler, 1999). The SRMR was 0.024, which was below the cutoff value of 0.08(Hu & Bentler, 1999). The TLI(NNFI) was 1.004, which was greater than the recommended cutoff value of 0.9(Hu & Bentler, 1999). The CFI was 1.000, higher than the recommended cutoff value of 0.9 (Hu & Bentler, 1999). Based on the recommended criteria of model fit indices, the results showed that the second-order CFA model of social support yielded a good fit to the data.

Table 6.16   Model Fit of the Second-order CFA Model of Social Support

Model Fit Index	Criterion	Research Model
Satorra-Bentler χ^2	smaller is better	21.664
df(Degree of Freedom)	bigger is better	24
Normed Chi-squared(χ^2/df)	$1<\chi^2/df<3$	0.903
RMSEA(90% confidence interval)	<0.08	0.000[0.000, 0.036]
Pr(RMSEA $\leqslant$ 0.05)	bigger is better	0.996
SRMR	<0.08	0.024
TLI(NNFI)	>0.9	1.004
CFI	>0.9	1.000

Notes: 1. Scaling correction factor for the research model is 1.5743.
2. p-Value of the Chi-Squared is 0.5993.

6.3   Measuring Social Media Use

Using the second group of samples（N = 403）, the author conducted a confirmatory factor analysis（CFA） of social media use to
validate the structure of social media use measurements. Test
of multivariate normality, parameter estimation, model fit assessment, and test of reliability and validity of the model were
conducted.

6.3.1   Normality Test

The normality of the variables of social media use is shown in
Table 6.17. It can be observed that the absolute values of the skewness were lower than 2 and the absolute values of the kurtosis were
lower than 7, thus indicating univariate normality. However, the
multivariate normality of the social media use indicators was violated, as evidenced by the C. R.（critical ratio） value of the multivariate kurtosis higher than 5. Therefore, the MLM estimation method
in Mplus 7.4 was used to estimate the parameters.

Table 6.17   Assessment of Normality of Social Media Use Indicators

Variable	Min	Max	Skewness	C.R.	Kurtosis	C.R.
smu6	1	9	− 1.422	− 11.657	2.216	9.079
smu1	1	9	− 1.414	− 11.59	2.47	10.121
smu2	1	9	− 1	− 8.199	0.695	2.849
smu3	1	9	− 0.642	− 5.264	0	0
smu4	1	9	− 0.639	− 5.236	0.087	0.355
smu5	1	9	− 0.855	− 7.005	0.37	1.518
Multivariate					16.585	16.99

6.3.2   Initial CFA Model of Social Media Use

Parameter estimation. The parameter estimates of the social
media use variables are presented in Table 6.18. The C.R. values of
the parameter estimates were all greater than 1.96, suggesting that

the parameters were statistically significant (p<0.001).

Table 6.18   Estimate Results of the Initial CFA Model of Social Media Use

	Sig. test of parameters				Std.
	Unstd.	S.E.	C.R.	P	
Regression weights					
smu1 ←- SMU	1				0.611
smu2 ←- SMU	1.072	0.141	7.611	***	0.526
smu3 ←- SMU	1.099	0.157	6.989	***	0.612
smu4 ←- SMU	0.958	0.154	6.223	***	0.486
smu5 ←- SMU	1.086	0.158	6.878	***	0.542
smu6 ←- SMU	1.033	0.121	8.511	***	0.636
Variances					
SMU	0.875	0.223	3.916	***	1.000
Residual Variances					
smu1	1.472	0.157	9.361	***	0.627
smu2	2.632	0.269	9.792	***	0.724
smu3	1.763	0.159	11.057	***	0.625
smu4	2.593	0.208	12.469	***	0.763
smu5	2.481	0.206	12.070	***	0.706
smu6	1.375	0.192	7.176	***	0.596

Note: *** p<0.001.

However, the factor loadings of the social media use variables were all below 0.7, which was not desirable. The factor loading of smu4 was below 0.5. It indicated that the indicators were not well explained by the latent factor.

Assessment of model fit. The model fit indices of the initial CFA model of social media use are reported in Table 6.19. According to the criteria of model fit evaluation, the measurement model did not fit the data well. The Normed Chi-squared (χ^2/df) was above the cutoff level of 3(Hair et al., 2010). The RMSEA value was greater than the threshold value of 0.08(Hu & Bentler, 1999). The TLI (NNFI) was smaller than the cutoff value of 0.9(Hu & Bentler, 1999).

Table 6.19   Model Fit of the Initial CFA Model of Social Media Use

Model Fit Index	Criterion	Initial Model
Satorra-Bentler χ^2	smaller is better	32.508
df(Degree of Freedom)	bigger is better	9
Normed Chi-squared(χ^2/df)	$1<\chi^2/df<3$	3.612
RMSEA(90% confidence interval)	<0.08	0.081[0.052, 0.111]
Pr(RMSEA $\leqslant$ 0.05)	bigger is better	0.041
SRMR	<0.08	0.044
TLI(NNFI)	>0.9	0.879
CFI	>0.9	0.927

Note: Scaling correction factor for the initial model is 1.3030.

Reliability and validity test. The composite reliability(CR) and the convergent validity of the CFA model of social media use were tested. The CR of the CFA model of social media use was 0.742, which was above the cutoff value of 0.7(Hair et al., 2010) and thus indicating good reliability of the CFA model. However, the AVE value was 0.326, which was below the recommended cutoff value of 0.36(Fornell & Larcker, 1981). Therefore, the convergent validity of the measurement model was not confirmed.

6.3.3   Model Modification

Given the poor model fit and the lack of convergent validity, the author considered deleting a few indicators with low factor loadings to modify the CFA model of social media use. After deleting ss4 and ss5, the parameter estimation was conducted again. As is shown in Table 6.20, the critical ratio(C.R.) of the parameter estimates were all greater than 5, indicating the statistical significance of the parameters($p<0.001$). The factor loadings of the retained indicators were all above 0.5, showing that the indicators of social media use can be explained by the latent variable. The modified model was reevaluated for their goodness of fit after deleting one indicator each time.

Table 6.20   Estimate Results of the Modified CFA Model of Social Media Use

	Sig. test of parameters				Std.
	Unstd.	S.E.	C.R.	P	
	Regression weights				
smu1 ← SMU	1				0.691
smu2 ← SMU	1.050	0.137	7.655	***	0.583
smu3 ← SMU	0.857	0.125	6.845	***	0.540
smu6 ← SMU	0.863	0.105	8.227	***	0.601
	Variances				
SMU	1.121	0.248	4.514	***	1.000
	Residual Variances				
smu1	1.226	0.175	7.004	***	0.522
smu2	2.401	0.285	8.430	***	0.660
smu3	1.997	0.194	10.284	***	0.708
smu6	1.474	0.200	7.377	***	0.638

Note: *** $p < 0.001$.

Table 6.21   Model Fit of the Modified CFA Model of Social Media Use

Model Fit Index	Criterion	Initial Model	Modified Model
Satorra-Bentler χ^2	smaller is better	32.508	1.216
df(Degree of Freedom)	bigger is better	9	2
Normed Chi-squared(χ^2/df)	$1 < \chi^2/df < 3$	3.612	0.608
RMSEA (90% confidence interval)	< 0.08	0.081 [0.052, 0.111]	0.000 [0.000, 0.085]
Pr(RMSEA $\leqslant$ 0.05)	bigger is better	0.041	0.783
SRMR	< 0.08	0.044	0.010
TLI(NNFI)	> 0.9	0.879	1.013
CFI	> 0.9	0.927	1.000

Note: Scaling correction factor for the modified model is 1.2406.

The model fit indices of the modified model are presented in Table 6.21. Based on the criteria of the fit indices, the modified model revealed a good fit to the data. The composite reliability (CR) value of the model was 0.698. According to Fornell and Larcker(1981), a CR value higher than 0.7 is adequate, and a CR value between 0.6 and 0.7 is acceptable. The AVE value of the model was 0.368, which was above the lowest acceptable level of 0.36 (Fornell & Larcker, 1981). Thus, the convergent validity of the CFA model of social media use was confirmed. After the model modification, the final model is presented in Figure 6.9.

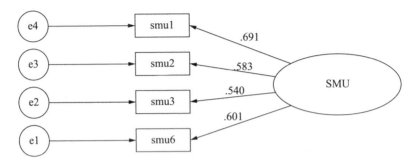

Figure 6.9   The Final CFA Model of Social Media Use

6.4   Measuring Acculturative Stress

Acculturative Stress is a multi-dimensional construct. Building on the literature review, the research identified four sub-constructs of acculturative stress of internal migrants in Shanghai: perceived discrimination(PD), homesickness(HS), cultural discomfort(CD) and economic strain(ES).

In this section, confirmatory factor analysis(CFA) of acculturative stress was conducted. First, a first-order CFA was conducted to validate the factorial structure of the four sub-constructs of acculturative stress(perceived discrimination, homesickness, cultural discomfort, and economic strain). Then, a second-order CFA was conducted to derive a higher-order construct of acculturative stress.

6.4.1   Normality Test

The normality of the acculturative stress indicators is presented in Table 6.22. It can be observed that the absolute values of the skewness were lower than 2 and the absolute values of the kurtosis were lower than 7, thus indicating univariate normality. As is shown in Table 6.21, the C.R. values of multivariate kurtosis of acculturative stress was 25.758, which was higher than the cutoff value of 5. It showed that the indicators of acculturative stress departed from multivariate normality. Thus, the MLM estimation method in Mplus 7.4 was used to estimate the parameters.

Table 6.22   Assessment of Normality of the Indicators of Acculturative Stress

Variable	Min	Max	Skewness	C.R.	Kurtosis	C.R.
as1	1	9	− 0.047	− 0.389	− 0.628	− 2.572
as2	1	9	− 0.177	− 1.454	− 0.877	− 3.595
as3	1	9	0.168	1.38	− 0.765	− 3.135
as4	1	9	0.228	1.87	− 0.715	− 2.93
as5	1	9	− 0.106	− 0.865	− 1.014	− 4.155
as6	1	9	0.136	1.115	− 0.881	− 3.61
as7	1	9	0.052	0.43	− 0.927	− 3.798
as8	1	9	0.201	1.644	− 0.794	− 3.252
as9	1	9	− 0.79	− 6.471	0.145	0.593
as10	1	9	− 0.136	− 1.118	− 0.847	− 3.469
as11	1	9	0.446	3.657	− 0.88	− 3.607
as12	1	9	0.354	2.899	− 0.704	− 2.885
as13	1	9	0.315	2.583	− 1.003	− 4.111
as14	1	9	− 0.004	− 0.033	− 0.901	− 3.692
as15	1	9	0.059	0.48	− 1.176	− 4.817
as16	1	9	− 0.8	− 6.559	− 0.22	− 0.9
as17	1	9	0.389	3.188	− 0.739	− 3.027
as18	1	9	− 0.166	− 1.363	− 0.814	− 3.336
Multivariate					68.859	25.758

6.4.2   First-order CFA of Acculturative Stress

Based on the previous literature, the author first specified a four-factor fist-order CFA model of acculturative stress using the second group of samples(N = 403), which involved four sub-constructs: perceived discrimination(PD), homesickness(HS), cultural discomfort(CD), and economic strain(ES).

6.4.2.1   Parameter Estimation

The parameter estimates of the first-order CFA model of acculturative stress are reported in Table 6.23. It can be observed that the C.R. values of the parameter estimates were all above 1.96, suggesting that parameters were statistically significant(p<0.001). The standardized factor loadings of most variables were high, but a few items had low factor loadings. For example, as17 had a factor loading of 0.272, which was much lower than the lowest acceptable level of 0.4.

Table 6.23   Estimate Results of the Initial CFA Model of Acculturative Stress

	Sig. test of parameters				Std.
	Unstd.	S.E.	C.R.	P	
Regression weights					
as1 ← PD	1.000				0.786
as2 ← PD	1.008	0.054	18.681	***	0.752
as3 ← PD	1.141	0.057	19.907	***	0.857
as4 ← PD	1.075	0.060	17.942	***	0.821
as5 ← PD	1.042	0.063	16.674	***	0.725
as6 ← PD	1.119	0.072	15.477	***	0.776
as7 ← HS	1.000				0.778
as8 ← HS	0.954	0.051	18.692		0.784
as9 ← HS	0.613	0.056	11.006	***	0.561
as10 ← HS	0.895	0.059	15.077	***	0.729
as11 ← CD	1.000				0.648
as12 ← CD	1.047	0.072	14.556	***	0.761
as13 ← CD	1.004	0.083	12.129	***	0.639
as14 ← CD	0.705	0.080	8.787	***	0.497
as15 ← ES	1.000				0.891
as16 ← ES	0.490	0.066	7.378	***	0.485
as17 ← ES	0.272	0.058	4.671		0.266
as18 ← ES	0.510	0.065	7.896	***	0.493
Variances					
PD	2.577	0.245	10.520	***	1.000
HS	3.201	0.323	9.924	***	1.000
CD	2.302	0.287	8.006	***	1.000
ES	4.957	0.581	8.533	***	1.000
Covariances					
PD ↔ HS	1.360	0.182	7.476	***	0.474
PD ↔ CD	1.643	0.177	9.286	***	0.675
PD ↔ ES	1.046	0.215	4.867	***	0.293
HS ↔ CD	1.401	0.182	7.684	***	0.516
HS ↔ ES	1.630	0.258	6.312	***	0.409
CD ↔ ES	1.448	0.234	6.192	***	0.429

continued

	Sig. test of parameters				Std.
	Unstd.	S.E.	C.R.	P	
	Residual Variances				
as1	1.589	0.148	10.766	***	0.382
as2	2.011	0.166	12.140	***	0.435
as3	1.217	0.120	10.130	***	0.266
as4	1.444	0.127	11.398	***	0.327
as5	2.521	0.200	12.580	***	0.474
as6	2.134	0.222	9.631	***	0.398
as7	2.086	0.247	8.432	***	0.394
as8	1.826	0.170	10.729	***	0.385
as9	2.624	0.206	12.726	***	0.685
as10	2.259	0.205	10.999	***	0.469
as11	3.174	0.276	11.508	***	0.580
as12	1.839	0.224	8.206	***	0.422
as13	3.361	0.294	11.431	***	0.592
as14	3.489	0.236	14.777	***	0.753
as15	1.283	0.509	2.518	**	0.206
as16	3.872	0.264	14.692	***	0.765
as17	4.812	0.269	17.887	***	0.929
as18	4.018	0.290	13.868	***	0.757

Note: ** $p < 0.05$, *** $p < 0.001$.

6.4.2.2   Assessment of Model Fit

The model fit indices of the first-order CFA model of acculturative stress are reported in Table 6.24. The Satorra-Bentler χ^2 value was 263.331 with 129 degree of freedom. The Normed Chi-squared (χ^2/df) was 2.041. The RMSEA was 0.051, which was below the cutoff value of 0.08 (Hair et al., 2010). The SRMR was 0.055, which was below the cutoff level of 0.08 (Hu & Bentler, 1999). The TLI(NNFI) was 0.934, greater than the cutoff value of 0.9 (Hu & Bentler, 1999). The CFI was 0.944, which was above the recommended cutoff value of 0.9 (Hu & Bentler, 1999). Based on the criteria of the model fit indices (see Table 6.24), the four-factor first-order model provided a good fit to the data.

Table 6.24   Model Fit of the Initial First-order CFA Model of Acculturative Stress

Model Fit Index	Criterion	Initial Model
Satorra-Bentler χ^2	smaller is better	263.331
df(Degree of Freedom)	bigger is better	129
Normed Chi-squared(χ^2/df)	$1<\chi^2/df<3$	2.041
RMSEA(90% confidence interval)	<0.08	0.051[0.042, 0.060]
Pr(RMSEA $\leqslant$ 0.05)	bigger is better	0.426
SRMR	<0.08	0.055
TLI(NNFI)	>0.9	0.934
CFI	>0.9	0.944

Note: Scaling correction factor for the initial model is 1.2357.

6.4.2.3   Reliability and Validity Test

The composite reliability(CR) was calculated to test the internal reliability of the four-factor CFA model of acculturative stress. According to the common rule of thumb, a CR value greater than 0.7 is considered adequate for the internal reliability of the measurement model, and a CR value between 0.6 to 0.7 is the lowest acceptable level(Fornell & Larcker, 1981). It is observed from Table 6.24 that the CR values of the four sub-constructs(PD, HS, CD, and ES) were all above 0.6, suggesting that the model was internally reliable.

The convergent validity of the first-order CFA model of acculturative stress was examined by computing the Average Variance Extracted(AVE) values of the four sub-constructs(PD, HS, CD, and ES). An AVE value greater than 0.5 is considered adequate to confirm the convergent validity and a value between 0.36 and 0.5 was considered the lowest acceptable level confirm the convergent validity(Fornell & Larcker, 1981). As can be seen from Table 6.25, the AVE value for economic strain was 0.31, less than the acceptable level of 0.36. It thus indicated that the sub-construct of economic strain did not explain its indicators well.

The discriminant validity of the initial first-order measurement model was examined by comparing the square root of AVE for each sub-construct and the correlation coefficients between it and any other sub-construct. As is shown in Table 6.25, the square root of the AVE for cultural discomfort was less than its correlation with perceived discrimination, indicating a lack of discriminant validity of the first-order CFA model of acculturative stress. Thus, in order to increase the discriminant validity of the first-order CFA model, the initial model needed to be modified by deleting the observed variables with low factor loadings.

Table 6.25   Reliability and Validity Test of the Initial CFA Model
of Acculturative Stress(First-order)

	CR	AVE	PD	HS	CD	ES
Perceived Discrimination (PD)	0.907	0.620	**0.787**			
Homesickness(HS)	0.808	0.517	0.474	**0.719**		
Cultural Discomfort(CD)	0.734	0.413	0.675***	0.516***	**0.643**	
Economic Strain(ES)	0.632	0.336	0.293***	0.409***	0.429***	**0.579**

Notes: 1. Square root of AVE in bold on diagonals.
2. Off diagonals are Pearson's correlation of constructs.

6.4.2.4   Model Modification

Based on the analysis mentioned above, the initial model was modified by deleting items with low factor loadings(as15 and as17). Besides, the model modification indices suggested a covariance of the standard errors between as9 and as10 be added, which would result in a decrease of 29.401 of Satorra-Bentler χ^2. Given that both as9("I miss my hometown and the people at my hometown.") and as10("I feel sad leaving my relatives behind.") were concerned with nostalgia, it was reasonable that the two variables had a covariance. Therefore, an error covariance between as9 and as10 was added.

Parameter estimation. After the model modification, the parameters were estimated again. It can be observed from Table 6.26

that the C.R. values of the factor loadings were above 5, which was indicative of the statistically significance of the factor loadings (p<0.001). The factor loadings were all above the cutoff level of 0.4, suggesting that the indicators can be explained by the latent factors.

Table 6.26   Estimate Results of the Final First-order CFA Model
of Acculturative Stress

	Sig. test of parameters				Std.
	Unstd.	S.E.	C.R.	P	
Regression weights					
as1 ← PD	1.000				0.786
as2 ← PD	1.007	0.055	18.178	***	0.751
as3 ← PD	1.142	0.057	19.890	***	0.857
as4 ← PD	1.077	0.060	18.023	***	0.821
as5 ← PD	1.043	0.063	16.506	***	0.725
as6 ← PD	1.119	0.071	15.680	***	0.776
as7 ← HS	1.000				0.761
as8 ← HS	1.034	0.057	18.062		0.831
as9 ← HS	0.533	0.059	9.050	***	0.476
as10 ← HS	0.847	0.063	13.375	***	0.675
as11 ← CD	1.000				0.665
as12 ← CD	1.046	0.076	13.850	***	0.779
as13 ← CD	0.950	0.081	11.684	***	0.620
as15 ← ES	1.000				0.872
as16 ← ES	0.500	0.073	6.848	***	0.484
as18 ← ES	0.534	0.069	7.715	***	0.505
Variances					
PD	2.574	0.251	10.258	***	1.000
HS	3.061	0.321	9.535	***	1.000
CD	2.418	0.310	7.796	***	1.000
ES	4.748	0.600	7.908	***	1.000
Covariances					
PD ↔ HS	1.407	0.185	7.585	***	0.501
PD ↔ CD	1.662	0.185	8.986	***	0.666
PD ↔ ES	1.069	0.218	4.907	***	0.306
HS ↔ CD	1.456	0.189	7.708	***	0.535
HS ↔ ES	1.694	0.252	6.709	***	0.444
CD ↔ ES	1.412	0.241	5.862	***	0.417
as9 ↔ as10	0.956	0.190	5.024	***	0.343

continued

	Sig. test of parameters				Std.
	Unstd.	S.E.	C.R.	P	
	Residual Variances				
as1	1.592	0.149	10.722	***	0.382
as2	2.019	0.168	12.047	***	0.436
as3	1.213	0.119	10.167	***	0.265
as4	1.438	0.125	11.458	***	0.325
as5	2.522	0.200	12.595	***	0.474
as6	2.136	0.231	9.257	***	0.398
as7	2.225	0.238	9.353	***	0.421
as8	1.468	0.179	8.217	***	0.310
as9	2.959	0.211	14.026	***	0.773
as10	2.627	0.249	10.540	***	0.545
as11	3.058	0.284	10.761	***	0.558
as12	1.714	0.244	7.038	***	0.393
as13	3.497	0.295	11.841	***	0.616
as15	1.492	0.527	2.832	**	0.239
as16	3.874	0.285	13.593	***	0.765
as18	3.957	0.294	13.479	***	0.745

Note: ** $p < 0.01$, *** $p < 0.001$.

Assessment of model fit. To determine how well the modified model represented the data, model fit was examined. Table 6.27 reports the model fit indices of the modified model. According to the criteria of model fit indices, the final first-order CFA model of acculturative stress exhibited a good fit: The Satorra-Bentler χ^2 was 187.643, with the $df = 97$. The Normed Chi-squared (χ^2/df) was 1.934. The RMSEA was 0.048. The SRMR was 0.044. The TLI (NNFI) was 0.951. The CFI was 0.961. The model fit indices of the final model improved compared with those of the initial model, which indicated that the final model better represented the data.

Reliability and validity test. The composite reliability(CR) of the modified model was examined. As is shown in Table 6.27, the CR values of the four sub-constructs(PD, HS, CD, and EC) were all above the benchmark of 0.6(Fornell & Larcker, 1981), thus demonstrating the internal consistency of the modified model.

Table 6.27   Model Fit of the Final First-order CFA Model of Acculturative Stress

Model Fit Index	Criterion	Initial Model	Final Model
Satorra-Bentler χ^2	smaller is better	263.331	187.643
df (Degree of Freedom)	bigger is better	129	97
Normed Chi-squared (χ^2/df)	$1 < \chi^2/df < 3$	2.041	1.934
RMSEA (90% confidence interval)	<0.08	0.051 [0.042, 0.060]	0.048 [0.038, 0.058]
Pr(RMSEA $\leqslant$ 0.05)	bigger is better	0.426	0.602
SRMR	<0.08	0.055	0.044
TLI(NNFI)	>0.9	0.934	0.951
CFI	>0.9	0.944	0.961

Note: Scaling correction factor for the final model is 1.2448.

The convergent validity of the modified model was examined by calculating the AVE values of the four sub-constructs. As is seen from Table 6.28, the AVE value of PD(perceived discrimination) was above 0.6. The AVE values of the three sub-constructs(HS, CD, and ES) were below 0.5 but above the lowest acceptable level of 0.36(Fornell & Larcker, 1981). Thus, the convergent validity of the first-order CFA model of acculturative stress was confirmed.

Table 6.28   Reliability and Validity Test of the Final CFA Model of Acculturative Stress(First-order)

	CR	AVE	PD	HS	CD	ES
Perceived Discrimination (PD)	0.907	0.620	**0.787**			
Homesickness(HS)	0.786	0.488	0.501	**0.698**		
Cultural Discomfort(CD)	0.731	0.478	0.666 ***	0.535 ***	**0.691**	
Economic Strain(ES)	0.664	0.417	0.306 ***	0.444 ***	0.417 ***	**0.646**

Note: 1. Square root of AVE in bold on diagonals.
2. Off diagonals are Pearson's correlation of constructs.
3. Significance of correlations: † p<0.100, * p<0.050, ** p<0.010, *** p< 0.001.

The discriminant validity of the modified model was examined by comparing the square root of AVE for each construct and the correlations between it and any other sub-construct. It can be observed from Table 6.28 that the square root of AVE for each sub-construct was above the correlation between it and any other sub-construct. Therefore, it is concluded that the final first-order CFA model of acculturative stress demonstrated discriminant validity. After the modification of the first-order CFA model of acculturative stress, the final model is presented in Figure 6.10.

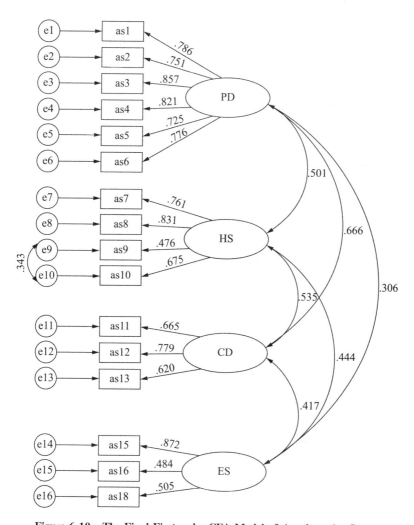

Figure 6.10   The Final First-order CFA Model of Acculturative Stress

6.4.3 Second-order CFA of Acculturative Stress

In this section, a second-order confirmatory factor analysis(CFA) was performed to develop a single second-order factor of acculturative stress. The second-order CFA included four first-order latent factors: perceived discrimination (PD), homesickness (HS) culture discomfort (CD), and economic strain(EC) (See Figure 6.11). The second-order CFA model was tested for its statistical significance, model fit, reliability, and validity.

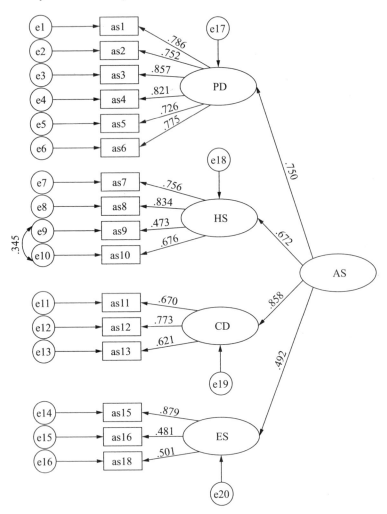

Figure 6.11   The Second-order CFA Model of Acculturative Stress

Parameter estimation. The parameter estimates of the second-order CFA model are reported in Table 6.29. It can be observed that the C.R. values of the parameter estimates were all above 1.96, which suggested that the parameters were statistically significant ($p<0.001$). Most of the factor loadings of the indicators were above 0.6, and a few were below 0.6 but above the cutoff level of 0.4. It suggested that the indicators can be explained by their correspondent sub-constructs, and the sub-constructs can be explained by the second-order construct of acculturative stress.

Table 6.29 Estimate Results of the Second-Order CFA Model of Acculturative Stress

	Sig. test of parameters				Std.
	Unstd.	S.E.	C.R.	P	
	Regression weights				
as1 ←- PD	1.000				0.786
as2 ←- PD	1.008	0.056	18.117	***	0.752
as3 ←- PD	1.142	0.058	19.836	***	0.857
as4 ←- PD	1.076	0.060	17.844	***	0.821
as5 ←- PD	1.044	0.063	16.555	***	0.726
as6 ←- PD	1.117	0.072	15.550	***	0.775
as7 ←- HS	1.000				0.756
as8 ←- HS	1.045	0.059	17.674	***	0.834
as9 ←- HS	0.532	0.060	8.882	***	0.473
as10 ←- HS	0.854	0.064	13.297	***	0.676
as11 ←- CD	1.000				0.670
as12 ←- CD	1.030	0.075	13.807	***	0.773
as13 ←- CD	0.944	0.080	11.734	***	0.621
as15 ←- ES	1.000				0.879
as16 ←- ES	0.493	0.075	6.603	***	0.481
as18 ←- ES	0.526	0.071	7.401	***	0.501
PD ←- AS	1.000				0.750
HS ←- AS	0.970	0.104	9.340	***	0.672
CD ←- AS	1.116	0.131	8.530	***	0.858
ES ←- AS	0.896	0.128	7.016	***	0.492
	Variances				
PD	1.449	0.226	6.416	***	1.000
	Covariances				
as9 ←→ as10	0.964	0.191	5.059	***	0.345

continued

	Sig. test of parameters				Std.
	Unstd.	S.E.	C.R.	P	
Residual Variances					
as1	1.591	0.148	10.722	***	0.382
as2	2.011	0.168	11.994	***	0.435
as3	1.216	0.119	10.186	***	0.266
as4	1.442	0.126	11.462	***	0.326
as5	2.512	0.200	12.561	***	0.472
as6	2.145	0.232	9.248	***	0.400
as7	2.265	0.236	9.584	***	0.429
as8	1.440	0.181	7.972	***	0.304
as9	2.971	0.212	14.034	***	0.776
as10	2.621	0.249	10.509	***	0.543
as11	3.020	0.285	10.600	***	0.552
as12	1.757	0.242	7.249	***	0.403
as13	3.490	0.296	11.801	***	0.615
as15	1.420	0.558	2.545	*	0.228
as16	3.888	0.291	13.360	***	0.768
as18	3.978	0.297	13.376	***	0.749
PD	1.126	0.198	5.689	***	0.437
HS	1.656	0.253	6.552	***	0.548
CD	0.650	0.239	2.717	**	0.265
ES	3.606	0.625	5.806	***	0.758

Note: *** $p<0.001$, ** $p<0.01$, * $p<0.05$.

Assessment of model fit. The model fit indices of the second-order CFA model of acculturative stress are reported in Table 6.30. The Satorra-Bentler χ^2 was 197.274. The df (Degree of Freedom) was 99. The Normed Chi-squared (χ^2/df) was 1.993. The RMSEA was 0.50, lower than the cutoff value of 0.08. The SRMR was 0.048, which was below the cutoff level of 0.08. And the TLI value and the CFA value were all above the cutoff level of 0.9. Based on the criteria of model fit indices, the second order CFA model exhibited a good fit to the data.

Table 6.30   Model Fit of the Second-order CFA Model of Acculturative Stress

Model Fit Index	Criterion	Initial Model
Satorra-Bentler χ^2	smaller is better	197.274
df(Degree of Freedom)	bigger is better	99
Normed Chi-squared(χ^2/df)	$1<\chi^2/df<3$	1.993
RMSEA(90% confidence interval)	<0.08	0.050[0.039, 0.060]
Pr(RMSEA$\leqslant$0.05)	bigger is better	0.509
SRMR	<0.08	0.048
TLI(NNFI)	>0.9	0.948
CFI	>0.9	0.957

Note: Scaling correction factor for the Second-Order CFA model is 1.2432.

Reliability and validity test. The reliability and validity of the second-order measurement model of acculturative stress was tested. As can be observed from Table 6.31, the Composite Reliability (CR) of the first-order sub-constructs were all above 0.6(Fornell & Larcker, 1981), indicating the internal consistence of the second-order CFA model of acculturative stress.

Table 6.31   Reliability and Validity Test of the Second-order CFA Model of Acculturative Stress

Construct	Indicator/ Sub-construct	Std.	Item reliability	Constructive reliability	Convergent Validity
			SMC	CR	AVE
PD	as1	0.786	0.618	0.907	0.62
	as2	0.752	0.566		
	as4	0.857	0.734		
	as5	0.821	0.674		
	as6	0.726	0.527		
HS	as7	0.775	0.601	0.785	0.487
	as8	0.756	0.572		
	as9	0.834	0.696		
	as10	0.473	0.224		
CD	as11	0.676	0.457	0.731	0.477
	as12	0.67	0.449		
	as13	0.773	0.598		

continued

Construct	Indicator/Sub-construct	Std.	Item reliability	Constructive reliability	Convergent Validity
			SMC	CR	AVE
ES	as15	0.621	0.386	0.665	0.418
	as16	0.879	0.773		
	as18	0.481	0.231		
AS	PD	0.501	0.251	0.793	0.498
	HS	0.75	0.563		
	CD	0.672	0.452		
	ES	0.858	0.736		

The convergent validity of the measurement model of acculturative stress was tested by calculating the AVE of the sub-constructs. As is shown in Table 6.31, the AVE values of the sub-constructs were all above the lowest acceptable value of 0.36 (Fornell & Larcker, 1981), thus confirming the convergent validity of the second-order CFA model of acculturative stress.

6.5   Measuring Local Cultural Identification

This section is focused on the first-order CFA of local cultural identification. First, the test of multivariate normality was confirmed. Second, the parameters were estimated. Third, the model fit was evaluated. Last, the reliability and validity of the CFA model were tested. Last, the model was modified and the final model was developed.

6.5.1 Normality Test

The normality of the indicators of local cultural identification is presented in Table 6.32. It can be observed that the absolute values of the skewness were lower than 2 and the absolute values of the kurtosis were lower than 7, thus indicating univariate normality. The multivariate normality of the variables was tested by examining the C. R. value of the multivariate kurtosis. A common rule of thumb is that C.R. values $>$ 5.00 are indicative of multivariate normality(Bentler, 2005). As is shown in Table 6.32, the C.R. value of the multivariate kurtosis was 16.124, which suggested that the data violated multivariate normality. Therefore, the MLM method in Mplus 7.4 was used for parameter estimation.

Table 6.32   Assessment of Normality of the Indicators of Local Cultural Identification

Variable	Min	Max	Skewness	C.R.	Kurtosis	C.R.
lci1	1	9	− 1.113	− 9.123	1.795	7.354
lci2	1	9	− 0.517	− 4.234	− 0.076	− 0.31
lci3	1	9	− 0.084	− 0.687	− 0.981	− 4.021
lci4	1	9	− 0.915	− 7.497	0.3	1.228
lci5	1	9	− 1.083	− 8.88	1.513	6.199
Multivariate					13.44	16.124

6.5.2   Initial CFA Model of Local Cultural Identification

Parameter estimation. The parameter estimates of the CFA model of local cultural identification are presented in Table 6.33. It can be observed that the C.R. values of the parameter estimates were higher than 1.96, indicating that the parameter estimates were statistically significant($p<0.001$). The standardized factor loadings of the indicators were all above 0.5, meaning that the construct of local cultural identification well explained its indicators.

Table 6.33   Estimate Results of the Initial CFA Model of Local Cultural Identification

	Sig. test of parameters				Std.
	Unstd.	S.E.	C.R.	P	
Regression weights					
lci1 ← LCI	1				0.531
lci2 ← LCI	1.670	0.221	7.540	***	0.751
lci3 ← LCI	1.810	0.275	6.590	***	0.615
lci4 ← LCI	1.704	0.232	7.336	***	0.667
lci5 ← LCI	1.254	0.190	6.608	***	0.628
Variances					
LCI	0.648	0.178	3.645	***	1

continued

	Sig. test of parameters				Std.
	Unstd.	S.E.	C.R.	P	
	Residual Variances				
lci1	1.649	0.162	10.150	***	0.718
lci2	1.395	0.171	8.154	***	0.436
lci3	3.483	0.278	12.551	***	0.622
lci4	2.343	0.289	8.117	***	0.555
lci5	1.565	0.205	7.617	***	0.606

Note: *** p<0.001.

Assessment of model fit. The model fit indices of the initial CFA model of local cultural identification are presented in Table 6.34. The model did not exhibit a good fit. The Satorra-Bentler χ^2 was 47.984. The df was 2. The Normed Chi-squared(χ^2/df) was 9.597, which was high above the cutoff level of 3(Hair et. al., 2010). The RMSEA was 0.146, which was greater than the recommended cut-off level of 0.08(Hu & Bentler, 1999). In addition, the values of TLI(NNFI)(0.779) and CFI(0.889) were below the lower accepta-ble level of 0.9(Hu & Bentler, 1999). Therefore, there was need to modify the initial model by deleting the indicators with low factor loadings.

Table 6.34   Model Fit of the Initial CFA Model of Local Cultural Identification

Model Fit Index	Criterion	Initial Model
Satorra-Bentler χ^2	smaller is better	47.984
df(Degree of Freedom)	bigger is better	5
Normed Chi-squared(χ^2/df)	$1<\chi^2/df<3$	9.597
RMSEA(90% confidence interval)	<0.08	0.146[0.110, 0.185]
Pr(RMSEA$\leqslant$0.05)	bigger is better	0.000
SRMR	<0.08	0.052
TLI(NNFI)	>0.9	0.779
CFI	>0.9	0.889

Note: Scaling correction factor for the initial model is 1.3185.

6.5.3 Model Modification

Given a poor model fit, the model needed to be modified by deleting indicators with low factor loadings. After comparing different modification solutions, it was found that the best solution was to remove lci3.

The parameter estimates of the modified model are reported in Table 6.35. It can be observed that the C.R. values of the factor loadings were higher than 1.96, showing that the factor loadings were statistically significant($p < 0.001$). The standardized factor loadings of the indicators were all higher than 0.5, suggesting that the construct of local cultural identification well explained the indicators.

Table 6.35 Estimate Results of the Final CFA Model of Local Cultural Identification

	Sig. test of parameters				Std.
	Unstd.	S.E.	C.R.	P	
	Regression weights				
lci1 ← LCI	1.000				0.597
lci2 ← LCI	1.328	0.180	7.386	***	0.672
lci3 ← LCI	1.472	0.205	7.171	***	0.648
lci4 ← LCI	1.243	0.187	6.647	***	0.700
	Variances				
LCI	0.819	0.207	3.955	***	1
	Residual Variances				
lci1	1.478	0.171	8.645	***	0.644
lci2	1.757	0.207	8.505	***	0.549
lci3	2.449	0.332	7.382	***	0.580
lci4	1.318	0.227	5.813	***	0.510

Note: *** $p < 0.001$.

Table 6.36 reports the model fit indices of the final CFA model of local cultural identification. As is shown in Table 6.36, the final model exhibited a better fit to the data than the initial model after deleting lci3.

Table 6.36   Model Fit of the Modified CFA Model of Local Cultural Identification

Model Fit Index	Criterion	Initial Model	Modified Model
Satorra-Bentler χ^2	smaller is better	47.984	0.179
df(Degree of Freedom)	bigger is better	5	2
Normed Chi-squared(χ^2/df)	$1<\chi^2/df<3$	9.597	0.0895
RMSEA (90% confidence interval)	<0.08	0.146 [0.110, 0.185]	0.000 [0.000, 0.037]
Pr(RMSEA $\leqslant$ 0.05)	bigger is better	0.000	0.967
SRMR	<0.08	0.052	0.004
TLI(NNFI)	>0.9	0.779	1.024
CFI	>0.9	0.889	1.000

Note: Scaling correction factor for the modified model is 1.2148.

Reliability and validity test. The modified model of local cultural identification was assessed for its composite reliability and convergent validity. The composite reliability was 0.75, greater than the benchmark of 0.6(Fornell & Larcker, 1981). Therefore, the internal consistency of the measurement model was adequate.

The convergent validity of the CFA model of local cultural identification was tested by calculating the AVE value. The AVE value of the model was 0.429, which was above the lower acceptable value of 0.36(Fornell & Larcker, 1981). As a result, the convergent validity of the CFA model of local cultural identification was confirmed. The final CFA model of local cultural identification is presented in Figure 6.12.

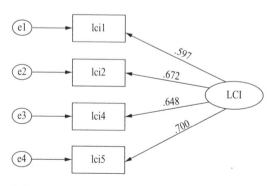

Figure 6.12   The Final CFA Model of Local Cultural Identification

6.6   Measuring Life Satisfaction

In this section, confirmatory factor analysis(CFA) of life satisfaction was performed. First, the test of multivariate normality was performed. Second, the parameter estimation was conducted. Third, the model fit was evaluated. Forth, the reliability and validity of the model were assessed. Last, the model was modified and the final model was developed.

6.6.1   Normality Test

The normality of the life satisfaction variables is presented in Table 6.37. It can be observed that the absolute values of the skewness were lower than 2 and the absolute values of the kurtosis were lower than 7, thus indicating univariate normality. Multivariate normality of the life satisfaction was tested by examining the C.R. value of the multivariate kurtosis. The rule of thumb is that the C.R. value of the multivariate kurtosis greater than 5 suggests departure from multivariate normality. As is seen from Table 6.36, the C.R. value of the multivariate kurtosis of life satisfaction was higher than 5, indicating a deviation from multivariate normality. Therefore, the MLM estimation method in Mplus 7.4 was used to test the significance of the parameters.

Table 6.37   Assessment of Normality of the Indicators of Life Satisfaction

Variable	Min	Max	Skewness	C.R.	Kurtosis	C.R.
ls1	1	9	− 0.321	− 2.627	− 0.258	− 1.056
ls2	1	9	− 0.395	− 3.238	− 0.149	− 0.609
ls3	1	9	− 0.421	− 3.45	− 0.4	− 1.638
ls4	1	9	− 0.575	− 4.713	− 0.098	− 0.4
ls5	1	9	0.275	2.255	− 0.793	− 3.249
Multivariate					5.807	6.967

6.6.2   Initial CFA Model of Life Satisfaction

Parameter estimation. The parameter estimates of the indicators are presented in Table 6.38. It can be observed that the C.R. values of the factor loadings were all above 1.96, suggesting that the parameters were statistically significant($p < 0.001$). The standardized factor loadings of the indicators were all above 0.5, suggesting that the indicators were adequately explained by the latent construct of life satisfaction.

Table 6.38   Estimate Results of the Initial CFA Model of Life Satisfaction

	Sig. test of parameters				Std.
	Unstd.	S.E.	C.R.	P	
	Regression weights				
ls1 ←- LS	1				0.862
ls2 ←- LS	1.044	0.044	23.941	***	0.866
ls3 ←- LS	1.082	0.046	23.436	***	0.865
ls4 ←- LS	0.877	0.066	13.198	***	0.684
ls5 ←- LS	0.772	0.068	11.341	***	0.529
	Variances				
LS	2.255	0.203	11.089	***	1
	Residual Variances				
ls1	0.780	0.083	9.407	***	0.257
ls2	0.822	0.107	7.667	***	0.251
ls3	0.886	0.096	9.234	***	0.251
ls4	1.969	0.177	11.113	***	0.532
ls5	3.463	0.278	12.451	***	0.721

Note: ** $p < 0.01$, *** $p < 0.001$.

Assessment of model fit. The model fit of the initial CFA model of life satisfaction was evaluated. The model fit indices are reported in Table 6.39. It can be observed that the initial model did not exhibit a good fit. The Normed Chi-squared (χ^2/df) was 0.5774, which was lower than the cutoff value of 1(Hair et. al., 2010). Therefore, there was need to modify the initial model by deleting the indicators with low factor loadings.

Table 6.39   Model Fit of the Initial CFA Model of Life Satisfaction

Model Fit Index	Criterion	Initial Model
Satorra-Bentler χ^2	smaller is better	2.887
df(Degree of Freedom)	bigger is better	5
Normed Chi-squared(χ^2/df)	$1<\chi^2/df<3$	0.5774
RMSEA(90% confidence interval)	<0.08	0.000[0.000, 0.051]
Pr(RMSEA $\leqslant$ 0.05)	bigger is better	0.946
SRMR	<0.08	0.008
TLI(NNFI)	>0.9	1.005
CFI	>0.9	1.000

Note: Scaling correction factor for the initial model is 1.3131.

6.6.3   Model Modification

As the factor loading of ls5 was a little lower than those of other indicators, the model was modified by deleting ls5. The parameter estimation was conducted again. As can be seen from Table 6.40, the C.R. values of the factor loadings were all above 1.96, which indicated that factor loadings were statistically significant ($p<0.001$). The standard factor loadings of the variables were all above 0.6, indicating that the indicators were well explained by the latent construct of local cultural identification.

Table 6.40   Estimate Results of the Modified CFA Model of Life Satisfaction

	Sig. test of parameters				Std.
	Unstd.	S.E.	C.R.	P	
	Regression weight				
ls1 ← LS	1.000				0.860
ls2 ← LS	1.046	0.046	22.581	***	0.865
ls3 ← LS	1.088	0.047	22.954	***	0.868
ls4 ← LS	0.879	0.067	13.048	***	0.684
	Variances				
LS	2.244	0.204	10.987	***	1

continued

	Sig. test of parameters				Std.
	Unstd.	S.E.	C.R.	P	
	Residual Variances				
ls1	0.791	0.087	9.118	***	0.261
ls2	0.823	0.113	7.290	***	0.251
ls3	0.871	0.100	8.716	***	0.247
ls4	1.971	0.177	11.145	***	0.532

Note: ** $p < 0.01$, *** $p < 0.001$.

The model fit indices of the modified model are reported in Table 6.41. The model fit of the modified model improved compared with those of the initial model. The Satorra-Bentler χ^2 was 2.449. The df was 2. The Normed Chi-squared (χ^2/df) was 1.2245, which was within the acceptable range between 1 and 3(Hair et.al., 2010). The RMSEA was 0.024, below the cutoff value of 0.08(Hu & Bentler, 1999). The SRMR was 0.008, which was deemed acceptable(Hu & Bentler, 1999). The TLI(NNFI) was 0.998 and the CFI was 0.999, all greater than the cutoff value of 0.9(Hu & Bentler, 1999). According to the criteria of model fit indices, the modified model of life satisfaction yielded a good fit to the data.

Table 6.41   Model Fit of the Modified CFA Model of Life Satisfaction

Model Fit Index	Criterion	Initial Model	Modified Model
Satorra-Bentler χ^2	smaller is better	2.887	2.449
df(Degree of Freedom)	bigger is better	5	2
Normed Chi-squared(χ^2/df)	$1 < \chi^2/df < 3$	0.5774	1.2245
RMSEA (90% confidence interval)	< 0.08	0.000 [0.000, 0.051]	0.024 [0.000, 0.105]
Pr(RMSEA $\leqslant$ 0.05)	bigger is better	0.946	0.589
SRMR	< 0.08	0.008	0.008
TLI(NNFI)	> 0.9	1.005	0.998
CFI	> 0.9	1.000	0.999

Note: Scaling correction factor for the modified model is 1.2334.

Reliability and validity test. The Composite Reliability(CR) of the modified model was tested. The CR value was 0.893, greater than the recommended level of 0.7(Fornell & Larcker, 1981). It is thus claimed that the modified CFA model of life satisfaction was internally consistent.

The convergent validity of the model was examined by calculating the AVE of the latent construct of life satisfaction. The AVE value was 0.677, which was higher than the lowest acceptable level of 0.36(Fornell & Larcker, 1981). Therefore, the convergent validity of the modified CFA model was confirmed. After the model modification, the final CFA model of life satisfaction is presented in Figure 6.13.

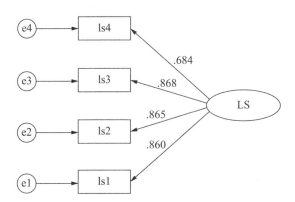

Figure 6.13   The Final CFA Model of Life Satisfaction

6.7   Validity and Reliability Test of the Overall CFA Model

After conducting the CFA of each latent construct, the overall CFA model is shown in Figure 6.14. The model fit, together with the construct validity and reliability of the overall CFA model were tested. As is shown in Table 6.42, the model fit indices met the recommended criteria, indicating that the overall CFA model exhibited a good fit to the data.

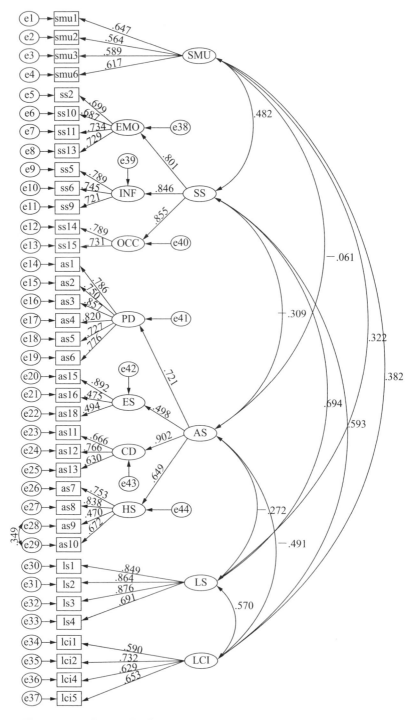

Figure 6.14   Overall Confirmatory Factory Analysis on the Latent Variables

Table 6.42 Model Fit of the Overall CFA Model

Model Fit Index	Criterion	Modified Model
Satorra-Bentler χ^2	smaller is better	866.289
df(Degree of Freedom)	bigger is better	611
Normed Chi-squared(χ^2/df)	$1<\chi^2/df<3$	1.4178
RMSEA(90% confidence interval)	<0.08	0.032[0.027, 0.037]
Pr(RMSEA $\leqslant$ 0.05)	bigger is better	1.000
SRMR	<0.08	0.056
TLI(NNFI)	>0.9	0.945
CFI	>0.9	0.949

Note: Scaling correction factor for the overall CFA model is 1.2537.

The validity and reliability of the overall CFA model were tested. As is shown in Table 6.43, The CR value for each latent construct was above 0.6(Fornell & Larcker, 1981), indicating that the overall CFA model was internally consistent. The AVE value for each construct was higher than the minimum threshold of 0.36(Fornell & Larcker, 1981), and thus confirming the convergent validity of the overall CFA model. The square root of AVE for each construct was above its correlation with any other construct. Thus, the discriminant validity of the overall CFA model was confirmed.

Table 6.43 Overall Validity and Reliability Test on the Latent Variables

	CR	AVE	SMU	LS	LCI	SS	AS
SMU	0.697	0.366	**0.605**				
LS	0.893	0.678	0.322 ***	**0.823**			
LCI	0.747	0.427	0.382 ***	0.570 ***	**0.653**		
SS	0.873	0.696	0.482 ***	0.694 ***	0.593 ***	**0.834**	
AS	0.794	0.501	$-$0.061	$-$0.272 ***	$-$0.491 ***	$-$0.309 ***	**0.708**

Note: 1. Square root of AVE in bold on diagonals.
2. Off diagonals are Pearson correlation of constructs.
3. Significance of correlations: † p<0.100, * p<0.050, ** p<0.010, *** p<0.001.

It can also be observed from the above table that the bivariate correlations among the latent constructs were all below 0.7. According to Hair et al.(2010), correlations among the constructs greater than 0.7 is indicative of multicollinearity. Therefore, there was no concern about multicollinearity among the latent constructs.

In addition, it can be observed from the above table that the bivariate correlations among the latent constructs were statistically significant except that between social media use and acculturative stress. The correlations among the latent constructs were consistent with the research hypotheses.

6.8   Common Method Variance(CMV) Test

Common method variance(CMV) is the "systematic error variance shared among variables measured with"(Richardson, Simmering, & Sturman, 2009, p.763). It is attributable to "the measurement method rather than to the constructs the measures represent" (Podsakoff, MacKenzie, Lee, & Podsakoff, 2003, p.879). It is likely to arise when the reserachers use self-reported questinnaires to collect data from the same respondents(Chang, Witteloostuijn, & Eden, 2010). CMV causes problems in determining the true interrelations among the constructs(Doty & Glick, 1998).

There are two basic methods to test the CMV. One is the Harman's single-factor test and the other is using the common latent factor(CLF). The Harman's single-factor test conducted factor analysis for all the varialbes with an unrotated factor solution(Podsakoff et al., 2003). There is potential concern for the CMV if there emerge factors that "explain the majority of the covariance among the measures"(Podsakoff et al., p.889). The author used the Harman's single-factor test to examine the CMV. Factor analysis with unrotated factor solution yielded 8 factors which accounted for 62.069% of the total variance. The first factor explained 22.431% of the variance, well below 50%. It hence indicated that the CMV was not a problem among the measures of the latent constructs.

The CLF method is using a common latent factor to capture the common variance among all observed variables in the model. According to Podsakoff et al.(2003), when using this method, add a latent factor to the CFA model(as in Figure 6.15), connect it to all

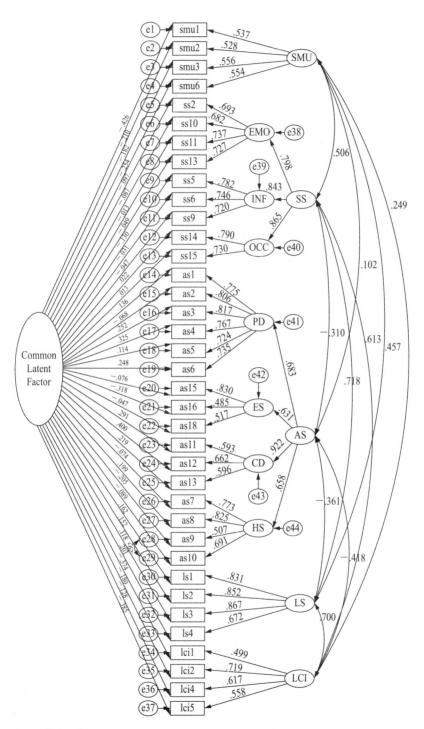

Figure 6.15   Common Latent Factor Test on Overall Confirmatory Factory Analysis

observed items in the model, and then compare the standardized regression weights from this model to the standardized regression weights of a model without the CLF. If there are large differences (like greater than 0.20), then the CLF should be retained in the structural model.

The author used the CLF to test the common method variance (CMV) by adding a latent factor to the overall CFA model (See Figure 6.15). Through the comparison between Figure 6.15 and Figure 6.14, it can be found that difference between the standardized estimates with CLF and without CLF was lesser than 0.20. It thus indicated that there was no concern of CMV.

6.9 Analyzing the Factor Scores of Adaption Variables

Based on the confirmatory factor analysis(CFA) of acculturative stress, life satisfaction, and local cultural identification, the factor scores of these three constructs were calculated. Then, respondents were divided into different groups according to their demographic information and the Independent Samples t test was carried out to compare the group differences in terms of the adaptation variables, so as to examine whether the demographic variables affected the adaptation of internal migrants in Shanghai or not.

6.9.1 Introduction of the Method of Analysis

Factor score is the numerical value that indicates a person's relative spacing or standing on a latent factor. CFA has identified the indicators of the latent variables. In order to obtain the factor score of a latent construct, the factor score weights of its indicator variables should be calculated. Through summing up the product of the factor score weight and raw value for each indicator variable, the regression-based factor score① for each latent construct is generated. Factor score is the composite value by integrating the value of each indicator variable for each respondent. Therefore, factor score is appropriate for assessing each latent variable for individual respondent. Based on the factor scores, the comparison among the individuals or the different groups can be conducted, so as to identify the causes for the differences on the factor scores. AMOS 24.0 provides the statistical analysis of the factor score weights and the factor scores on the basis of the confirmatory factor analysis(CFA) models.

In order to determine whether there are differences among the factor scores for each respondent from different groups, the Independent Samples t Test on the factor scores of the latent variables was carried out based on some demographic factors, including gender, educational level, length of stay, Hukou status, and Housing conditions.

The Independent Samples t Test is used to compare whether the means of a specific variable for two independent groups are statistically significant. Suppose that the means of Group 1 and Group 2 were μ_1 and μ_2 respectively. The null hypothesis H_0 of the Independent Samples t Test was $\mu_1 = \mu_2$ and the alternative hypothesis H_1 was $\mu_1 \neq \mu_2$. A basic assumption of the Independent Samples t Test is the homogeneity of variance.

Therefore, before the Independent Samples t Test, it is necessary to test the homogeneity of variance of Group 1 and Group 2, so as to examine whether the degrees of dispersion of the variables of the two groups are the same. SPSS provides the Levene's Test for Equality of Variances to test the homogeneity of variance of two groups of samples.

---

① Regression approach produces factor score estimates that maximize determinacy. The factor score determinacy is the correlation between the estimated and true factor scores. It ranges from zero to one and describes how well the factor is measured with one being the best value.

If the assumption of the homogeneity of variance is met, i.e., $\sigma_1^2 = \sigma_2^2$, the conventional Independent Samples t Test is carried out to examine the differences of the means of the variables. If the assumption of the homogeneity of variance is not met, i.e., $\sigma_1^2 \neq \sigma_2^2$, the scaled Independent Samples t Test should be used.

The criterion to determine whether there are differences of the means between independent groups is to examine whether the absolute p-value of t-test is below a certain significance level (usually 0.05). When $|p| < 0.05$, it shows that the differences of the means between independent groups are significant. On the contrary, when the absolute p-value is greater than 0.05, it indicates that there is no statistical significance in the differences of the means between different groups.

The assumptions of the Independent Samples t Test also include independence and normality. Independence refers that the value of the sample is not affected by the values of other samples. Normality means that the data of the two independent samples should be normally distributed. It is common that the data obtained from the questionnaires are independent, but they are not normally distributed. However, the Independent Samples t Test compares the means of the samples. According to the Central Limit Theorem CLT, the distribution of the mean of the sample approaches normal distribution as sample size increases no matter whether the raw data was normal or not. And the consensus among experts is that when the sample size is bigger than 30, even though the data violates normality, the Independent Samples t Test can be conducted.

6.9.2   The Factor Score of Life Satisfaction

First, the indicators of life satisfaction have been identified through confirmatory factor analysis (CFA), and then the factor score weights of the indicators are presented in Table 6.44. To be specific, the factor score of life satisfaction (FS_LS) was calculated through the formula as follows:

Table 6.44   Factor Score Weights of LS

	ls4	ls3	ls2	ls1
FS_LS	.093	.261	.265	.264

$$FS\_LS = 0.264 \times ls1 + 0.265 \times ls2 + 0.261 \times ls3 + 0.093 \times ls4$$

$$(6\text{-}1)$$

According to the afore-mentioned formula, the factor score of life satisfaction for each respondent was generated. After that, the descriptive analysis of *FS_LS* of the respondents was conducted(see Table 6.45).

Table 6.45   Descriptive Analysis of the Factor Score of LS

	N	Min	Max	Mean	SD	Skewness	Kurtosis
FS_LS	403	0.88	7.95	5.2166	1.42842	-0.447	-0.175

The descriptive analysis indicated that the range of the *FS_LS* of the respondents was large, which showed that the *FS_LS* of the respondents was significantly different. Based on the method of normality test provided by Hair(2014)[1], the $z_{skewness}$ and $z_{kurtosis}$ of the *FS_LS* were 3.6634 and 11.5762 respectively[2]. If either calculated z value exceeds the specified critical value, then the distribution is non-normal. The most commonly used critical values are ± 2.58(at the 1% level of significance) and ± 1.96(at the 5% level of significance), which corresponds to a 0.05 error level. With these simple tests, the researcher can easily assess the degree to which the skewness and peakedness of the distribution vary from

---

[1]   According to Hair(2014), the statistic value(z) for the skewness value and the kurtosis value are calculated as:

$$z_{skewness} = \frac{skewness}{\sqrt{\dfrac{6}{N}}}, \; z_{kurtosis} = \frac{kurtosis}{\sqrt{\dfrac{24}{N}}}.$$

[2]   In SPSS, a correction term of-3 is added to the kurtosis formula so that a normal distribution has a kurtosis of 0. The kurtosis formula with a term of-3 is called excess kurtosis. When calculating $z_{kurtosis}$, we need to add 3 to excess kurtosis reported by SPSS to turn it into a normal one.

the normal distribution. Because the $z_{skewness}$ was lower than -2.58 and the $z_{kurtosis}$ was greater than 2.58, it showed that the FS_LS was not normally distributed.

Table 6.46 presents the results of the Independent Samples t Test. First, the differences of the means among the respondents were analyzed according to their gender. The Levene's Test for Equality of Variances indicated that F 1.880, $p = 0.171 > 0.05$. Therefore, the null hypothesis $H_0: \sigma^2_{female} = \sigma^2_{male}$ was not rejected. Results of the Independent Samples t Test showed that $t = df = 401$, $df = 401$, and $p = 0.064$. It indicated that "life satisfaction" experienced by male and female migrants differed at a 10% level. The mean of FS_LS of female migrants (M = 5.3240) was significantly higher than that of male migrants (M = 5.0552). It might be because that people have higher expectations on men's social roles and their responsibilities for raising the family than on women. Normally, men are supposed to work hard to provide good material comfort to their family whereas women are expected to play the role of supporting their husbands and bringing up their children.

In addition, in order to examine whether there were differences on FS_LS among internal migrants with different educational levels, the author divided the respondents into two groups: respondents with "college diploma or below" and respondents with "bachelor degree or above." The results of the Independent Samples t Test indicated that although the mean of the group of "college diploma or below" (M = 4.9612) was below "bachelor degree or above" (M = 5.2779), but the p-value of t was above than 0.1 ($p = 0.126$). Therefore, it indicated that there were no significant differences between the two groups regarding FS_LS, i.e., educational level did not have significant influences on respondents' life satisfaction.

In addition, the author conducted the Independent Samples t Test according to the length of the respondents' stay in Shanghai. The respondents were divided into two groups: "short-term

Table 6.46 Independent Samples _t_ Tests of the Factor Score of Life Satisfaction

Grouping		N	Mean	SD	Levene's Test		t-test		
					F-value	p	t-value	df	p
Gender	Male	161	5.0552	1.50969	1.880	0.171	-1.856	401	0.064
	Female	242	5.3240	1.36431					
Educational Attainment	College degree or below	78	4.9612	1.68859	8.859	0.003	-1.542	102.037	0.126
	Bachelor Degree or above	325	5.2779	1.35442					
Length of Stay	66 months or below	207	4.9872	1.39717	0.044	0.833	-3.356	401	0.001
	Above 66 months	196	5.4589	1.42451					
Household Registration Status	Non-Shanghai Hukou	160	4.6792	1.49013	3.847	0.050	-6.428	401	0.000
	Shanghai Hukou	243	5.5704	1.27038					
Housing Conditions	Owing a house	204	5.7565	1.23390	2.603	0.107	8.308	401	0.000
	Not owing a house	199	4.6631	1.40475					

migrants"(those whose length of stay was less than 66 months) and
"long-term migrants"(those whose length of stay was more than 66
months). Results of the Independent Samples t Test showed that
the mean of the short-term migrants($M = 4.9872$) was significantly
lower than that of the "long-term migrants"($M = 5.4589$), with a
p-value lower than 0.05. It indicated that the longer internal migrants stayed in Shanghai, the more they were satisfied with their
lives. The results are in consistent with the argument that adaptation is a long-term process(Kim, 2001). Internal migrants who have
been staying in Shanghai longer will be more adaptive to the local
environment and will thus have higher levels of life satisfaction. On
the contrary, the shorter the internal migrants stay in Shanghai,
the more cultural discomfort they might encounter. It makes their
life satisfaction lower than those who have been staying in Shanghai
for a longer period of time.

Last, the author analyzed the effects of respondents' Hukou
status and housing conditions on their life satisfaction. The Independent Samples t Test indicated the mean of FS_LS($M = 4.6792$)
of the respondents who did not have Shanghai Hukou was significantly lower than the mean of FS_LS of those who had Shanghai
Hukou ($M = 5.5704$). In addition, the mean of FS_LS of the respondents who owned their houses in Shanghai was significantly
higher than the mean of FS_LS of those who did not own their houses in Shanghai($M = 4.6631$). It might be because traditionally Hukou and self-owned houses have significant meanings in Chinese
people's mind. Obtaining the Hukou and owing houses in their migration destination are the criteria based on which internal migrants
are judged as settling in the migration destination. In addition, internal migrants who have obtained the Hukou and the houses tend
to identify themselves as locals. Internal migrants have to make
great efforts to obtain Hukou and buy houses in first-tier cities like
Shanghai, and the fact that obtaining Hukou and self-owned houses
in Shanghai makes internal migrants have the feeling of stability

and accomplishment of taking root in the local environment, which will increase their satisfaction towards life.

6.9.3   Factor Score of Local Cultural Identification

In addition to life satisfaction, local cultural identification is another construct that represents internal migrants' outcome of adaptation. Based on the confirmatory factor analysis(CFA) of LCI, the indicators of LCI are lci1, lci2, lci4, and lci5. Then the factor score weights of LCI are shown in Table 6.47. The factor score of LCI(FS_LCI) was calculated as follows:

Table 6.47   Factor Score Weights of LCI

	lci5	lci4	lci2	lci1
LCI	0.190	0.121	0.152	0.136

$$FS\_LCI = 0.136 \times lci1 + 0.152 \times lci2 + 0.121 \times lci4 + 0.190 \times lci5$$

(6-2)

The descriptive statistics of FS_LCI was conducted. The results are shown in Table 6.48. The minimum value of FS_LCI was 0.60, and the maximum value of FS_LCI was 5.40. The mean was 4.0465, and the standard deviation was 0.78660. It showed that the FS_LCI had good discrimination. Using Hair(2014)'s method, the $z_{skewness}$ and the $z_{kurtosis}$ were -7.8349 and 19.4275 respectively. Because their absolute values were more than 2.58, so FS_LCI was not normally distributed at a 0.01 level of significance.

Table 6.48   Descriptive Analysis of the Factor Score of LCI

	N	Min	Max	Mean	SD	Skewness	Kurtosis
FS_LCI	403	0.60	5.40	4.0465	0.78660	-0.956	1.741

The Independent Samples t Test was conducted on the differences of the means of FS_LCI. For the group of different gender, the mean of FS_LCI of the female migrants was 4.0810 which was slightly higher than the mean of FS_LCI of the male migrants (M = 3.9946). But there were no significant differences on local cultural identification between male and female migrants. Similarly, there were no statistically differences on *FS_LCI* between respondents whose educational levels were low(below college diploma) and respondents whose educational levels were high(above bachelor degree).

Length of stay had significant influences on internal migrants' local cultural identification. The mean of *FS_LCI* (M = 3.9018) of internal migrants who stayed for a short period of time was significantly lower than the mean of *FS_LCI* (M = 4.1993). It further indicates that adaptation is a long-term process, and it needs time for internal migrants to perceive, understand, and identify with the culture of their migration destination.

Results indicated that internal migrants' Hukou status affected their identification with the local culture. Respondents who have obtained the Shanghai Hukou had higher levels of identification with the local culture than those who haven't obtained the Shanghai Hukou. For a long time, the Hukou system determines the affiliation of the residents and affects their entitlement to the social welfare, which makes Hukou closely connect with the local identity. Kang(2017) pointed out that the local Hukou and use of the local dialect are of great significance to migrants' sense of belonging. Therefore, internal migrants who have obtained Shanghai Hukou tend to have a higher level of sense of belonging to Shanghai. They are more likely to change their self-identification from "*waidiren*" to "*the locals*," have higher levels of identification with the local culture, and will be more willing to become "*the locals*."

What's more, housing conditions significantly affected local cultural identification of internal migrants. The mean value of *FS_LCI* (M = 4.2599) of the respondents who owned houses in Shanghai was significantly higher than those who did not own houses in Shanghai(M = 3.8277) at a 0.001 level of significance. In Chinese people's mind, "house" is not only limited to an architectural concept, it has been extended to reflect the meaning of "home." As the

Table 6.49   Independent Samples *t* Tests of the Factor Score of LCI

Grouping		N	Mean	SD	Levene's Test		*t*-test		
					F-value	p	*t*-value	df	p
Gender	Male	161	3.9946	0.85872	2.418	0.121	− 1.080	401	0.281
	Female	242	4.0810	0.73453					
Educational Attainment	College degree or below	78	4.0095	0.80953	0.305	0.581	− 0.461	401	0.645
	Bachelor Degree or above	325	4.0553	0.78201					
Length of Stay	66 months or below	207	3.9018	0.78395	0.002	0.968	− 3.859	401	0.000
	Above 66 months	196	4.1993	0.76197					
Household Registration Status	Non-Shanghai Hukou	160	3.8905	0.82628	0.840	0.360	− 3.269	401	0.001
	Shanghai Hukou	243	4.1492	0.74334					
Housing Conditions	Owing a house	204	4.2599	0.70271	1.538	0.216	5.728	401	0.000
	Not owing a house	199	3.8277	0.80928					

saying goes, "One shall have his piece of mind when he possesses a piece of land." Internal migrants who have purchased their houses in their migration destination are more determined to settle in their current residence. The stability of settling down and their desire to integrate into the local society contribute to their identification with the local culture.

6.9.4 Factor Score of Acculturative Stress

Acculturative stress is the stress migrants experienced, caused by the challenges they are faced with when they enter to a new environment. It reflects how well internal migrants adapt to the local society and also affects two outcome variables: life satisfaction and local cultural identification. Through confirmatory factor analysis (CFA), the sub-constructs of acculturative stress have been identified: PD(perceived discrimination), HS(homesickness), CD(cultural discomfort), and ES(economic strain). The factor weights of the four sub-constructs were calculated by AMOS 24(See Table 6.50). The factor score of acculturative stress (FS_AS) was calculated based on the factor score weights of the indicator variables:

$$
\begin{aligned}
FS\_AS = {} & 0.040 \times as1 + 0.032 \times as2 + 0.060 \times as3 + 0.048 \times as4 \\
& + 0.027 \times as5 + 0.033 \times as6 + 0.044 \times as7 + 0.072 \times as8 \\
& + 0.008 \times as9 + 0.029 \times as10 + 0.074 \times as11 + 0.131 \times as12 \\
& + 0.060 \times as13 + 0.055 \times as15 + 0.010 \times as16 + 0.010 \times as18
\end{aligned}
$$

$$(6\text{-}3)$$

In this section, the factor scores of PD(perceived discrimination), HS(homesickness), CD(cultural discomfort), ES(economic strain), and AS(acculturative stress) were calculated one by one. Then, the Independent Samples t Test was conducted according to the demographic variables, in order to examine the effects of the demographic variables on the afore-mentioned constructs.

Table 6.50   Factor Score Weights of AS and Its Sub-constructs

	as18	as16	as15	as10	as9	as8	as7	as6
AS	.010	.010	.055	.029	.008	.072	.044	.033
ES	.121	.117	.647	.006	.002	.016	.010	.007
HS	.003	.003	.015	.149	.042	.366	.222	.009
PD	.002	.002	.010	.005	.001	.013	.008	.112
CD	.007	.006	.035	.018	.005	.045	.027	.021
	as5	as4	as3	as2	as1	as13	as12	as11
AS	.027	.048	.060	.032	.040	.060	.131	.074
ES	.006	.011	.013	.007	.009	.013	.029	.016
HS	.007	.013	.017	.009	.011	.017	.036	.021
PD	.089	.160	.202	.108	.135	.011	.024	.013
CD	.017	.030	.038	.020	.025	.137	.297	.168

6.9.4.1   Factor Score of Perceived Discrimination(PD)

Using AMOS 24, the factor score of PD(FS_PD) for each respondent was calculated and the descriptive analysis of FS_PD was conducted. It can be observed from Table 6.51 that the minimum value of FS_PD was 0.92, and the maximum value of FS_PD was 7.79. The mean was 4.1449 and the standard deviation was 1.53816. It showed that there was a large degree of dispersion of FS_PD, indicating large differences of FS_PD among respondents. Because $z_{kurtosis} > 2.58$, it can be claimed with 99% confidence that the distribution of FS_PD was non-normal.

Table 6.51   Descriptive Analysis of the Factor Score of PD

	N	Min	Max	Mean	SD	Skewness	Kurtosis
FS_PD	403	0.92	7.79	4.1449	1.53816	−0.026	−0.792

Because the number of the respondents of each group was more than 30, the Independent Samples t Test was conducted. Results based on gender indicated that the p-value was more than 0.1, which showed that there was no statistical significance of the mean value of FS_PD between the male and female respondents.

Results of the Independent Samples t Test based on educational level showed that although the mean of *FS_PD* of respondents of low educational levels($M = 4.2800$) was higher than the mean of *FS_PD* of respondents of high educational levels($M = 4.1125$), but the p-value of the Independent Samples *t* Test was more than 0.1. Therefore, there was no significant difference on the mean of *FS_PD* between the two groups, indicating that educational level had no significant effect on perceived discrimination.

Results of the Independent Samples *t* Test based on the length of stay showed that the mean of *FS_PD* of the short-term migrants (the length of stay in Shanghai was less than or amounted to 66 months)($M = 4.4746$) was much greater than that of the long-term migrants(the length of stay in Shanghai was more than 66 months). The difference of the mean of *FS_PD* between the two groups was significant at the 0.001 level of significance, which indicated that respondents' length of stay in Shanghai had significant negative effects on their perceived discrimination. That is to say, the shorter internal migrant stayed in Shanghai, the higher level of perceived discrimination they reported.

As for the group difference based on the Hukou status, despite the mean of *FS_PD* of the respondents who did not have the Shanghai Hukou was lower than that of the respondents who had the Shanghai Hukou, the difference was not statistically significant. It indicated that even though internal migrants have obtained Shanghai Hukou and can be viewed as "the new Shanghainese" nominally, they might still think they are treated differently as the locals.

Last, the housing conditions affected perceived discrimination of internal migrants. The mean of *FS_PD* of the respondents who owned houses in Shanghai($M = 3.9688$) was obviously lower than that of the respondents who did not own houses in Shanghai($M = 4.3255$). In China, houses are associated with some social issues such as social satisfaction, marriage and spouse selection, and happiness. Having self-owned houses in Shanghai might have enhanced internal migrants' sense of superiority and hence they reported a low level of perceived discrimination.

Table 6.52   Independent Samples *t* Tests of the Factor Score of PD

Grouping		N	Mean	SD	Levene's Test		t-test		
					F-value	p	t-value	df	p
Gender	Male	161	4.1289	1.58411	0.516	0.473	−0.170	401	0.865
	Female	242	4.1555	1.51004					
Educational Attainment	College degree or below	78	4.2800	1.49495	0.580	0.447	0.863	401	0.388
	Bachelor Degree or above	325	4.1125	1.54885					
Length of Stay	66 months or below	207	4.4746	1.43661	3.417	0.065	4.528	401	0.000
	Above 66 months	196	3.7967	1.56842					
Household Registration Status	Non-Shanghai Hukou	160	4.2903	1.52724	0.623	0.430	1.543	401	0.124
	Shanghai Hukou	243	4.0491	1.54095					
Housing Conditions	Owing a house	204	3.9688	1.60393	5.945	0.015	−2.343	398.692	0.020
	Not owing a house	199	4.3255	1.44957					

6.9.4.2   Factor Score of Economic Strain

First, according to the factor weights of the observed variables of economic strain, the factor score of economic strain(FS_ES) was calculated. The results of the descriptive analysis are shown in Table 6.53. The minimum value of FS_ES was 1.05, and the maximum value of FS_ES was 8.88. The mean was 5.1175 and the standard deviation was 1.9776.

Table 6.53   Descriptive Analysis of the Factor Score of ES

	N	Min	Max	Mean	SD	Skewness	Kurtosis
FS_ES	403	1.05	8.88	5.1175	1.97760	− 0.015	− 1.051

Next, the Independent Samples t Test was conducted according to the demographic variables, so as to examine whether gender, educational level, length of residence, Hukou status, and housing conditions have significant effects on FS_ES. As is seen in Table 6.54, respondents' gender and educational level did not cause differences of FS_ES. Even though the male respondents' economic strain was higher than the female respondents, but there was no statistical significance.

Similarly, respondents who had a low educational level(college diploma or lower) perceived more economic strain than respondents who had a high educational level. But there was no statistical significance. The mean value of FS_ES of short-term migrants(M = 5.6274) was significantly higher than the mean value of FS_ES of long-term migrants(M = 4.5791), which showed that short-term migrants experienced more economic strain than long-term migrants. The reason might be that short-term migrants who migrated to the current residence are faced with high living expense at the beginning(such as purchasing houses and goods for daily use), which makes them experience higher levels of economic strain.

Household status had significant influences on the economic strain of internal migrants. The mean of respondents who had Shanghai Hukou(M = 4.8143) was obviously lower than that of

Table 6.54　Independent Samples *t* Tests of the Factor Score of ES

Grouping		N	Mean	SD	Levene's Test		*t*-test		
					F-value	p	*t*-value	df	p
Gender	Male	161	5.1515	2.05980	2.001	0.158	0.281	401	0.779
	Female	242	5.0950	1.92497					
Educational Attainment	College degree or below	78	5.2689	2.03432	0.232	0.630	0.752	401	0.452
	Bachelor Degree or above	325	5.0812	1.96521					
Length of Stay	66 months or below	207	5.6274	1.79633	4.761	0.030	5.492	389.498	0.000
	Above 66 months	196	4.5791	2.02144					
Household Registration Status	Non-Shanghai Hukou	160	5.5781	1.91165	0.092	0.762	3.859	401	0.000
	Shanghai Hukou	243	4.8143	1.96546					
Housing Conditions	Owing a house	204	4.5006	1.90136	0.044	0.834	−6.676	401	0.000
	Not owing a house	199	5.7500	1.85463					

respondents who did not have Shanghai Hukou. It should be noted
that Hukou is closely related with some social welfare issues such as
children's education opportunities, medical care etc. Internal migrants who have the Shanghai Hukou are more likely to enjoy more
social welfares, which will indirectly reduce the cost of their living
in Shanghai. Therefore, internal migrants who have the Shanghai
Hukou are likely to experience less economic strain than those who
do not have the Shanghai Hukou.

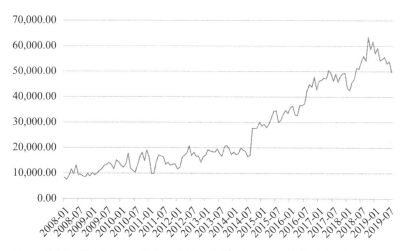

Figure 6.16   The Average Price of Shanghai's Commercial Residential Housing
Unit: yuan per square meter.
Source: Wind.

As previously discussed, purchasing one's own houses is viewed
as a mark that internal migrants settle down in the migration destination. However, the housing prices are expensive in first-tier cities
like Shanghai. As is shown in Figure 6.16, according to the statistics
of Centaline Property, there was a drastic increase in the average
price of Shanghai's commercial residential housing within 10 years,
which rose from 8314.66 yuan per square meter in 2008 to 63.449
thousand yuan per square meter in 2018, and decreased to 50 thousand yuan per square meter in the first half year of 2019. High
housing prices have definitely increased the economic strain of internal migrants who have not purchased their own houses yet. No

matter whether they are renting houses or saving money to buy the houses, expenditure on living accounts for a large part of their income. It made the mean of *FS_ES* (M = 4.5006) of the respondents who own a house significantly lower than that of the respondents who do not have their self-owned houses.

6.9.4.3   Factor Score of Homesickness(HS)

According to the factor score weights of homesickness, the factor score of *FS_HS* was calculated, and the descriptive analysis was conducted. As is seen from Table 6.55, the maximum value of *FS_HS* was 8.05 and the minimum value of *FS_HS* was 1.03. The mean was 4.4952 and the standard deviation was 1.58869.

Table 6.55   Descriptive Analysis of the Factor Score of HS

	N	Min	Max	Mean	SD	Skewness	Kurtosis
FS_HS	403	1.03	8.05	4.4952	1.58869	− 0.092	− 0.735

Based on respondents' demographic variables, the Independent Samples *t* Test was conducted. The results are shown in Table 6.56. Gender, educational level, and Hukou status did not have significant effects on *FS_HS* of the respondents, but length of stay in Shanghai and housing conditions significantly affected *FS_HS* of the respondents.

The mean of *FS_HS* of the short-term migrants(M = 4.8617) was significantly higher than that of the long-term migrants(M = 4.1082). Internal migrants who have migrated to Shanghai for a short period of time are faced with challenges of integrating to the local society. Their social networks of the migration destination have not been established and they depend largely on the emotional support from their family and relatives at their hometowns, and therefore, they are likely to experience higher levels of homesickness.

For the long-term migrants, most of them have probably gone through the period of "adjustment pain," and their focus of social interaction has shifted from their hometown-based social networks to the local social networks. For some of them, their family members

Table 6.56 Independent Samples t Tests of the Factor Score of HS

Grouping		N	Mean	SD	Levene's Test		t-test		
					F-value	p	t-value	df	p
Gender	Male	161	4.4219	1.53202	0.907	0.342	-0.755	401	0.451
	Female	242	4.5440	1.62660					
Educational Attainment	College degree or below	78	4.7179	1.65193	0.074	0.785	1.380	401	0.168
	Bachelor Degree or above	325	4.4418	1.57105					
Length of Stay	66 months or below	207	4.8617	1.56931	0.158	0.691	4.893	401	0.000
	Above 66 months	196	4.1082	1.51932					
Household Registration Status	Non-Shanghai Hukou	160	4.5640	1.58870	0.089	0.765	0.705	401	0.481
	Shanghai Hukou	243	4.4499	1.59033					
Housing Conditions	Owing a house	204	4.2775	1.55523	0.015	0.903	-2.810	401	0.005
	Not owing a house	199	4.7184	1.59548					

might have moved to Shanghai, which helps alleviate their home-sickness. Results also indicated that respondents' housing conditions affected their homesickness. When internal migrants have pur-chased their own houses in their migration destination, they have feelings of settling down and sense of belongings to the migration destination. However, those who have not purchased houses in the migration destination tend to view themselves as drifters in the mi-gration destination, and have more intense feelings that "home is the root." It may account for the reasons why the mean of *FS_HS* (M = 4.2775) of respondents who owned houses in Shanghai was significantly lower than that of the respondents who did not own houses in Shanghai.

6.9.4.4 Factor Score of Cultural Discomfort

The descriptive statistics of the factor score of cultural discom-fort(*FS_CD*) are presented in Table 6.57. The minimum value of *FS_CD* was 0.96 and the maximum value of *FS_CD* was 7.46. The mean was 3.8389 and the standard deviation was 1.39773.

Table 6.57 Descriptive Analysis of the Factor Score of CD

	N	Min	Max	Mean	SD	Skewness	Kurtosis
FS_CD	403	0.96	7.46	3.8389	1.39773	0.145	− 0.594

Table 6.58 presents the results of the Independent Samples *t* Test on the groups categorized according to the demographic varia-bles. Results indicated that respondents' gender and educational lev-el did not have significant effects on the value of *FS_CD*, but their length of stay and housing conditions significantly affected the val-ue of *FS_CD*. And Hukou had a weak influence on the value of *FS_CD*. It can be observed from Table 6.58 that the mean of *FS_CD* of the short-term migrants(M = 4.2216) was significantly higher than that of the long-term migrants(M = 3.4347). Internal migrants who have been staying in the host place for a long period of time are likely to have more understanding and deeper perceptions of the lo-cal culture, and are more adaptive to the differences between the

Table 6.58   Independent Samples t Tests of the Factor Score of CD

Grouping		N	Mean	SD	Levene's Test		t-test		
					F-value	p	t-value	df	p
Gender	Male	161	3.8800	1.47424	1.914	0.167	0.482	401	0.630
	Female	242	3.8115	1.34685					
Educational Attainment	College degree or below	78	3.9610	1.29105	1.748	0.187	0.859	401	0.391
	Bachelor degree or above	325	3.8096	1.42246					
Length of Stay	66 months or below	207	4.2216	1.29096	2.969	0.086	5.880	401	0.000
	Above 66 months	196	3.4347	1.39543					
Household Registration Status	Non-Shanghai Hukou	160	3.9874	1.35968	1.185	0.277	1.735	401	0.084
	Shanghai Hukou	243	3.7411	1.41651					
Housing Conditions	Owing a house	204	3.6083	1.47673	7.362	0.007	−3.403	395.025	0.001
	Not owing a house	199	4.0753	1.27270					

host culture and culture of their hometowns. Therefore, their cultural discomfort will decrease. On the contrary, internal migrants who stayed in the migration destination for a short period of time are more likely to be faced with some culture shock and will thus experience higher levels of cultural discomfort.

The difference between the mean of *FS_CD* of the respondents who had the Shanghai Hukou(M = 3.7411) and those who did not have the Shanghai Hukou(M = 3.7411) was at a 0.1 level of significance and passed the Independent Samples *t* Test. It indicates that even though Hukou is a system of population regulation, which institutionally assigns individuals into different geographic areas, internal migrants who have obtained the local Hukou has a higher sense of identification with the local culture and are more willing to actively adapt to the local culture.

The mean of *FS_CD* of the respondents who had purchased their own houses in Shanghai(M = 3.6083) was significantly lower than that of the respondents who did not own houses in Shanghai (M = 4.0753). It indicates that owing houses brings about a sense of stability to internal migrants. They are likely to have higher levels of sense of belongings and are more adaptable to the cultural differences. In contrast, those who do not own houses in Shanghai tend to have lower levels of sense of belonging and a lack of determination and motivation to overcome the cultural differences. Therefore, they will report higher levels of cultural discomfort.

6.9.4.5 Factor Score of Acculturative Stress

Last, the author calculated the factor score of acculturative stress(*FS_AS*) according to the factor score weights of all the observed variables and conducted descriptive statistics. As is shown in Table 6.59, the minimum value of *FS_AS* was 0.83, and the maximum value of *FS_AS* was 5.94.The mean was 3.3063 and the standard deviation was 1.04786.

Table 6.59   Descriptive Analysis of the Factor Score of AS

	N	Min	Max	Mean	SD	Skewness	Kurtosis
FS_AS	403	0.83	5.94	3.3063	1.04786	-0.009	-0.561

Then, the Independent Samples t Test was conducted to analyze the effects of the demographic variables on FS_AS. As is shown in Table 6.60 the effects of gender and educational level on FS_AS were not statistically significant. Yet respondents' length of stay in Shanghai, Hukou status, and housing conditions significantly affected FS_AS.

To be specific, the mean of FS_AS of long-term migrants (M = 2.9883) was significantly lower than that of short-term migrants (M = 3.6074). The mean of FS_AS of the respondents who had obtained Shanghai Hukou (M = 3.2237) was significantly lower than that of the respondents who did not have Shanghai Hukou. The mean of FS_AS of who had purchased their houses in Shanghai (M = 3.1122) was significantly lower than that of the respondents who did not own houses in Shanghai (M = 3.5053).

The above findings were in consistent with the factor scores of the sub-constructs of acculturative stress. To sum up, as internal migrants' stay in the migration destination increases, their perceived discrimination, cultural discomfort, economic strain, and homesickness will decrease, which will alleviate their acculturative stress. And those who have obtained the local Hukou have higher levels of sense of belonging in the local residence, will experience less economic strain and cultural discomfort, and will thus alleviate their acculturative stress. In addition, for internal migrants who have purchased their own houses in the migration destination, they have higher sense of stability of settling down in Shanghai, which helps reduce their perceived discrimination, cultural discomfort, economic strain, and homesickness, and thus alleviate their overall acculturative stress.

Table 6.60   Independent Samples *t* Tests of the Factor Score of AS

Grouping		N	Mean	SD	Levene's Test		t-test		
					F-value	p	t-value	df	p
Gender	Male	161	3.3114	1.08194	0.145	0.704	0.080	401	0.936
	Female	242	3.3029	1.02682					
Educational Attainment	College degree or below	78	3.4224	0.97930	0.788	0.375	1.090	401	0.276
	Bachelor Degree or above	325	3.2784	1.06321					
Length of Stay	66 months or below	207	3.6074	0.95134	2.514	0.114	6.199	401	0.000
	Above 66 months	196	2.9883	1.05337					
Household Registration Status	Non-Shanghai Hukou	160	3.4318	0.98888	1.971	0.161	1.957	401	0.05
	Shanghai Hukou	243	3.2237	1.07899					
Housing Conditions	Owing a house	204	3.1122	1.12379	9.152	0.003	-3.837	390.039	0.000
	Not owing a house	199	3.5053	0.92516					

6.10   Chapter Summary

This chapter introduced the process of testing the measurement models of the latent constructs. First, an exploratory factor analysis (EFA) of the perceived social support scale was performed using a number of 300 samples randomly drawn by SPSS 24.0. Through Principal Axis Factoring(PAF) with Oblique Rotation(Promax with Kaiser Normalization), three factors were extracted from the 15-item perceived social support scale developed by the author: emotional support, informational support, and occupational support. Then, the remaining 403 samples were used to conduct a second-order confirmatory factor analysis(CFA) of social support. A second-order CFA model of social support was derived, which comprised three sub-constructs: emotional support, informational support, and occupational support. In a similar vein, CFA of the other four latent constructs were conducted, including social media use, acculturative stress, local cultural identification, and life satisfaction. A second-order CFA was conducted for acculturative stress, and a second-order CFA model of acculturative stress with four sub-constructs (perceived discrimination, homesickness, cultural discomfort, and economic strain) was derived.

After the CFA of each latent construct, the author tested the model fit and the reliability and validity of the overall CFA model. Results indicated that the overall CFA model yielded a good fit to the current data. Besides, the overall CFA model was internally consistent, and demonstrated adequate convergent and discriminant validity. Then, as the current data was collected from the self-reported questionnaires, the author tested the common method variance(CMV) of the overall model. Results indicated that the overall CFA model did not have CMV.

Last, the factor scores of the latent contructs were calculated, and the Independent Samples t Test was carried out to examine the effects of the demographic factors on the varialbes of adaptation. The smmary of the results of respondents' demographic factors on their adaptation is listed in Table 6.61. Results indicated that respondents' length of stay in Shanghai, whether they have the Shanghai Hukou or not, and whether they have purchased their houses in Shanghai are important factors affecting their adaption. In the next chapter, the structural model will be tested to examine whether or not the hypothesized relationships among the constructs in the proposed model are supported.

Table 6.61   Summary of Independent Samples t Tests

	FS_LS	FS_LCI	FS_PD	FS_ES	FS_HS	FS_CD	FS_AS
Gender	*						
Educational Attainment							
Length of Stay	***	***	***	***	***	***	***
Household Registration Status	***	***		***		*	*
Housing Conditions	***	***	*	***	**	***	***

Note: * p<0.1, ** p<0.01, *** p<0.001.

Chapter Seven
Data Analysis: The Structural Model

In the previous chapter, the measurement models of the latent constructs in the hypothesized structural model were developed. This chapter focuses on the estimation of the structural model. It comprises four sections. The first section describes the respecification of the hypothesized model based on the CFA. The second section describes the structural model fitting process. The third section presents the hypotheses test of the direct effects among the constructs in the structural model. The fourth section describes the robustness test of the structural model. The fifth section describes the item parceling process, which aims at deriving a simplified structural model. The last section describes the test of the mediation effects in the structural model.

7.1 Respecification of the Hypothesized Model

In the previous chapter, an exploratory factor analysis(EFA) on the self-developed perceived social support scale was performed and three factors were extracted: emotional support, occupational support, and informational support. Then a second-order CFA model of social support comprising three sub-constructs(emotional support, occupational support, and informational support) was built. Likewise, a second-order CFA model of acculturative stress comprising four sub-constructs (perceived discrimination, cultural discomfort, homesickness, and economic strain) was constructed. Building on the previous work, the hypothesized model was respecified and is presented in Figure 7.1.

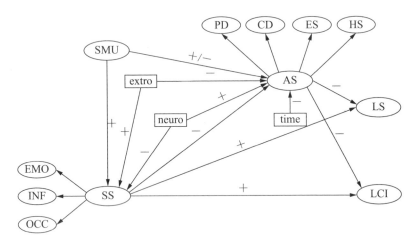

Figure 7.1   Respecified Hypothesized Model

Notes: SMU: Social Media Use, SS: Social Support, AS: Acculturative Stress, LS: Life Satisfaction, LCI: Local Cultural Identification, extro: extroversion, neuro: neuroticism, EMO: Emotional Support, INF: Informational Support, OCC: Occupational Support, PD: Perceived Discrimination, CD: Cultural Discomfort, ES: Economic Strain, HS: Homesickness.

In the preliminary analysis in Chapter Five, Pearson's correlation analysis was performed to examine the bivariate relationships among the study variables(See Appendix 3). The results revealed that the correlation coefficient between extroversion and neuroticism was -0.706 and was statistically significant at the 0.01 level. As noted earlier, correlations between two variables greater than 0.7 is indicative of multicollinearity(Hair et al., 2010). However, it should be noted that the correlation coefficient in the preliminary analysis was derived using the total samples of 703. As the structural model was to be estimated using a number of 403 samples, would there still be a high correlation between extroversion and neuroticism?

In order to avoid multicollinearity in the structural model, it was necessary to conduct Pearson's correlation analysis again using the second group of samples(N = 403) to test the correlations among the study variables. The results of the correlation between extroversion and neuroticism was -0.733, and was statistically significant at the 0.01 level. The high correlation between extroversion and neuroticism was indicative of a high degree to which the two variables could explain each other. In order to avoid multicollinearity, these two observed variables should not be in the structural model together. Therefore, the author first kept extroversion and removed neuroticism from the structural model. The modified hypothesized model with extroversion is presented below(See Figure 7.2).

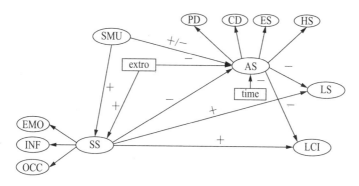

Figure 7.2 Modified Hypothesized Model

Notes: SMU: Social Media Use, SS: Social Support, AS: Acculturative Stress, LS: Life Satisfaction, LCI: Local Cultural Identification, extro: extroversion, EMO: Emotional Support, INF: Informational Support, OCC: Occupational Support, PD: Perceived Discrimination, CD: Cultural Discomfort, ES: Economic Strain, HS: Homesickness.

7.2 Fitting the Structural Model

7.2.1 The Initial Structural Model

The measurement models of the latent constructs in the hypothesized model have been established in the previous chapter. As the data violated multivariate normality, the MLM estimation method in Mplus 7.4 was used for structural model estimation. The model fit indices of the initial structural model are presented in Table 7.1. According to the model fit criteria, the model yielded a good fit. Table 7.2 presents the estimate results of the initial structural model. The results indicated that all path coefficients among the variables were statistically significant at a p<0.001 level, except for the direct effect of social media use on acculturative stress(AS – SMU). Figure 7.3 presents the initial structural model with path coefficients among the latent constructs and the factor loadings of the observed variables.

Table 7.1   Model Fit of the Initial Structural Model

Model Fit Index	Criterion	Initial Model
Satorra-Bentler χ^2	smaller is better	1016.421
df(Degree of Freedom)	bigger is better	650
Normed Chi-squared(χ^2/df)	$1<\chi^2/df<3$	1.564
RMSEA(90% confidence interval)	<0.08	0.037 [0.033, 0.042]
Pr(RMSEA $\leqslant$ 0.05)	bigger is better	1.000
SRMR	<0.08	0.062
TLI(NNFI)	>0.9	0.922
CFI	>0.9	0.928

Note: Scaling correction factor for the structural model is 1.2253.

Table 7.2   Selected Output of the Initial Structural Model

	Sig. test of parameters				Std.
	Unstd.	S.E.	C.R.	P	
Regression Weights: Factor Loadings					
smu1 – SMU	1.000				0.656 ***
smu2 – SMU	1.093	0.110	9.968	***	0.576 ***
smu3 – SMU	0.953	0.102	9.336	***	0.571 ***
smu6 – SMU	0.931	0.096	9.709	***	0.616 ***
ss2 – EMO	1.000				0.692 ***
ss10 – EMO	1.092	0.097	11.311	***	0.679 ***
ss11 – EMO	0.990	0.080	12.360	***	0.731 ***
ss13 – EMO	0.973	0.076	12.879	***	0.729 ***
ss5 – INF	1.000				0.783 ***
ss6 – INF	1.043	0.075	13.928	***	0.741 ***
ss9 – INF	1.080	0.075	14.424	***	0.717 ***
ss14 – OCC	1.000				0.791 ***
ss15 – OCC	0.959	0.075	12.807	***	0.721 ***
EMO – SS	1.000				0.807 ***
INF – SS	1.055	0.097	18.875	***	0.822 ***

continued

	Sig. test of parameters				Std.
	Unstd.	S.E.	C.R.	P	
Regression Weights: Factor Loadings					
OCC ←- SS	1.074	0.096	11.159	***	0.846 ***
as1 ←- PD	1.000				0.786 ***
as2 ←- PD	1.006	0.051	19.879	***	0.751 ***
as3 ←- PD	1.139	0.054	21.140	***	0.855 ***
as4 ←- PD	1.074	0.055	19.598	***	0.820 ***
as5 ←- PD	1.045	0.059	17.769	***	0.727 ***
as6 ←- PD	1.118	0.066	16.894	***	0.775 ***
as7 ←- HS	1.000				0.759 ***
as8 ←- HS	1.041	0.059	17.714	***	0.834 ***
as9 ←- HS	0.530	0.059	9.028	***	0.472 ***
as10 ←- HS	0.845	0.067	12.619	***	0.671 ***
as11 ←- CD	1.000				0.668 ***
as12 ←- CD	1.018	0.066	15.467	***	0.762 ***
as13 ←- CD	0.957	0.076	12.526	***	0.628 ***
as15 ←- ES	1.000				0.887 ***
as16 ←- ES	0.482	0.068	7.100	***	0.475 ***
as18 ←- ES	0.518	0.065	7.952	***	0.498 ***
PD ←- AS	1.000				0.716 ***
HS ←- AS	0.980	0.096	10.239	***	0.646 ***
CD ←- AS	1.202	0.121	9.911	***	0.884 ***
ES ←- AS	0.998	0.124	8.062	***	0.518 ***
lci1 ←- LCI	1.000				0.590 ***
lci2 ←- LCI	1.432	0.157	9.120	***	0.718 ***
lci4 ←- LCI	1.443	0.158	9.114	***	0.628 ***
lci5 ←- LCI	1.173	0.163	7.205	***	0.653 ***
ls1 ←- LS	1.000				0.845 ***
ls2 ←- LS	1.059	0.043	24.749	***	0.862 ***
ls3 ←- LS	1.113	0.045	24.880	***	0.873 ***
ls4 ←- LS	0.900	0.061	14.643	***	0.687 ***
Regression Weights: Path Coefficients					
SS ←- SMU	0.447	0.074	6.020	***	0.438 ***
AS ←- SMU	0.078	0.084	0.926		0.068
SS ←- extro	0.142	0.018	7.785	***	0.450 ***
AS ←- SS	− 0.226	0.101	− 2.232	†	− 0.202†
AS ←- time	− 0.004	0.001	− 5.480	***	− 0.306 ***
AS ←- extro	− 0.071	0.022	− 3.233	***	− 0.201 ***
LCI ←- AS	− 0.281	0.052	− 5.386	***	− 0.362 ***
LCI ←- SS	0.438	0.078	5.636	***	0.505 ***
LS ←- SS	0.958	0.099	9.675	***	0.673 ***
LS ←- AS	− 0.134	0.065	− 2.065	†	− 0.105†

Note: *** p<0.001, ** p<0.01, † p<0.05, * p<0.1.

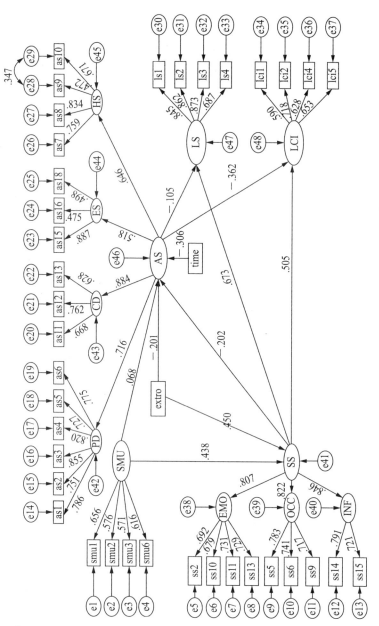

Figure 7.3   Estimate Results of the Initial Structural Model

In order to control the negative impact of multicollinearity on the model estimation, the correlation analysis among the main variables(social media use, social support, extroversion, acculturative stress, length of stay, life satisfaction, and local cultural identification) were conducted. The correlations among the afore-mentioned variables reported by Mplus 7.4 are presented in Table 7.3. The correlation coefficients among the main study variables were highlighted in bold. The estimation results suggested that the correlation coefficients among the main variables were all below 0.7. Therefore, multicollinearity would not substantially impact the estimation results. It can also be observed that the correlations among the main study variables were all statistically significant at a $p < 0.001$ level, except for the correlation between social media use and acculturative stress(AS — SMU).

The correlation coefficients among the sub-constructs of social support(emotional support, informational support, and occupational support) and social support were 0.807, 0.822, and 0.846 respectively. The high correlations among social support and the three sub-constructs indicated that the second-order construct of social support explained its sub-constructs well. Likewise, the correlation coefficients between acculturative stress and the four sub-constructs (perceived discrimination, cultural discomfort, homesickness, and economic strain) were 0.716, 0.884, 0.646, and 0.518 respectively. It indicated that the second-order construct of acculturative stress could explain its sub-constructs well.

7.2.2 Model Modification

As is shown in Table 7.3, the correlation coefficient between local cultural identification (LCI) and life satisfaction (LS) was 0.456 and exhibited a statistical significance at a $p < 0.001$ level. The dependence relationship between these two variables was not considered when the hypothesized model was constructed, as the dependence relationship between these two variables was unclear due

Table 7.3   Estimated Correlation Matrix for the Variables of the Initial Structural Model

	SMU	EMO	INF	OCC	SS	PD	CD	HS	ES	AS	LCI	LS	time	extro
SMU	1.000													
EMO	0.353***	1.000												
INF	0.360***	0.663***	1.000											
OCC	0.370***	0.682***	0.695***	1.000										
SS	0.438***	0.807***	0.822***	0.846***	1.000									
PD	-0.014	-0.152***	-0.155***	-0.159***	-0.188***	1.000								
CD	-0.018	-0.188***	-0.191***	-0.197***	-0.232***	0.633***	1.000							
HS	-0.013	-0.137***	-0.140***	-0.144***	-0.170***	0.463***	0.571***	1.000						
ES	-0.010	-0.110***	-0.112***	-0.115***	-0.136***	0.371***	0.458***	0.334***	1.000					
AS	-0.020	-0.212***	-0.216***	-0.222***	-0.263***	0.716***	0.884***	0.646***	0.518***	1.000				
LCI	0.228***	0.484***	0.493***	0.507***	-0.600***	-0.354***	-0.437***	-0.319***	0.256***	0.495***	1.000			
LS	0.242***	0.561***	0.545***	0.593***	0.684***	-0.202***	-0.249***	-0.182***	-0.146***	-0.282***	0.456***	1.000		
time	0.000	0.000	0.000	0.000	0.000	-0.219***	-0.270***	-0.197***	-0.158***	-0.306***	0.111***	0.032*	1.000	
extro	0.000	0.363***	0.370***	0.380***	0.450***	-0.209***	-0.258***	-0.189***	-0.151***	-0.292***	0.333***	0.334***	0.000	1.000

Note: *** $p < 0.001$, ** $p < 0.01$, * $p < 0.1$.

to a lack of the empirical research basis. Given the significant correlation between LCI and LS, it was necessary to add a covariance of the residual errors of LCI and LS, and then test the error covariance between LCI and LS to see whether the model fit would improve or not.

In addition, a review of the modification indices of the initial structural model indicated that adding a direct path from length of stay(time) to local cultural identification(LCI←time) into the model would result in a decrease of the Satorra-Bentler χ^2 of 15.728. Cultural identification is a process, and it takes time for internal migrants to develop their identification with the local culture. The longer internal migrants stay in the local society, the more they are exposed to the local culture. Increased contact with the local culture will increase their knowledge of the local culture and facilitate their sociocultural adaptation, which will in turn strengthen their identification with the local culture. Therefore, the author added a direct path from time to local cultural identification(LCI←time) into the structural model to examine the relationship between length of stay and local cultural identification.

Table 7.4   Model Fit of the Overall Structural Model(a)

Model Fit Index	Criterion	Overall Model(a)
Satorra-Bentler χ^2	smaller is better	994.776
df(Degree of Freedom)	bigger is better	684
Normed Chi-squared(χ^2/df)	$1<\chi^2/df<3$	1.454
RMSEA(90% confidence interval)	<0.08	0.034[0.029, 0.038]
Pr(RMSEA $\leqslant$ 0.05)	bigger is better	1.000
SRMR	<0.08	0.058
TLI(NNFI)	>0.9	0.936
CFI	>0.9	0.941

Note: Scaling correction factor for the structural model is 1.2232.

The model fit of the modified structural model(a) was evaluated. The model fit indices are reported in Table 7.4. It can be observed that the model fit improved compared with the initial model (See Table 7.1 and Table 7.4). The estimate results of the modified model are reported in Table 7.5. The path coefficients of the direct effects among the variables were similar to those of the initial model, and were all statistically significant except for the direct effect of social media use on acculturative stress(AS→SMU).

Table 7.5   Selected Output of the Overall Structural Model(a)

	Sig. test of parameters				Std.
	Unstd.	S.E.	C.R.	P	
Regression Weights: Path Coefficients					
SS←SMU	0.448	0.075	5.962	***	0.434***
AS←SMU	0.090	0.085	1.061		0.078
SS←extro	0.146	0.018	7.948	***	0.459***
AS←SS	−0.246	0.101	−2.437	†	−0.221†
AS←time	−0.004	0.001	−5.120	***	−0.281***
AS←extro	−0.069	0.022	−3.116	**	−0.195**
LCI←AS	−0.209	0.051	−4.142	***	−0.282***
LCI←SS	0.409	0.079	5.205	***	0.494***
LCI←time	0.002	0.000	4.701	***	0.210***
LS←SS	0.927	0.100	9.267	***	0.658***
LS←AS	−0.115	0.064	−1.796	*	−0.091*
Covariance					
LS↔LCI	0.154	0.061	2.519	†	0.234**

Note: *** p<0.001, ** p<0.01, † p <0.05, * p<0.1.

The added direct path from length of stay(time) to local cultural identification(LCI) yielded a coefficient of 0.209 and was statistically significant at a p<0.001 level, which indicated that length of stay(time) had a positive impact on local cultural identification (LCI). In addition, the error covariance between LS(life satisfaction) and LCI was 0.154, indicative of a positive correlation between these two variables. The estimate results of the overall structural model are presented in Figure 7.4.

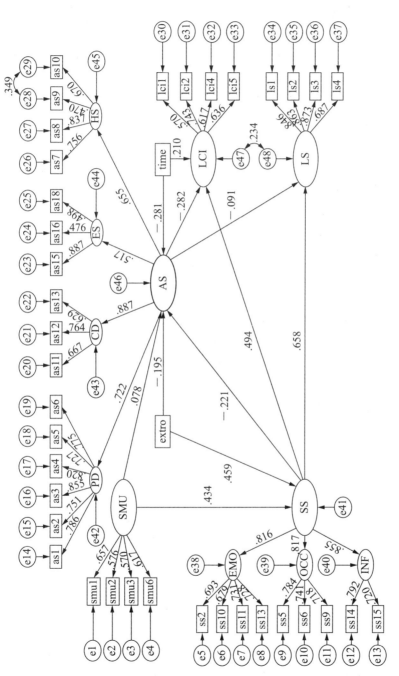

Figure 7.4   Estimate Results of the Overall Structural Model(a)

7.3   Direct Effects Test

Based on the estimate results of the overall structural model
(a), the findings concerning the hypothesized direct relationships
among the variables are presented as follows:

Social Media Use and Social Support. Social media use was expected to have a positive relationship with social support. The research
hypothesis was:

H1: The more that internal migrants use social media, the
higher the level of social support they will perceive.

As is shown in Table 7.5, the path coefficient of the direct
effect from social media use to social support(SS ← SMU) was 0.434
and was significant at the 0.001 level, showing that social media use
had a positive effect on social support. It is thus confirmed that respondents who used social media more perceived higher level of social support. H1 was supported.

Social Media Use and Acculturative Stress. Social media use was
expected to have either a negative or a positive effect on acculturative stress. The research hypothesis was:

H2a: The more that internal migrants use social media, the
less acculturative stress they will experience.

H2b: The more that internal migrants use social media, the
more acculturative stress they will experience.

The path coefficient of the direct effect of social media use on
acculturative stress(AS ← SMU) was 0.078. However, the critical
ratio(C.R.) of the path coefficient(AS ← SMU) was below 1.96, indicating that the direct effect of social media use on acculturative
stress was not significantly different from zero. Therefore, H2a and
H2b were both rejected.

Extroversion and Social Support. Extroversion was expected to
have a positive association with social support. The research hypothesis was presented as follows:

H3: Internal migrants high in extroversion will have higher levels of perceived social support.

As is shown in Table 7.5, the path coefficient of the direct effect of extroversion on social support(SS←extro) was 0.459 and had a significant value of 0.001, indicating that extroversion positively affected social support. Therefore, it is confirmed that respondents who were more extroverted had higher levels of perceived social support. H3 was supported.

Extroversion and Acculturative Stress. Extroversion was expected to negatively impact social support. The research hypothesis was presented as follows:

H5: The more extroverted internal migrants are, the less acculturative stress they will experience.

The path coefficient of the direct effect of extroversion on acculturative stress(AS←extro) yielded a significant value of -0.195 (p< 0.01), showing that extroversion was negatively associated with acculturative stress. It is confirmed that respondents who were more extroverted had lower levels of acculturative stress. H5 was supported.

Social Support and Acculturative Stress. Social support was expected to have a negative association with acculturative stress. The research hypothesis were:

H7: The more that internal migrants perceive the availability of social support, the less acculturative stress they will experience.

The path coefficient of the direct effect of social support on acculturative stress(AS←SS) was -0.221 and had a significant level of 0.1, indicating that social support had a negative effect on acculturative stress. It is thus confirmed that respondents who perceived higher levels of social support had lower levels of acculturative stress. H7 was supported.

Length of Stay and Acculturative Stress. Respondents' length of stay was expected to have a negatively association with the acculturative stress they experienced. The research hypothesis was presented as follows:

H8: The longer that internal migrants stay in the new residence, the less acculturative stress they will experience.

The path coefficient of the direct effect of the length of stay on acculturative stress(AS -- time) was − 0.281 and was significant at a 0.001 level, suggesting that length of stay was positively associated with acculturative stress. It indicated that respondents who stayed longer in Shanghai perceived less acculturative stress. H8 was supported.

Acculturative Stress and Local Cultural Identification. Acculturative stress was expected to have a negative effect on local cultural identification. The research hypothesis was presented as follows:

H9: Internal migrants who experience higher levels of acculturative stress will have lower levels of local cultural identification.

The path coefficient of the direct effect of acculturative stress on local cultural identification(LCI -- AS) was − 0.282 and was significant at a 0.001 level, indicating that acculturative stress had a negative effect on local cultural identification. It is thus confirmed that respondents who reported higher levels of acculturative stress had lower levels of local cultural identification. H9 was supported.

Social Support and Local Cultural Identification. Social support was expected to have a positive association with local cultural identification. The research hypothesis was presented as follows:

H10: The more that internal migrants perceive social support, the higher level of local cultural identification they will have.

The path coefficient of the direct effect of social support on local cultural identification(LCI -- SS) was 0.494 and had a significant level of 0.001, which showed that social support had a negative effect on local cultural identification. It is thus confirmed that respondents who reported higher levels of perceived social support had higher levels of local cultural identification. H10 was supported.

Social Support and Life Satisfaction. Social support was expected to have a positive association with life satisfaction. The research hypothesis was presented as follows：

H11：The more that internal migrants perceive social support, the higher levels of life satisfaction they will have.

The path coefficient between social support and life satisfaction was 0.661（LS<—SS）（p<0.001）, which was indicative of a positive and statistically significant association between social support and life satisfaction. Therefore, respondents who reported higher levels of perceived social support had higher levels of life satisfaction. H11 was supported.

Acculturative Stress and Life Satisfaction. Acculturative stress was expected to have a negative association with life satisfaction. The research hypothesis was：

H12：Internal migrants who experience higher levels of acculturative stress will have lower levels of life satisfaction.

The path coefficient of the direct effect of acculturative stress on life satisfaction was −0.091（LS<—AS) and was significant at a 0.1 level, which indicated that acculturative stress had a negative effect on life satisfaction. It is confirmed that respondents who reported higher levels of acculturative stress had lower levels of life satisfaction. Therefore, H12 was supported.

7.4 Robustness Test

In order to test the robustness of the statistical results of structural model（a）, the author replaced the variable "extroversion" with "neuroticism" and estimated the model again. The estimate results of the overall structural model（b）with neuroticism is presented in Figure 7.5. The model fit indices of the structural model（b）with "neuroticism" are reported in Table 7.6. It can be observed that the structural model（b）yielded a good fit.

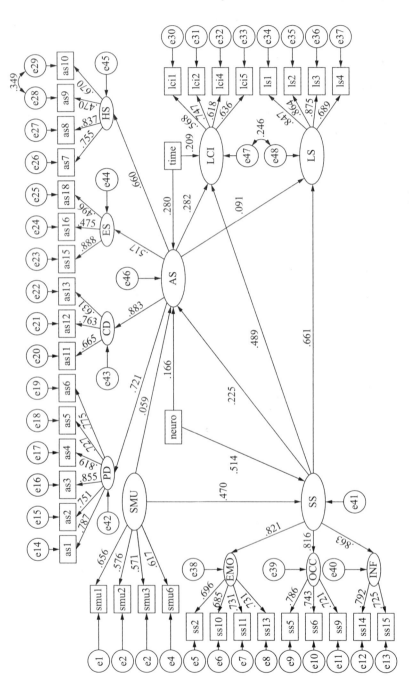

Figure 7.5 Estimate Results of the Overall Structural Model(b)

Table 7.6   Model Fit of the Overall Structural Model(b)

Model Fit Index	Criterion	Full Model(b)
Satorra-Bentler χ^2	smaller is better	1001.074
df(Degree of Freedom)	bigger is better	684
Normed Chi-squared(χ^2/df)	$1 < \chi^2/df < 3$	1.464
RMSEA(90% confidence interval)	< 0.08	0.034[0.029, 0.038]
Pr(RMSEA $\leqslant$ 0.05)	bigger is better	1.000
SRMR	< 0.08	0.057
TLI(NNFI)	> 0.9	0.935
CFI	> 0.9	0.940

Note: Scaling correction factor for the structural model is 1.2271.

The estimate results of the overall structural model(b) are reported in Table 7.7. It can be observed that the path coefficients of the direct effects among the latent constructs in the overall structural model(b) did not change significantly compared with the path coefficients in the overall structural model(a), which indicated that the dependence relationships among the latent variables specified in the overall structural model(a) were stable.

Table 7.7   Selected Output of the Overall Structural Model(b)

	Sig. test of parameters				Std.
	Unstd.	S.E.	C.R.	P	
Regression Weights: Path Coefficients					
SS←SMU	0.493	0.076	6.502	***	0.470***
AS←SMU	0.067	0.090	0.750		0.059
SS←neuro	−0.169	0.019	−8.920	***	−0.514***
AS←SS	−0.247	0.109	−2.265	†	−0.225†
AS←time	−0.004	0.001	−5.070	***	−0.280***
AS←neuro	0.060	0.025	2.426	†	0.166†
LCI←AS	−0.209	0.050	−4.149	***	−0.282***
LCI←SS	0.397	0.075	5.283	***	0.489***
LCI←time	0.002	0.000	4.707	***	0.209***
LS←SS	0.922	0.098	9.437	***	0.661***
LS←AS	−0.115	0.065	−1.782	*	−0.091*
Covariance					
LS↔LCI	0.162	0.061	2.677	**	0.246**

Note: *** p<0.001, ** p<0.01, † p<0.05, * p<0.1.

As can be seen from Table 7.7, the path coefficient of the direct effect of neuroticism on social support(SS ← neuro) was − 0.514 and was significant at a 0.001 level, indicating that neuroticism had a negative effect on perceived social support. It means the more neurotic the respondents were, the less social support they perceived. The path coefficient of the direct effect of neuroticism on acculturative stress(AS ← neuro) was 0.166 and was significant at a 0.1 level. It shows neuroticism had a significantly positive effect on acculturative stress, thereby indicating that the more neurotic the respondents were, the more acculturative stress they experienced. Therefore, H4 and H6 were supported.

7.5   Simplifying the Structural Model Through Item Parceling

In the previous chapter, two second-order CFA models of social support and acculturative stress were derived. In order to develop a more parsimonious model, item parceling was conducted on the second-order latent constructs of social support and acculturative stress.

Item parceling is a common practice in structural equation modeling analysis. It is a method of "summing or averaging the original item scores from two or more items and using these parcel scores in place of the original individual item scores as new indicators of the underlying constructs/factors" (Wang & Wang, 2012, p.37). Item parceling is recommend in SEM. First, compared with the treatment of individual items as indicators, composite indicators are more likely to yield a better model fit. It has been confirmed in several studies(Landis, Beal, and Tesluk 2000; Bandalos, 2002). Second, item parceling increase the likelihood of the normality of data, as it may "well distinguish individuals at subtly varying levels in regard to that construct"(Matsunaga, 2008, p.267).

The author used isolated parceling method to create item par-

cels of the second-order constructs of social support and acculturative stress. Isolated parceling is the method of grouping items into
parcels on the basis of content similarity and factor structure
(Wang, 2012, p.244). Based on the prior confirmatory factor anal-
ysis(CFA) of social support, three item parcels were created as indicators to measure social support. Each set of the items belong to
the three first-order constructs(emotional support, informational
support, and occupational support) was summed and their means
were calculated to form three measured indicators. For example,
for the item parcel of social support, the means of emotional support items were calculated in this way: EMO = (ss2 + ss10 + ss11 +
ss13)/4. In a similar vein, four item parcels of the second-order
construct of acculturative stress were created, which were perceived
discrimination(PD), cultural discomfort(CD), homesickness(HS),
and economic strain(ES).

The model fit of the simplified structural model(a) was evaluated and is presented in Table 7.8. It can be observed that the simplified structural model(a) yielded a good fit. A comparison of the
model fit between the simplified structural model(a) and the overall structural model(a)(see Table 7.4 and Table 7.8) and that of the
simplified structural model(see Table 7.8) indicated that the simplified model(a) fitted the data better.

Table 7.8   Model Fit of the Simplified Structural Model(a)

Model Fit Index	Criterion	Simplified Model(a)
Satorra-Bentler χ^2	smaller is better	293.825
df(Degree of Freedom)	bigger is better	179
Normed Chi-squared(χ^2/df)	$1<\chi^2/df<3$	1.641
RMSEA(90% confidence interval)	<0.08	0.040[0.032, 0.048]
Pr(RMSEA $\leqslant$ 0.05)	bigger is better	0.982
SRMR	<0.08	0.053
TLI(NNFI)	>0.9	0.941
CFI	>0.9	0.957

Note: Scaling correction factor for the structural model is 1.2311.

In addition, the estimation results of the path coefficients of the simplified structural model(a) are reported in Table 7.9. Compared with the path coefficients of the overall structural model(a), the path coefficients of the simplified structural model(a) were nearly the same. There was an increase in the significance of the path coefficients. For example, the path coefficient of the direct effect of acculturative stress on life satisfaction (LS -- AS) in the overall structural model(a) was significant at a p<0.1 level, whereas the path coefficient of the direct effect of acculturative stress on life satisfaction(LS -- AS) in the simplified model(a) was statistically significant at a p<0.05 level. The estimation results of the simplified structural model(a) showed that the dependence relationships among the variables were stable, and the research hypotheses confirmed in the overall structural model(a) were still supported. The estimate results of the simplified structural model(a) are presented in Figure 7.6.

Table 7.9   Selected Output of the Simplified Structural Model(a)

	Sig. test of parameters				Std.
	Unstd.	S.E.	C.R.	P	
Regression Weights: Factor Loadings					
smu1 -- SMU	1.000				0.657 ***
smu2 -- SMU	1.092	0.126	8.659	***	0.576 ***
smu3 -- SMU	0.952	0.119	7.979	***	0.571 ***
smu6 -- SMU	0.930	0.104	8.962	***	0.616 ***
EMO -- SS	1.000				0.727 ***
INF -- SS	1.076	0.087	12.374	***	0.731 ***
OCC -- SS	1.043	0.094	11.143	***	0.730 ***
PD -- AS	1.000				0.693 ***
HS -- AS	0.733	0.079	9.337	***	0.529 ***
CD -- AS	1.110	0.107	10.402	***	0.763 ***
ES -- AS	0.614	0.085	7.224	***	0.425 ***
lci1 -- LCI	1.000				0.570 ***
lci2 -- LCI	1.532	0.178	8.586	***	0.743 ***
lci4 -- LCI	1.472	0.180	8.182	***	0.619 ***
lci5 -- LCI	1.179	0.166	7.091	***	0.634 ***

continued

	Sig. test of parameters				Std.
	Unstd.	S.E.	C.R.	P	
Regression Weights: Factor Loadings					
ls1 ←- LS	1.000				0.846 ***
ls2 ←- LS	1.060	0.043	24.375	***	0.863 ***
ls3 ←- LS	1.113	0.047	23.927	***	0.874 ***
ls4 ←- LS	0.899	0.067	13.356	***	0.687 ***
Regression Weight: Path Coefficients					
SS ←- SMU	0.458	0.081	5.683	***	0.439 ***
AS ←- SMU	0.139	0.093	1.503		0.113
SS ←- extro	0.146	0.019	7.841	***	0.453 ***
AS ←- SS	− 0.259	0.107	− 2.436	†	− 0.219†
AS ←- time	− 0.004	0.001	− 5.320	***	− 0.289 ***
AS ←- extro	− 0.074	0.024	− 3.067	**	− 0.194 **
LCI ←- AS	− 0.192	0.049	− 3.929	***	− 0.278 ***
LCI ←- SS	0.410	0.083	4.926	***	0.501 ***
LCI ←- time	0.002	0.000	4.570	***	0.210 ***
LS ←- SS	0.916	0.092	9.997	***	0.658 ***
LS ←- AS	− 0.120	0.059	− 2.021	†	− 0.102†
Covariance					
LS ←→ LCI	− 0.150	0.065	2.287	†	0.228 **

Note: *** p<0.001, ** p<0.01, † p<0.05, * p<0.1.

Likewise, the correlation analysis was conducted to examine multicollinearity. Table 7.10 reports the correlation matrix. It can be observed that the correlation coefficients were all below 0.7, showing that multicollinearity would not substantially affect the estimate results. Just like the overall structural model(a), all the correlation coefficients among the latent variables in the simplified structural model(a) were statistically significant except for the correlation between social media use and acculturative stress. Thus, it can be concluded that the correlation patterns of the latent variables did not change after item parceling, which indicated that the simplified structural model(a) was effective.

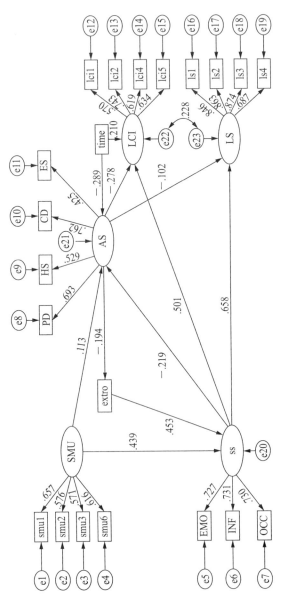

Figure 7.6   Estimate Results of the Simplified Structural Model(a)

Table 7.10   Estimated Correlation Matrix for the Variables
of the Simplified Structural Model(a)

	SMU	SS	AS	LS	LCI	time	extro
SMU	1.000						
SS	0.439 ***	1.000					
AS	0.017	− 0.258 ***	1.000				
LS	0.287 ***	0.684 ***	− 0.271 ***	1.000			
LCI	0.215 ***	0.573 ***	0.468 ***	0.543 ***	1.000		
time	0.000	0.000	− 0.289 ***	0.029 *	0.290 ***	1.000	
extro	0.000	0.453 ***	− 0.294 ***	0.328 ***	0.309 ***	0.000 ***	1.000

Note: *** $p<0.001$, ** $p<0.01$, * $p<0.1$.

The author further replaced extroversion with neuroticism and developed a simplified structural model(b). The model fit indices of the simplified structural model(b) are reported in Table 7.11. It can be observed that the simplified structural model(b) also yielded a good fit to the data.

Table 7.11   Model Fit of the Simplified Structural Model(b)

Model Fit Index	Criterion	Simplified Model(b)
Satorra-Bentler χ^2	smaller is better	294.584
df(Degree of Freedom)	bigger is better	179
Normed Chi-squared(χ^2/df)	$1<\chi^2/df<3$	1.646
RMSEA(90% confidence interval)	<0.08	0.040[0.032, 0.048]
Pr(RMSEA $\leqslant$ 0.05)	bigger is better	0.980
SRMR	<0.08	0.058
TLI(NNFI)	>0.9	0.941
CFI	>0.9	0.950

Note: Scaling correction factor for the structural model is 1.2375.

Table 7.12 reports the estimate results of the simplified structural model(b). It can be observed that the relationships among the variables did not change in the simplified structural model(b), indicating that results of the overall structural model(a) were robust. The estimate results of the simplified structural model(b) are presented in Figure 7.7.

Table 7.12   Selected Output of the Simplified Structural Model(b)

| | Sig. test of parameters | | | | Std. |
	Unstd.	S.E.	C.R.	P	
	Regression Weights: Path Coefficients				
SS←SMU	0.503	0.080	6.257	***	0.474 ***
AS←SMU	0.115	0.099	1.166		0.093
SS←neuro	− 0.170	0.019	− 9.064	***	− 0.511 ***
AS←SS	− 0.259	0.117	− 2.210	†	− 0.222†
AS←time	− 0.004	0.001	− 5.290	***	− 0.287 ***
AS←neuro	0.064	0.028	2.312	†	0.165†
LCI←AS	− 0.191	0.048	− 3.938	***	− 0.278 ***
LCI←SS	0.397	0.080	4.982	***	0.495 ***
LCI←time	0.002	0.000	4.561	***	0.209 ***
LS←SS	0.910	0.089	10.189	***	0.661 ***
LS←AS	− 0.120	0.060	− 2.000	†	− 0.101†
	Covariance				
LS↔LCI	0.159	0.065	2.450	†	0.241 **

Note: *** p <0.001, ** p<0.01, † p<0.05, * p<0.1.

7.6   Mediation Effects Test

In this section, the hypothesized mediation effects among the latent variables proposed in Chapter Three were tested. Using bootstrap method, the author first tested the mediation effects in the proposed overall structural model(a), and then tested the mediation effects in the simplified structural model(a) to examine the robustness of the findings.

7.6.1   Introduction of the Methods of Mediation Analysis

Mediation analysis is common in SEM. It explains the process how an independent variable affects the dependent variable. A

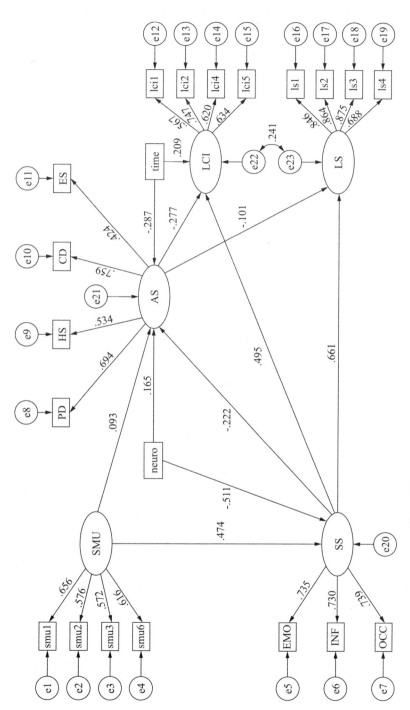

Figure 7.7   Estimate Results of the Simplified Structural Model(b)

mediating variable, i. e. a mediator, is an intervening or intermedi-
ate variable through which an independent variable X affects an
outcome variable Y(Baron & Kenny, 1986; Hayes, 2009; Gunzler,
Chen, Wu, &, Zhang, 2013). In a causal relationship, change of
the independent variable X affects the mediator, which will in turn
affects the dependent variable Y (Wang & Wang, 2012; Hayes,
Preacher, & Myers, 2011). In a structural model, one or more mediators might be found(Hayes, 2009).

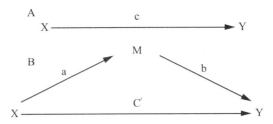

Figure 7.8   The Mediation Model Requirements(Baron & Kenny, 1986)

Note: A: The direct effect. B: The mediation effect.
Source: Mallinckrodt, Abraham, Wei, & Russell, 2006, p.373.

One of the most widely used approach to test mediating effect
is the causal steps approach proposed by Baron and Kenny(1986).
In this approach, the researcher conducts a four-step regression
equation to test the significance of the mediating effects(Hayes,
2009)(See Figure 7.8). First, the total effect of X on Y, which is
represented as c, should be significant. Otherwise, the mediation
test should not be proceeded. Second, path coefficient a, which represents the regression coefficient between the independent variable X and the mediating variable Y, should be significant. Third,
path coefficient b, which represents the regression coefficient between the mediating variable M and the dependent variable Y(con-
trolling for the independent variable X) should be significant.
Fourth, when path coefficient b is significant, path coefficient c',
which represents the regression coefficient of Y on X after control-
ling for the mediating variable M, will be examined. When path coefficient c' is not significant, the researcher claims that M com-

pletely mediates the effect of X on Y. When path coefficient c' is significant less than path coefficient c, it supports a claim of partial mediation, i.e., some but not all of the effects of X on Y is carried through M(Preacher & Hayes, 2004; Rucker, Preacher, Tormala, & Petty 2011; Baron & Kenny, 1986).

However, Baron and Kenny(1986)'s causal steps approach is critiqued by some scholars (MacKinnon, Lockwood, Hoffman, West, & Sheets, 2002; Hayes, 2009). First, the requirement that a total X to Y effect be present before assessing mediation is questioned as there is evidence of significant indirect effects in the absence of significant total or direct effects(Rucker et al., 2011). Second, it is difficult to extend the causal steps method to models incorporating multiple mediating variables and to evaluate each of the mediating variable effects separately in a model with more than one mediating variables(MacKinnon et al., 2002).

Recently, the Bootstrap method is used more often in testing the indirect effects(Shrout & Bolger, 2002). Bootstrap method is a computer-based resampling method, which draws samples repeatedly from the original sample set to obtain an estimate's empirical sampling distribution(Hayes et al., 2011; Nevitt & Hancock, 2001). The software treats the original samples as a pseudo population, and draws randomly samples of size n from the original samples with replacement(Hayes et al., 2011). Size n is usually the same with the number of the original cases(Kline, 2011). As for the times of the sample replacements, some scholars argue that it should be at least 5000, and the larger the better(Hayes, 2009). Mallinckrodt et al.(2006) note that it will be more desirable if 10000—20000 times of sample replacements be conducted. Bootstrap analysis generates a CI confidence interval of the indirect effects via empirical approximation of the sampling distribution (Hayes, 2009).

Bootstrap method has some advantages over Baron and Kenny (1986)'s causal steps approach. As noted by Hayes(2009), it makes no assumptions of the distribution of the data and thus can be used when multivariate normality of the data is violated. Besides, bootstrap method can estimate the mediating effects of two or more intervening variables in a multi-step mediation model. Thus, bootstrapping is considered as more valid and powerful in testing mediation effects(MacKinnon, Lockwood, & William, 2004).

7.6.2   Hypotheses of the Mediation Effects

Parametric bootstrapping method was used to examine the hypothesized mediation effects. The bootstrap analysis was performed using the Maximum likelihood(ML) estimation method by default provided by Mplus 7.4. The author requested 10000 bootstrapping samples drawn with replacement from the full data set of 403 cases. Mplus provides two types of bootstrap confidence intervals: the percentile confidence interval and bias-corrected bootstrap confidence interval. As the percentile-based bootstrap confidence interval retains bias, it is suggested that the bias-corrected bootstrap confidence interval be estimated.(Mallinckrodt, Abraham, Wei, & Russell, 2006). The author selected "CINT(bcbootstrap)" from the "OUTPUT" command to generate the bias-corrected bootstrap confidence intervals for the indirect effects.

To facilitate the mediation analysis, the author coded the paths in the overall structural model(a)(see Figure 7.9). The hypotheses of the mediating effects in the structural model(a) are presented in Table 7.13. It can be observed that there were nine mediation effects to be tested.

In addition, the hypotheses (h10—h14) regarding the total effect in the structural model were tested(see Table 7.14). The purpose of examining the total effects was to decompose the total effects into direct and indirect(mediation) effects and calculate the proportion of the indirect effects over the total effects, so as to compare the effects of specific mediators.

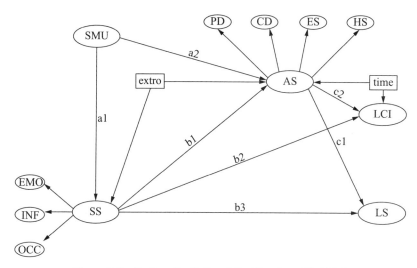

Figure 7.9　Coding the Paths of the Structure Model(a)

Notes: SMU: Social Media Use, SS: Social Support, AS: Acculturative Stress, LS: Life Satisfaction, LCI: Local Cultural Identification, extro: extroversion, EMO: Emotional Support, INF: Informational Support, OCC: Occupational Support, PD: Perceived Discrimination, CD: Cultural Discomfort, ES: Economic Strain, HS: Homesickness.

Table 7.13　Hypotheses of the Mediation Effects

Hypothesis	Path	Coefficient
h1: Social support will mediate the relationship between social media use and acculturative stress.	SMU→SS→AS	$a_1 b_1$
h2: Acculturative stress will mediate the relationship between social support and life satisfaction.	SS→AS→LS	$b_1 c_1$
h3: Acculturative stress will mediate the relationship between social support and local cultural identification.	SS→AS→LCI	$b_1 c_2$
h4: Acculturative stress will mediate the relationship between social media use and life satisfaction.	SMU→AS→LS	$a_2 c_1$
h5: Social support will mediate the relationship between social media use and life satisfaction.	SMU→SS→LS	$a_1 b_2$
h6: Social support and acculturative stress will mediate the relationship between social media use and life satisfaction.	SMU→SS→ AS→LS	$a_1 b_1 c_1$
h7: Acculturative stress will mediate the relationship between social media use and local cultural identification.	SMU→AS→LCI	$a_2 c_2$
h8: Social support will mediate the relationship between social media use and local cultural identification.	SMU→SS→LCI	$a_1 b_3$
h9: Acculturative stress and social support will mediate the relationship between social media use and local cultural identification.	SMU→SS→ AS→LCI	$a_1 b_1 c_2$

Table 7.14   Hypotheses of the Total Effects

Hypothesis	Path	Coefficient
h10: The total effect from social media use to acculturative stress will be significant.	IE: SMU→SS→AS	$a_1 b_1 + a_2$
	DE: SMU→AS	
h11: The total effect from social support to life satisfaction will be significant.	IE: SS→AS→LS	$b_1 c_1 + b_2$
	DE: SS→LS	
h12: The total effect from social support to local cultural identification will be significant.	IE: SS→AS→LCI	$b_1 c_2 + b_3$
	DE: SS→LCI	
h13: The total effect from social media use to life satisfaction will be significant.	IE: SMU→AS→LS	$a_2 c_1 + a_1 b_2 + a_1 b_1 c_1$
	IE: SMU→SS→LS	
	IE: SMU→SS→AS→LS	
h14: The total effect from social media use to local cultural identification will be significant.	IE: SMU→AS→LCI	$a_2 c_2 + a_1 b_3 + a_1 b_1 c_2$
	IE: SMU→SS→LCI	
	IE: SMU→SS→AS→LCI	

Notes: IE: Indirect Effect, DE: Direct Effect.

7.6.3   Mediation Effects Test on the Overall Structural Model(a)

First, the mediation effects in the overall structural model(a) were examined. Table 7.15 shows the model fit indices of the overall structural model(a) using bootstrap method. It can be observed that the model fit indices met the criteria, indicating that the overall structural model(a) using the bootstrap estimation fitted the data well.

Table 7.15   Model Fit of the Overall Structural Model(a) Using Bootstrap

Model Fit Index	Criterion	Overall Model(a)
χ^2	smaller is better	1216.763
df(Degree of Freedom)	bigger is better	684
Normed Chi-squared(χ^2/df)	$1<\chi^2/df<3$	1.857
RMSEA(90% confidence interval)	<0.08	0.044[0.040, 0.048]
Pr(RMSEA $\leqslant$ 0.05)	bigger is better	0.994
SRMR	<0.08	0.058
TLI(NNFI)	>0.9	0.913
CFI	>0.9	0.919

For illustration purpose, the regression results and the bootstrap estimates of path coefficients are presented in Table 7.16. It can be observed that regression and bootstrap estimation yielded the same coefficients of the indirect effects. However, as the MLM estimation method adopted in regression analysis corrected the standard errors, it yielded smaller standard errors than the standard errors estimated by the bootstrap method.

Table 7.16 also shows the bias-corrected bootstrap confidence intervals. To be specific, the bias-corrected 99% confidence interval for the direct effect a_1 (SMU→SS), b_2 (SS→LS), b_3 (SS→LCI) and c_2 (AS→LCI) excluded zero, indicating that the aforementioned direct effects were statistically significant. The bias-corrected 95% confidence interval for the direct effect b_1 (SS→AS) did not include zero, indicating a statistical significant direct effect from social support to acculturative stress. However, the bias-corrected 90% confidence interval for the direct effect a_2 (SMU→AS) and c_1 (AS→LS) included zero, indicating that the direct effects from social media use to acculturative stress and the direct effects from acculturative stress to life satisfaction were insignificant. The bootstrap estimates were inconsistent with the z-statistic. Next, the indirect effects and the total effects in the structural model(a) were examined.

Table 7.17 reports the bootstrap confidence intervals for the indirect and total effects. The hypotheses of the mediation effects (h1—h9) were examined.

It can be observed that the bias-corrected 95% confidence level for the indirect effect $a_1 b_1$ (SMU→SS→AS) was between -0.256 and -0.015. As zero was not in this interval, we can conclude that the indirect effect of social media on acculturative stress through social support was statistically significant. It means that with 95% confidence we can say that the social media use had a significantly negative effect on acculturative stress through social support. h1 was supported.

Table 7.16   Test Significance of Direct Effects of the Overall Structural Model(a)

Direct effects	Regression result		Bootstrap estimate			Bias-corrected Bootstrap		
	B	SE	B	SE	90% CI	95% CI	99% CI
a_1 (SMU→SS)	0.448***	0.075	0.448***	0.107	[0.307, 0.654]	[0.283, 0.704]	[0.241, 0.827]
a_2 (SMU→AS)	0.090	0.085	0.090	0.111	[−0.091, 0.269]	[−0.132, 0.306]	[−0.216, 0.396]
b_1 (SS→AS)	−0.246†	0.101	−0.246†	0.121	[−0.448, −0.054]	[−0.495, −0.018]	[−0.596, 0.066]
b_2 (SS→LS)	0.927***	0.100	0.927***	0.118	[0.763, 1.154]	[0.734, 1.207]	[0.674, 1.301]
b_3 (SS→LCI)	0.409***	0.079	0.409***	0.092	[0.278, 0.576]	[0.255, 0.613]	[0.217, 0.696]
c_1 (AS→LS)	−0.115*	0.064	−0.115	0.080	[−0.249, 0.012]	[−0.282, 0.038]	[−0.347, 0.083]
c_2 (AS→LCI)	−0.209***	0.051	−0.209***	0.065	[−0.330, −0.115]	[−0.354, −0.098]	[−0.405, −0.060]

Notes: 1. The reported estimates are unstandardized ones.

2. *** $p<0.001$, † $p<0.05$, * $p<0.1$.

Table 7.17   Test Significance of Mediation and Total Effects
of the Overall Structural Model(a)

	Bias-corrected Bootstrap			
	Estimate	90% CI	95% CI	99% CI
Indirect(Mediation) effects				
$a_1 b_1$ (SMU→SS→AS)	-0.110	$[-0.228, -0.030]$	$[-0.256, -0.015]$	$[-0.323, 0.021]$
$b_1 c_1$ (SS→AS→LS)	0.028	$[0.000, 0.092]$	$[-0.004, 0.106]$	$[-0.018, 0.151]$
$b_1 c_2$ (SS→AS→LCI)	0.051	$[0.017, 0.108]$	$[0.010, 0.122]$	$[-0.006, 0.154]$
$a_2 c_1$ (SMU→AS→LS)	-0.010	$[-0.055, 0.006]$	$[-0.069, 0.010]$	$[-0.105, 0.022]$
$a_1 b_2$ (SMU→SS→LS)	0.415	$[0.282, 0.607]$	$[0.260, 0.653]$	$[0.222, 0.750]$
$a_1 b_1 c_1$ (SMU→SS→AS→LS)	0.013	$[0.001, 0.045]$	$[-0.001, 0.053]$	$[-0.008, 0.076]$
$a_2 c_2$ (SMU→AS→LCI)	-0.019	$[-0.054, 0.017]$	$[-0.062, 0.027]$	$[-0.083, 0.049]$
$a_1 b_3$ (SMU→SS→LCI)	0.183	$[0.111, 0.295]$	$[0.100, 0.323]$	$[0.080, 0.373]$
$a_1 b_1 c_2$ (SMU→SS→AS→LCI)	0.023	$[0.008, 0.054]$	$[0.005, 0.061]$	$[-0.002, 0.078]$
Total effects				
$Total_1$ (SMU→AS)	-0.020	$[-0.161, 0.114]$	$[-0.189, 0.143]$	$[-0.248, 0.196]$
$Total_2$ (SS→LS)	0.955	$[0.791, 1.178]$	$[0.765, 1.232]$	$[0.706, 1.322]$
$Total_3$ (SS→LCI)	0.460	$[0.320, 0.640]$	$[0.298, 0.675]$	$[0.254, 0.764]$
$Total_4$ (SMU→LS)	0.417	$[0.282, 0.611]$	$[0.259, 0.656]$	$[0.214, 0.756]$
$Total_5$ (SMU→LCI)	0.187	$[0.108, 0.301]$	$[0.096, 0.327]$	$[0.072, 0.379]$

Notes：The reported estimates are unstandardized ones.

The bias-corrected 90% confidence level for the indirect effect of social support on life satisfaction through acculturative stress ($b_1 c_1$) was 0.000 to 0.092. As zero was included in this interval, it is thus concluded that the indirect effect of social support on life satisfaction through acculturative stress was not satisfactorily significant. h2 should be rejected.

The bias-corrected 95% confidence level for the indirect effect of social support on local cultural identification through acculturative stress($b_1 c_2$) was 0.010 to 0.122. It did not include zero, and thus confirming that the indirect effect of social support on local cultural identification through acculturative stress was statistically significant. h3 was supported.

The bias-corrected 90% confidence level for the indirect effect of social media use on life satisfaction through acculturative stress ($a_2 c_1$) was -0.055 to 0.006. As zero was included in this interval, it can be concluded that the indirect effect of social media use on life satisfaction through acculturative stress was not statistically significant. h4 was not supported.

The bias-corrected 99% confidence level for the indirect effect of social media use on life satisfaction through social support($a_1 b_2$) was 0.222 to 0.750. As zero was excluded from this interval, it can be claimed that the indirect effect of social media use on life satisfaction through social support was statistically significant. h5 was supported.

The bias-corrected 90% confidence level for the indirect effect of social media use on life satisfaction through social support and acculturative stress($a_1 b_1 c_1$) was 0.001 to 0.045. As zero was excluded in this interval, it can be concluded that social media use had a significant indirect effect on life satisfaction through social support and acculturative stress, and the indirect effect was positive. h6 was supported.

The bias-corrected 90% confidence level for the indirect effect of social media use on local cultural identification through acculturative stress($a_2 c_2$) was -0.054 to 0.017. As zero was contained in this interval, it is thus concluded that the indirect effect of social media use on local cultural identification through acculturative stress was not statistically significant. Therefore, acculturative stress did not mediate the relationship between social media use and local cultural identification. h7 was not supported.

The bias-corrected 99% confidence level for the indirect effect of social media use on local cultural identification through social support($a_1 b_3$) was between 0.080 to 0.373. As zero was not contained in this interval, it can thus be claimed that the indirect effect of social media use on local cultural identification through social support was statistically significant. h8 was supported.

The bias-corrected 95% confidence level for the indirect effect of social media use on local cultural identification through social support and acculturative stress($a_1 b_1 c_2$) was 0.005 to 0.061. As zero was not included in this interval, we can claim that the indirect effect of social media use on local cultural identification through social support and acculturative stress was statistically significant. h9 was supported.

In a similar vein, the total effects in the overall structural model(a) were tested. The key to claim the significance of the total effects is to examine the bias-corrected bootstrap confidence intervals for the total effects($Total_1 \sim Total_5$). If zero is not included in a specific bias-corrected bootstrap confidence interval, it can be claimed that the total effect is statistically significant. If zero is included in the specific bias-corrected bootstrap confidence interval, the total effect does not exist.

As can be seen from Table 7.17, the bias-corrected 90% confidence interval for the total effect of social media use on acculturative stress($Total_1$) was -0.161 to 0.114. As zero was included in the interval, it can be claimed that the total effect of social media use on acculturative stress was not statistically significant. It might be due to the fact that the negative effect of $a_1 b_1$ (SMU→SS→AS) neutralized the positive effect of a_2 (SMU→AS).

The bias-corrected 99% confidence interval for the total effect of social support on life satisfaction($Total_2$) was 0.706 to 1.322. Because zero was excluded, it can be claimed that the total effect of social support on life satisfaction was statistically significant. Social sup-

port had a significantly positive effect on life satisfaction(0.955).
As can be seen from Table 7.16 and Table 7.17, the total effect of
social support on life satisfaction was the sum of the indirect effect
of $b_1 c_1$ (SS→AS→LS) and the direct effect of b_2 (SS→LS). The indirect effect of $b_1 c_1$ (SS→AS→LS) was 0.028(2.618%), and the direct effect of b_2 (SS→LS) was 0.927(97.382%). Therefore, the indirect effect of $b_1 c_1$ (SS→AS→LS) was weak whereas the direct
effect of b_2 (SS→LS) was strong.

The bias-corrected 99% bootstrap confidence interval for the
total effect of social support on local cultural identification($Total_3$)
was 0.254 to 0.764. As zero was not included in the interval, it can
be claimed that the total effect of social support on local cultural
identification($Total_3$) was statistically significant. Social support
had a significantly positive effect on local cultural identification
(0.460). It can be observed from Table 7.16 and Table 6.17 that
$Total_3$(SS→LCI) was divided into the indirect effect of $b_1 c_2$ (SS→
AS→LCI) and b_3 (SS→LCI). The indirect effect of $b_1 c_2$ (SS→AS→
LCI) yielded a value of 0.051(11.087%), and the direct effect of
b_3 (SS→LCI) yielded a value of 0.409(88.913%). As the indirect
effect of $b_1 c_2$ (SS→AS→LCI) was weak, it is thus concluded that
the total effect of social support on local cultural identification was
largely derived from the direct effect of social support on local cultural identification(b_3).

The total effect of social media use on life satisfaction ($Total_4$)
was significant as the bias-corrected bootstrap 99% CI for $Total_4$
(SMU→LS) was 0.214 to 0.756 and excluded zero. Social media use
had a positive total effect on life satisfaction(0.417). As can be seen
from Table 7.16 and Table 7.17, $Total_4$(SMU→LS) is derived from
three parts: the indirect effect of $a_2 c_1$ (SMU→AS→LS) was −0.010
(2.398%), the indirect effect of $a_1 b_2$ (SMU→SS→LS) was 0.415
(99.520%), and $a_1 b_1 c_1$ (SMU→SS→AS→LS) was 0.013(3.118%).
It indicated that the indirect effect of $a_1 b_2$ (SMU→SS→LS) was
the strongest. The negative indirect effects of social media use on

life satisfaction through acculturative stress($a_2 c_1$) and the positive indirect effect of social media use on life satisfaction through social media use and acculturative stress($a_1 b_1 c_1$) were rather weak, and the two indirect effects nearly offset each other.

The bias-corrected 99% confidence interval for the total effect of social media use on local cultural identification($Total_5$) was 0.072 to 0.379. As zero was excluded, it is thus confirmed that the total effect of social media use on local cultural identification($Total_5$) was statistically significant. Social media use had a significant positive effect on local cultural identification. The total effect of social media use on local cultural identification($Total_5$) was divided into three parts: $a_2 c_2$(SMU→AS→LCI) was -0.019(10.160%), $a_1 b_3$ (SMU→SS→LCI) was 0.183(97.816%), and $a_1 b_1 c_2$(SMU→SS→ AS→LCI) was 0.023(12.299%). It can be easily observed that the indirect effect of social media use on local cultural identification through social support, i.e., $a_1 b_3$(SMU→SS→LCI) played a dominant role.

7.6.4   Mediation Effects Test on the Simplified Structural Model(a)

After the mediation test on the overall structural model(a), the mediation effects in the simplified structural model(a) were tested. The mediation hypotheses on the indirect and total effects (h1—h14) were tested again to derive robust findings.

Through item parceling, the simplified structural model(a) had fewer parameters to be estimated. The model fit indices of the simplified structural model(a) yielded from bootstrapping are reported in Table 7.18. Through a comparison between Table 7.18 and Table 7.15, it can be observed that most of the fit indices of the simplified structural model(a) were better than the overall structural model (a), which indicated that the simplified structural model(a) fit the data better. It provided basis for further analysis of the indirect and total effects in the simplified structural model(a).

Table 7.18   Model Fit of the Simplified Structural Model(a) Using Bootstrap

Model Fit Index	Criterion	Simplified Model(a)
χ^2	smaller is better	361.719
df(Degree of Freedom)	bigger is better	179
Normed Chi-squared(χ^2/df)	$1<\chi^2/df<3$	2.021
RMSEA(90% confidence interval)	<0.08	0.050[0.043, 0.058]
Pr(RMSEA $\leqslant 0.05$)	bigger is better	0.460
SRMR	<0.08	0.059
TLI(NNFI)	>0.9	0.926
CFI	>0.9	0.936

The bootstrap estimates of the direct effects in the simplified structural model(a) are presented in Table 7.19. Through a comparison of Table 7.19 and Table 7.16, it can be observed that the bootstrap estimates of the direct effects in the simplified structural model(a) yielded similar values to those in the overall structural model (a). However, the statistical significance of the direct effects in the simplified structural model(a) improved. For example, the direct effect of acculturative stress on life satisfaction c_1 (AS→LS) in the simplified model(a) was significant at a p<0.05 level, whereas the direct effect of acculturative stress on life satisfaction c_1 (AS→LS) in the overall structural model(a) was significant at a p<0.1 level.

The author then examined the bias-corrected bootstrap confidence intervals for the indirect effects in the simplified structural model(a) to test the hypotheses of the mediation effects. As can be seen from Table 7.19, the bias-corrected 99% confidence intervals for the indirect effects of $a_1 b_2$ (SMU→SS→LS) and $a_1 b_3$ (SMU→ SS→LCI) excluded zero, thus indicating the significance of the indirect effects of $a_1 b_2$ (SMU→SS→LS) and $a_1 b_3$ (SMU→SS→LCI). Therefore, h5 and h8 were confirmed. The indirect effects of $a_1 b_1$ (SMU→SS→AS), $b_1 c_2$ (SS→AS→LCI), and $a_1 b_1 c_2$ (SMU→SS→ AS→LCI) were statistically significant, evidenced by the exclusion of zero in their respective bias-corrected 95% confidence intervals. h1, h3, and h9 were thus supported. The bias-corrected 90% confidence

Table 7.19 Test Significance of Direct Effects of the Simplified Structural Model(a)

Direct effects	Regression result		Bootstrap estimate			Bias-corrected Bootstrap		
	B	SE	B	SE	90% CI	90% CI	95% CI	99% CI
a_1(SMU→SS)	0.458***	0.081	0.458***	0.099	[0.326, 0.650]	[0.301, 0.695]	[0.257, 0.801]
a_2(SMU→AS)	0.139	0.093	0.139	0.121	[−0.055, 0.340]	[−0.095, 0.383]	[−0.175, 0.484]
b_1(SS→AS)	−0.260†	0.107	−0.260†	0.125	[−0.459, −0.055]	[−0.505, −0.017]	[−0.590, 0.071]
b_2(SS→LS)	0.917***	0.092	0.917***	0.094	[0.776, 1.088]	[0.752, 1.119]	[0.703, 1.194]
b_3(SS→LCI)	0.410***	0.083	0.410***	0.088	[0.282, 0.570]	[0.260, 0.604]	[0.220, 0.681]
c_1(AS→LS)	−0.120†	0.059	−0.120*	0.071	[−0.236, −0.004]	[−0.263, 0.019]	[−0.320, 0.064]
c_2(AS→LCI)	−0.192***	0.049	−0.192***	0.060	[−0.306, −0.106]	[−0.327, −0.089]	[−0.371, −0.054]

Notes: 1. The reported estimates are unstandardized ones.
2. *** p<0.001, † p<0.05, * p<0.1.

interval for the indirect effects of $b_1 c_1$ (SS→AS→LS) and $a_1 b_1 c_1$ (SMU→SS→AS→LS) did not include zero, indicating a statistical significance for the indirect effects of $b_1 c_1$ (SS→AS→LS) and $a_1 b_1 c_1$ (SMU→SS→AS→LS). h2 and h6 were thus supported. However, as zero was included in the bias-corrected 90% confidence intervals for the indirect effects of $a_2 c_1$ (SMU→AS→LS) and $a_2 c_2$ (SMU→AS→LCI), it is thus claimed that the indirect effects of $a_2 c_1$ (SMU→AS→LS) and $a_2 c_2$ (SMU→AS→LCI) were not statistically significant. Therefore, h4 and h7 were not confirmed.

In addition, the hypotheses regarding the total effects in the simplified structural model(a) were tested. As is shown in Table 7.19, the bias-corrected bootstrap 90% confidence interval for the total effect of social media use on acculturative stress $Total_1$ (SMU→AS) included zero, thus indicating that the total effect for $Total_1$ (SMU→AS) was not statistically significant. The bias-corrected bootstrap 99% confidence intervals for the total effects of $Total_2$ (SS→LS), $Total_3$ (SS→LCI), $Total_4$ (SMU→LS), and $Total_5$ (SMU→LCI) excluded zero, thus confirming that the total effects of $Total_2$ (SS→LS), $Total_3$ (SS→LCI), $Total_4$ (SMU→LS), and $Total_5$ (SMU→LCI) were statistically significant. Therefore, h11—h14 were supported.

From Table 7.19 and Table 7.20, we can see the composition of the total effects in the simplified structural model(a). The total effect of social support on life satisfaction($Total_2$) was divided into b_2 (SS→LS) and $b_1 c_1$ (SS→AS→LS). The bootstrap estimates showed that the direct effect of b_2 (SS→LS) largely accounted for the total effect of social support on life satisfaction($Total_2$). Likewise, the total effect of social support on local cultural identification($Total_3$) was largely accounted for by the direct effect of b_3 (SS→LCI). However, the indirect effects of $a_1 b_2$ (SMU→SS→LS) and $a_1 b_3$ (SMU→SS→LCI) largely accounted for the total effect of $Total_4$ (SMU→LS) and $Total_5$ (SMU→LCI) respectively. Through the comparison of the total effects between the simplified structural model(a) and the overall structural model(a) and the decomposition of the total effects in the two models, it can be observed that the estimate results of the simplified structural model(a) were highly consistent with those of the overall structural model(a). It can thus be concluded that the findings on the total effects in the overall structural model(a) were robust.

Table 7.20　Significance Test of Mediation and Total Effects in the Simplified Structural Model(a)

	Bias-corrected Bootstrap			
	Estimate	90% CI	95% CI	99% CI
Indirect(Mediation) effects				
$a_1 b_1$ (SMU→SS→AS)	−0.119	[−0.247, −0.033]	[−0.277, −0.015]	[−0.352, 0.024]
$b_1 c_1$ (SS→AS→LS)	0.031	[0.003, 0.091]	[−0.001, 0.106]	[−0.013, 0.143]
$b_1 c_2$ (SS→AS→LCI)	0.050	[0.016, 0.106]	[0.010, 0.119]	[−0.005, 0.149]
$a_2 c_1$ (SMU→AS→LS)	−0.017	[−0.067, 0.003]	[−0.079, 0.007]	[−0.113, 0.019]
$a_1 b_2$ (SMU→SS→LS)	0.419	[0.287, 0.611]	[0.265, 0.655]	[0.225, 0.745]
$a_1 b_1 c_1$ (SMU→SS→AS→LS)	0.014	[0.002, 0.047]	[0.000, 0.056]	[−0.005, 0.077]
$a_2 c_2$ (SMU→AS→LCI)	−0.027	[−0.064, 0.005]	[−0.073, 0.014]	[−0.096, 0.035]
$a_1 b_3$ (SMU→SS→LCI)	0.187	[0.114, 0.301]	[0.104, 0.328]	[0.083, 0.378]
$a_1 b_1 c_2$ (SMU→SS→AS→LCI)	0.023	[0.008, 0.055]	[0.005, 0.062]	[−0.002, 0.079]
Total effects				
$Total_1$ (SMU→AS)	0.020	[−0.130, 0.166]	[−0.161, 0.195]	[−0.223, 0.256]
$Total_2$ (SS→LS)	0.948	[0.810, 1.112]	[0.786, 1.146]	[0.737, 1.220]
$Total_3$ (SS→LCI)	0.459	[0.322, 0.629]	[0.298, 0.663]	[0.258, 0.740]
$Total_4$ (SMU→LS)	0.417	[0.281, 0.612]	[0.258, 0.656]	[0.214, 0.753]
$Total_5$ (SMU→LCI)	0.184	[0.105, 0.297]	[0.092, 0.323]	[0.068, 0.376]

Notes：The reported estimates are unstandardized ones.

7.7   Chapter Summary

This chapter described the structural model estimating process. In the previous chapter, confirmatory factor analysis(CFA) of the latent variables in the proposed hypothesized model was conducted. A second-order CFA model of social support was derived, which comprised three first-order sub-constructs: emotional support, informational support, and occupational support. Likewise, a second-order CFA model of acculturative stress with four first-order sub-constructs(perceived discrimination, cultural discomfort, economic strain, and homesickness) was developed. Based on the CFA results, the hypothesized model was modified.

In examining the multicollinearity in the structural model, it was found that extroversion and neuroticism had a correlation higher than 0.7.Thus, the author first retained extroversion in the structural model, and tested the hypotheses regarding the dependence relationships among the variables in the structural model. Results indicated that respondents' social media use had a positive effect on their perceived social support but had no significant effects on the acculturative stress they experienced. The results also showed that respondents' acculturative stress negatively affected their life satisfaction and local cultural identification. In addition, respondents' perceived social support was found positively associated with their life satisfaction and local cultural identification but negatively associated with their acculturative stress. As for the effects of extroversion, results showed that it had some positive impacts on social support and had negative influence on acculturative stress. In order to confirm the robustness of the findings, the author replaced extroversion with neuroticism and estimated the overall structural model again. The SEM analysis yielded similar results regarding the relationships among the variables. Neuroticism was found to be negatively associated with perceived social support and acculturative stress.

In order to derive a more parsimonious structural model, the author conducted item parceling on the first-order sub-constructs of social support and acculturative stress. The simplified structural model was tested and research results indicated that the hypothesized relationships among the variables were stable.

Then, the author conducted bootstrap analysis to test the mediation effects in the overall structural model. Research results indicated that social support served as a mediator of the relationship between social media use and life satisfaction, as well as the relationship between social media use and local cultural identification. Additionally, social support and acculturative stress served as the serial mediators of the relationship between social media use and life satisfaction, as well as the relationship between social media us and local cultural identification. What's more, acculturative stress served as the mediator of the relationship between social support and life satisfaction, as well as the relationship between social support and local cultural identification.

Last, the mediation effects in the simplified structural model were tested. Similar results were yielded, which led to the conclusion that the mediation effects in the overall structural model were robust. In the next chapter, the major research findings and implications of the findings will be discussed.

Chapter Eight

Discussion and Conclusions

This chapter first summarizes the present study. Then it discusses the major findings and implications of the major findings. In the following, it discusses the contributions of the study. Last, it puts forward some research limitations and offers some directions for future research.

8.1 Summary of the Present Study

The main objective of the present study was to examine how social media use affected the overall adaptation of internal migrants in China. Building on a thorough literature review of related theories and empirical studies at home and abroad, a hypothesized model describing factors affecting internal migrants' adaptation was proposed, with a focus on the effects of social media use on adaptation. More specifically, three key adaptation variables were identified as indicators to assess internal migrants' adaptation process and outcomes: acculturative stress, life satisfaction, and local cultural identification. Additionally, the present study identified social support as an important mediator linking social media use and the adaptation variables. Certain individual factors affecting the adaptation variables were also included in the hypothesized model as covariates in order to make the research results robust, including two personality variables (extroversion and neuroticism) and internal migrants' length of stay in their current residence.

The author then conducted a quantitative survey study to test the hypothesized model. The research sample was drawn from internal migrant population living in Shanghai(N = 703). An online survey was conducted to collect the data. After the data collection, the author examined the questionnaires carefully and retained a number of 703 questionnaires for further analysis. Structural equation modeling(SEM) was used to test the relationships among the variables in the hypothesized model. First, 300 samples were randomly drawn from the total sample and were used to conduct an exploratory factor analysis(EFA) on the self-developed perceived social support scale for internal migrants. Three factors were extracted: emotional support, informational support, and occupational support. Then, with the remaining 403 questionnaires, Confirmatory factor analysis(CFA) was conducted to establish the measurement models of the five latent variables(social media use, social support, acculturative stress, life satisfaction, and local cultural identification). Two second-order constructs were derived. The first was a second-order construct of social support which comprised three first-order sub-constructs(emotional support, informational support, and occupational support). The second was acculturative stress comprising four first-order sub-constructs(perceived discrimination, cultural discomfort, homesickness, and economic strain). Then, based on the factor scores of the latent variables, the Independent Samples *t* Test on the factor scores of the latent constructs was carried out to examine the effects of demographic variables on adaptation. Finally, the hypothesized structural model was tested. Path coefficients were examined to see whether the research hypotheses on the direct effects were supported or not. The Bootstrap method was adopted to examine the mediation effects among the variables. Item parceling was conducted to derive a more parsimonious structural model and to test the robustness of the hypothesized relationships among the variables. The main findings of the present study are listed as follows:

First, the perceived social support scale for internal migrants was developed and validated. Results indicated that three types of social support were important, including emotional support, informational support, and occupational support.

Second, three important constructs were identified to assess the overall adaptation of internal migrants: acculturative stress, life satisfaction, and local cultural identification. The measurements of these latent constructs were established. A second-order CFA model of acculturative stress was derived. Research results showed that internal migrants experienced stressors involving perceived discrimination, cultural discomfort, homesickness, and economic strain.

Third, research results indicated that there were some factors that have some significant effects on the adaptation of internal migrants, including a few demographic factors(gender, Local Hukou, Housing conditions, and length of stay in Shanghai) and two personality variables(extroversion and neuroticism).

Fourth, through SEM analysis, the study found the paths through which internal migrants' social media use affected their adaptation. To be specific, social media use affected adaptation variables through social support: (1) internal migrants' social media use increased their perceived social support, and in turn increased their life satisfaction; and (2) internal migrants' social media use increased their perceived social support, and in turn increased their local cultural identification. In addition, social support and acculturative stress served as serial mediators of the effects of social media use on adaptation variables: (1) internal migrants' social media use increased their perceived social support, and in turn decreased their acculturative stress, which in turn increased their life satisfaction; and(2) internal migrants' social media use increased their perceived social support, and in turn decreased their acculturative stress, which in turn increased their local cultural identification.

8.2   Discussion of Main Research Findings

8.2.1   The Development and Validation of Social Support Scales for Internal Migrants

Most domestic studies on adaptation of internal migrants examine their social support using the Social Support Rating Scales (SSRS)(Xiao, 1993) which measures the general perceived social support from two aspects: the social support network size and density. However, for internal migrants who relocate themselves in a new environment, they may need support that are specifically related to their needs of fitting into the new environment(e.g., learning about the cultural norms and practices of the local society). Therefore, the present study developed a perceived social support scale specific to internal migrants.

Through an exploratory factor analysis(EFA), the self-developed perceived social support scale was developed and three factors were extracted: emotional support, informational support, and occupational support. Then, the self-developed scale was validated through a second-order confirmatory factor analysis(CFA). Statistical analysis indicated the self-developed perceived social support scale was reliable and valid.

The results of the EFA and CFA indicate that the aforementioned three types of social support are important to internal migrants' adaptation. Similar to other establishes perceived social support scales, emotional support is the comfort and emotional support internal migrants could obtain when they are in need. Migration may bring about some acculturative stress such as perceived discrimination or homesickness, and emotional support boosts internal migrants' confidence to cope with the stress and is thus beneficial to their adaptation outcomes. Informational support contains some items that are specifically related to the knowledge of the local culture and rules and regulations. Despite internal migrants move within China, they may still face some challenges in fitting into the local society due to regional variations. As adaptation is a cultural learning process, they need to get some information on the local culture and rules and regulations of the local society to facilitate their adaptation process.

Compared with other perceived social support scales, the results of the present study indicate that occupational support is important to internal migrants and is of great significance to their adaptation outcomes. It is because that respondents of the present study are internal migrants who have jobs. According to the theories of the origins of migration(Lee,1966), one of the primary causes of migration is economic improvement. Internal migrants who move to the new environment are motivated by the opportunities to improve their economic conditions. Therefore, they desire to find good jobs which render high earnings and reward. However, they may face some difficulties in their occupation-related issues. For example, previous studies found that some internal migrants experienced difficulties in finding their jobs and had low earnings due to lack of skills(Wong & Song, 2008). What's more, some were discriminated against regarding their employment opportunities and working conditions(Yang et al., 2012). As a consequence, internal migrants are in need of social support to deal with the difficulties related to their occupation.

8.2.2   The Measurement of Adaptation of Internal Migrants

As previously discussed, adaptation is both a process during which migrants fit into their new residence and an outcome from their adjustive behavior(Kim, 2001; Searle & Ward, 1990). The present study identified three important variables to examine the overall adaptation of internal migrants in China: acculturative stress, life satisfaction, and local cultural identification. Life satisfaction and local cultural identification can be viewed as final adaptation outcomes. These two variables can reflect the psychological adaptation of internal migrants and their inner transformation after the process of their adjusting to the local culture.

Acculturative stress is a crucial factor affecting adaptation outcomes. Meanwhile, it is also an indicator of transitional outcome of adaptation which reflects how well internal migrants fit into the new environment after a certain period of stay in the new environment. In domestic studies, there is a lack of measurement of the stress internal migrants experienced in their adaptation process. In the present study, a second-order CFA model of internal migrants' acculturative stress was proposed, which comprised four sub-constructs (perceived discrimination, cultural discomfort, homesickness, and economic strain). The validation of the second-order CFA model of acculturative stress indicates that internal migrants experience the aforementioned stressors. Perceive discrimination is a common stressor in adaption process. Internal migrants may perceive discrimination from the local society due to their identity as "*waidiren*." Cultural discomfort is the negative feelings internal migrants have in adapting to some local customs or social practices. These research findings indicate that some internal migrants in Shanghai have some discomfort in adjusting themselves to the local food, and have some difficulties in understanding the Shanghai dialect or following some local cultural customs. It indicates that cultural differences do not only exist at a macro level, i.e., national differences. Internal migrants who are moving within a large nation like China may experience cultural differences at regional levels and have some adaptation problems. In addition, as relationships based on geographic proximity and kinship are important in the traditional Chinese values, internal migrants who move to a new location may experience some feelings of homesickness brought about by their separation from the families or close relationships at the places of origin. Last, economic strain is a major stressor experienced by internal migrants. Economic factor is one of the major reasons driving migration. Some migrants move from underdeveloped regions to developed ones in the hope of improving their economic conditions. However, there exist possibilities that some internal migrants experience economic strain due to changes of socioeconomic status or the economic disparity between the local residence and their places of origin.

8.2.3 Factors Affecting Adaptation of Internal Migrants

Adaptation is an umbrella term. Drawing upon the existing literature, the present study identified three important constructs to assess the adaptation of internal migrants in Shanghai: acculturative stress, life satisfaction, and local cultural identification. Through the Independent Samples t Test and the Structural Equation Modeling (SEM) analysis, the research findings indicated that internal migrants' adaptation was affected by multiple factors.

8.2.3.1 The Effects of Demographic Factors on Adaptation of Internal Migrants

Results indicated that a few demographic factors had significant influence on internal migrants' adaptation, including respondents' gender, hukou status, housing conditions, and their length of stay in Shanghai. First, respondents' gender affected their life satisfaction in Shanghai. Compared with female migrants, male migrants experienced less life satisfaction. It might be because that people have higher expectations on men's social roles and their responsibilities for raising the family, which is likely to cause more stress and will thus negatively affect their life satisfaction.

Second, respondents who had been staying in Shanghai for a longer time reported less acculturative stress, higher level of life satisfaction, and identification with the local culture. As Kim (2001) argues, adaptation is a long-process, and individuals who encounter a new culture are likely to go through the process of the stress-adaptation-growth. As internal migrants' length of stay in Shanghai increases, they will be more adaptive to the local culture, and acquire more skills to help them solve the difficulties of fitting in. In addition, they will establish more social networks and perceive more social support, which has positive effects on their adaptation.

Third, research results indicated that internal migrants' Hukou status and housing conditions had significant influences on their adaptation. To be specific, respondents who had obtained the Shanghai Hukou had less acculturative stress, higher level of life satisfaction and local cultural identification. And compared with those who had not purchased their own houses in Shanghai, those who had purchased their own houses in Shanghai had lower levels of acculturative stress, higher levels of life satisfaction and identification with local culture. These findings suggest that obtaining the local Hukou and having self-owned houses in the local residence are very important in internal migrants' adaptation. Traditionally Hukou and self-owned houses have significant meanings in Chinese people's mind. Obtaining the local Hukou and owing houses in the migration destination are the criteria based on which internal migrants are judged as settlers in their migration destinations. Those who have the local Hukou and their own houses in Shanghai tend to have more sense of the stability of taking root in the local society, which will have positive influence on their life satisfaction. In addition, internal migrants who have the local Hukou and self-owned houses tend to self-identify themselves as the locals. Meanwhile, they will have higher levels of sense of belongings to the local society and higher levels of identification with the local society.

8.2.3.2   The Effects of Personality Variables on Adaptation of Internal Migrants

The present study also examined the influence of two personality variables (neuroticism and extroversion) on social support and acculturative stress. Research results indicated that extroversion was positively associated with internal migrants' perceived social support but negative associated with their acculturative stress. By contrast, neuroticism was negatively associated with internal migrants' perceived social support while positively associated with their acculturative stress. The research results were in consistent with some previous literature(e.g., Poyrazli et al., 2007). Internal migrants who are more extrovert tend to be more active, cheerful and less sensitive to stressors(Carver & Connor-Smith, 2010; Roesch et al., 2006). Thereby, they will experience less acculturative stress in their adaptation process. Besides, they are more active in social interactions and social support seeking, and are more likely to have higher levels of perceived social support. On the contrary, migrants who are more neurotic are more pre-dispositioned to negative affect and are more susceptible to stress, and will experience higher levels of acculturative stress. In addition, they are less involved in social interactions and support seeking, and will thus have lower levels of perceived social support.

8.2.4 The Effects of Social Media Use on Adaptation of Internal Migrants

The research results of the present study indicated that social media use had some positive effects on the adaptation of internal migrants. The ways through which social media use affected the adaptation of internal migrants are presented as follows:

First, research results indicated that social media use positively affected internal migrants' adaptation through its effects on their perceived social support. To be specific, internal migrants' social media use increased their perceived social support, and in turn decreased their acculturative stress. In addition, internal migrants' social media use increased their perceived social support, and in turn increased their life satisfaction and local cultural identification.

These findings have confirmed the positive relationship between social media use and perceived social support and are consistent with some previous literature(Ellison et al., 2017; Liu & Yu, 2013). The current research results indicated that internal migrants'

social media use was positively correlated with the three types of
perceived social support: informational support, emotional support, and occupational support(See Table 7.3). This is most likely
due to social media's function in maintaining and expanding
individuals' social networks. As previous noted, social support is
considered as resources embedded in an individual's social networks
(Lin, 2008). Traditionally, internal migrants' social support is
mostly obtained via certain offline social networks, such as their
family members, friends, and neighbors they know about. However, the acquisition of traditional social support is limited by time
and space. Also, some studies indicated that internal migrants have
difficulties expanding their pre-existing networks that are restricted
by face-to-face encounters(Dong, 2009). Therefore, internal migrants may perceive inadequate access to the support they need. Social media facilitates communication among people by breaking
time and geographic boundaries and is conducive to the maintenance of their pre-existing social networks. In the present study, respondents reported using different types of social media(e.g., We-
Chat and QQ) to keep in contact with their family and communicate with their friends. As suggested by Ye(2006b), migrants' pre-
existing social networks characterized by strong ties are important
sources of emotional and instrumental support(e.g., financial support). In addition to maintaining pre-existing offline social networks, social media provides platforms(e.g., online communities)
for internal migrants to contact different groups of people, and
helps establish new social networks which would otherwise be difficult to be formed via face-to-face encounters. Internal migrants can
seek social support from their online connections that provide
"new, more appropriate or more matching networks of support,
such as others facing the same or similar transitions and stressors"
(Mikal, Rice, Abeyta, & DeVilbiss, 2013, p.A47). Chen and Choi
(2011) also argue that seeking social support from one's online social networks is flexible and efficient. According to Granovetter

(1973), diverse social networks are extremely helping in proving informational support and support for finding jobs. Therefore, internal migrants' use of social media helps maintain and expand their social networks both offline and online, and in turn increases their perceived availability of different types of social support.

Consistent with some previous literature (He & Wang, 2016; Wong et al., 2012), the current research results suggested that internal migrants' perceived social support was also positively associated with their life satisfaction. An individual's life satisfaction is understood as an individual's assessment on his overall life conditions. Cohen and Wills(1985, p.311) noted that social support "provides positive affect, a sense of predictability and stability in one's life situation, and a recognition of self-worth." Therefore, perceptions of adequate social support will increase internal migrants' positive assessment on their lives. Results of the present research indicated that internal migrant's occupational support had the highest correlation with their life satisfaction (See Table 7.3). Previous studies found that internal migrants' life satisfaction was related with their job conditions(Chen & Zhu, 2008; Wen & Wang, 2009). Some studies suggested that internal migrants moving to Shanghai reported experiencing difficulties in finding jobs or other work-related issues, such as job instability and unsatisfactory working conditions(Wong & Song, 2008; Yang et al., 2012). Therefore, when internal migrants perceive more occupational support, they will have enhanced confidence in handling job-related stress, thereby increasing their satisfaction towards life.

Likewise, research findings indicated that internal migrants' perceived social support helped increase their local cultural identification. This is consistent with Brisset et al. 's(2012) study. The current research results indicated that the three types of internal migrants' perceived social support(emotional support, informational support, and occupational support) were all positively correlated with their local cultural identification (See Table 7.3). Social support provides both tangible and intangible resources which help internal migrants deal with the difficulties in adapting to the local society. For example, in the present research, the items of internal migrants' perceived informational support are mainly related to where they could obtain information about the local culture or the local rules and regulations. These kinds of informational support help increase their cultural knowledge about Shanghai, and will contribute to their adoption of cultural practices in Shanghai. Additionally, emotional support can alleviate some negative feelings experienced by internal migrants, e.g., perceived discrimination. When internal migrants experience lower levels of discrimination from the local people, they will feel more accepted by the local society and will thus have a higher sense of belonging to the local culture.

Second, in Chapter Three, it was hypothesized that social media use would have both positive and negative effects on acculturative stress, and that social media use would have some indirect effects on life satisfaction and local cultural identification through its effects on acculturative stress. However, the direct relationship between social media use and acculturative stress was not found significant, nor were the indirect relationships between social media use and life satisfaction or local cultural identification via the mediating role of acculturative stress. This is perhaps because internal migrants' social media use has mixed effects on acculturative stress, depending on the different purposes of their social media use. On one hand, social media use facilitates internal migrants' social support acquisition, which will reduce their adaptation difficulties and in turn reduce their acculturative stress. On the other hand, using social media may contribute to the acculturative stress internal migrants experienced. As suggested in the study conducted by Park et al.(2014), migrants who use social media to increase connections with their family and friends at their home culture might strengthen their endorsement of the home cultural identity or activities, which will cause difficulties in their psychological or behavioral adjustments and thus lead to more acculturative stress. There is also likelihood that internal migrants who use social media to contact with their home culture experience some aspects of stress such as homesickness. In addition, according to Hampton et al. (2016), exposures to social media could increase social media users' awareness towards the stressful life events experienced by others and thus lead to greater level of stress among its users. When internal migrants learn about other people's negative experience in adapting to the new environment (e.g., perceived discrimination), they will probably be negatively affected and will experience more acculturative stress. Thus, the research findings suggest that in future, it is important for researchers to examine internal migrants' specific use of social media and its relation with different aspects of acculturative stress. As the author did not ask the respondents about their particular use of social media related with each of the four dimensions of acculturative stress, it is therefore difficult to determine the exact relationship between social media use and the four sub-dimensions of acculturative stress.

Third, despite acculturative stress did not mediate the relationship between social media use and life satisfaction, nor the relationship between social media use and local cultural identification, research results indicated that social support and acculturative stress served as serial mediators of the relationship between social media use and life satisfaction, and that of social media use and local cultural identification. More specifically, internal migrants' social media use increased their perceived social support and in turn decreased their acculturative stress, which further increased their life satisfaction. Likewise, internal migrants' social media use increased their perceived social support and in turn decreased their acculturative stress, which further increased their local cultural identification.

As previously discussed, social media use of the respondents increased their perceived social support and in turn reduced their acculturative stress. The research results of the present study revealed that decreased levels of acculturative stress was negatively related with respondents' life satisfaction, which were in line with some previous research findings(Chow, 2007; Pan, Wong, Joubert, & Chan, 2008). The results of the present research indicated that the four sub-constructs of acculturative stress were all negatively related with life satisfaction(See Table 7.3). As previously reviewed, internal migrants' life satisfaction is associated with some factors such as their income, housing, and working conditions(Chen & Zhu, 2008; Wen & Wang, 2009). Thus, higher levels of acculturative stress are associated with more difficulties in internal migrants' lives(e.g., experiencing economic strain), which will negatively affect internal migrants' assessment on their life and result in lower levels of life satisfaction. On the contrary, when internal migrants experience lower levels of acculturative stress, their life satisfaction will increase. Therefore, the above reasons could explain why social media use affects life satisfaction through its effects on perceived social support and acculturative stress.

Likewise, the research results suggested that the four sub-constructs of internal migrants' acculturative stress were negatively correlated with their local cultural identification(See Table 7.3). Previous studies found that certain objective factors(e.g., Hukou status, housing conditions, and employment) and subjective factors (e.g., discrimination from the locals and lack of social interactions with the locals) affected internal migrants' local cultural identification(Dong, 2009; Xu, 2007; Zhao & Li, 2013). When internal migrants experience acculturative stress in their adaptation process, they tend to feel upset by the discrepancy between reality and their previous expectations, which can negatively impact their attachment to the local society. Other stressors, such as cultural discomfort, also affect internal migrants' willingness to adopt the local cultural practices. Therefore, when internal migrants experience higher levels of acculturative stress, they will have lower levels of local cultural identification. On the contrary, when internal migrants experience lower levels of acculturative stress, they will have higher levels of local cultural identification.

8.3   Implications of the Research Findings

Based on the main research findings of the present study, a few implications are presented as follows:

8.3.1   Deepen the Reform on Hukou Registration System

First, as the research findings indicate that internal migrants who have the Shanghai Hukou experience less acculturative stress and higher levels of life satisfaction and local cultural identification, it is important for the government to formulate some policies to deepen the reform on China's Hukou system. China' Hukou system was established in 1958 as a means of regulating the population movement from rural areas to urban cities. According to the Hukous system, an individual is assigned to a residence and certain requirements need to be fulfilled for a change of Hukou registration. In recent years, a series of reforms have been implemented to decrease the restrictions of Hukou registration. However, in some meta cities like Shanghai, there are rigorous restrictions on obtaining a local Hukou. The research findings of the present study show that obtaining a local Hukou has some positive effects on internal migrants' adaptation outcomes. Hukou is an objective indicator of whether internal migrants have taken root in the local society and is related to many aspects of their lives such as social welfare, employment, and education opportunities for their children. Meanwhile, it is a criterion of their avowed identity(self-identification) and ascribed identity(perception of others). Therefore, the government should promote the household registration in the local residence for internal migrants who meet certain requirements. Additionally, some measures should be taken to optimize the social welfare enjoyed by residence permit holders as well as facilitate the transfer from residence permit to a local Hukou for internal migrants who are eligible. By doing so, internal migrants' life satisfaction will increase, so will their identification with the local society.

8.3.2   Promote the Establishment of Housing Security System

The research findings of the present study indicate that economic strain is one of the main acculturative stressors experienced by internal migrants. It is also found internal migrants' housing conditions have a significant effect on internal migrants' adaptation. Migrating to a new location implies a change of one's economic status. For internal migrants who have medium or low earnings, housing is a great concern because of the high expenses needed to purchase a house, especially in large cities like Shanghai. Therefore, the government could take more measures to promote the housing security system, which will help solve the difficulties of internal migrants who have difficulties purchasing their own houses. Different types of houses are now provided by the government to people in need, including public rental houses, low-rent houses, residence houses for low-and-medium wage, and talent apartments for professionals. The government should increase the provision of these types of houses to internal migrants who have different purchasing needs. Meanwhile, it should enlarge the coverage of the housing security system, facilitate internal migrants' application of these types of houses. Through this way, internal migrants' economic strain could be alleviated, which is conductive to the enhancement of their life satisfaction and their sense of stability of living in the local environment.

8.3.3   Provide Social Support for Internal Migrants Through Social Media

As research findings demonstrate that social media plays some positive roles during internal migrants' adaptation process, it is important to think how social media can be used to facilitate internal migrants' adaptation. One possible way is to provide internal migrants some kinds of social support they need in adapting to the local environment via various types of social media. The government or institutions concerned could establish some official platforms to provide more information or policies on migration-related issues that are of vital importance to internal migrants' adaptation, such as Hukou policies, employment regulations, social welfare, house purchasing, and education opportunities for internal migrants' children. Take a WeChat public account named "Household Registration in Shanghai" for example. It informs internal migrants about the policies on how to obtain the Shanghai Hukou or the Shanghai residence permit. It also provides some information on public rental housing for internal migrants who have not purchased their own houses in Shanghai yet. Through such platforms, internal migrants can obtain vitally important information which can help them practically adapt more efficiently. In addition to providing policies and regulations, other platforms on social media with more information on the local culture could be provided, so as to help internal migrants have better understanding of the local cultural values and norms, the local dialect, and so on. For example, an official WeChat account named "Caohejing Community Service" provides some courses and activities on learning how to speak the Shanghai dialect. Adequate cultural knowledge of the local society and the ability to understand and speak the Shanghai dialect could decrease internal migrants' adjustment difficulties, and will have positive influence on their adaptation outcomes.

8.3.4 Establish "Contact Space" Between Internal Migrants and the Locals

In addition, social media is also able to provide a "contact space"(Harwood, 2010)(e.g., virtual communities) for internal migrants to maintain their home-based social networks and increase contact with the locals. As previously reviewed, internal migrants depend largely on social networks established based on geographic proximity and kinship, which could provide important emotional and instrumental support(e.g., financial help)(Zhu & Liu, 2007). However, traditional social support networks based on face-to-face encounters are restricted by time and space. Online contact transcends these limitations and can maintain ties between migrants and their networks in their hometowns. Increased contact with home-based networks can provide support to relieve certain aspects of internal migrants' acculturative stress, such as homesickness. Besides, maintenance of the strong ties with home-based networks is also helpful in providing emotional and tangible support, which may help reduce acculturative stress like perceived discrimination and economic strain.

However, some studies point out that internal migrants' social networks based on geographic proximity and kinship tend to restrict their social network expansion(Zhu, 2002). Additionally, according to the theory of weak ties(Granovetter, 1973), these social networks based on geographic proximity and kinship are likely to provide redundant information, while heterogeneous networks are more helpful in providing informational support. Thus, it is important for internal migrants to have social contact with the locals. However, previous studies showed that internal migrants had limited social contact with the locals in face-to-face encounters(Wei & Chen, 2015). It is possible that online interaction may more easily facilitate contact and communication between internal migrants and the locals. Increased contact with the locals via social media could provide more sources of social support from the locals, and increased social support will help facilitate the adaptation of internal migrants.

What's more, the "contact space"(Harwood, 2010) provided by social media will increase mediated contact between internal migrants and the locals, and is more likely to contribute to positive intergroup relations and will in turn increase internal migrants' local culture identification. When internal migrants enter the new residence, they may have some problems in intergroup relations. For example, previous studies have shown that internal migrants experience discrimination from the locals(Wang et al., 2010). Negative interaction between internal migrants and the local people may hinder internal migrants' adaptation to the local society. According to Intergroup Contact Theory (Pettigrew, 1997), the quantity and quality of intergroup contact help to reduce intergroup barriers (e.g., discrimination, outgroup barriers) and improve intergroup relations. According to Shim, Zhang and Harwood(2012), both direct and mediated contact between migrants and the locals have positive effects on intergroup attitudes. Also, as Wei and Chen (2015) point out, the openness and anonymity of social media communication enable internal migrants and the locals to participate on an equal footing. Therefore, some forms of "contact space"(Harwood, 2010) could be provided by communities or non-governmental institutions to increase online contact between internal migrants and the locals. For example, there is an online forum named "Rongcheng Forum" which is based in Songjiang, a district in Shanghai. It enables internal migrants to communicate with the locals online. With increased mediated contact between internal migrants and the locals beyond traditional face-to-face encounters, both groups will be able to learn more about each other's cultural values and practices, which is conductive to their mutual understanding. It helps improve intergroup relations and will increase internal migrants' local cultural identification. However, despite that social media could increase mediated contact between internal migrants and the locals, it should be noted that the relationships fostered via social media are usually "weak ties," which may lack duration and solidarity compared with face-to-face contact (Wang & Chen, 2014). Therefore, it is better to foster both online and offline communication between internal migrants and the locals.

8.3.5   Strengthen the Supervision on Information and Opinion Dissemination on Social Media

Despite the positive role of social media use on the adaptation of internal migrants, it also brings about some negative outcomes on the adaptation of internal migrants, which can't be neglected. As has been discussed above, social media use might enhance the acculturative stress of internal migrants in their adaptation process. Additionally, there is abundant information on social media, some of which are false and misleading. Use of social media exposes people to such information, and may increase the difficulties of discerning true information from the false one. In this sense, use of social media has some side effects of generating "information fatigue"(Liu, Zhang, & Sun, 2019) and will thereby causing anxiety and stress to social media users. What's more, despite social media enables people to express their opinions and thus enlarging the scale of public participation into the social affairs, there exist some problems brought about by the disorder and non-irrational dissemination of the opinions. Wei and Chen(2015) argue that exposure to negative opinions on social media increase internal migrants' worries about the social issues, which will cause their worries about their lives and the situations they are in. And when these negative aspects are concerned with the image of the local society, internal migrants' cultural identification with the local culture might be negatively affected. Therefore, the government should strengthen social media governance by carrying out regulations on the dissemination of information and opinions via social media. Additionally, the government should play a leading role in orienting the public opinions regarding some sensitive issues towards a positive direction, increase its authority on the supervision of the false information and negative events or public opinions that may cause anxiety and stress of internal migrants, and make the best use of social media to increase internal migrants' life satisfaction and their identification with the local culture.

In sum, based on the research findings, it is suggested that measures should be taken to promote the local Hukou registration among internal migrants and improve the housing security system to provide support for those who have difficulties in house purchasing. Because the present study indicates that internal migrant's use of social media has some positive effects on their adaptation, the government and the institutions concerned could make the best of use of social media to provide official platforms to release migration-related information and policies, and to provide support to address internal migrants' needs specific to their adaptation in the local residence. It will facilitate their adaptation in the local society. Moreover, communities or non-government institutions could establish "contact space" (Harwood, 2010) (e.g., online forum) to help internal migrants maintain their home-based social networks and increase their communication with the locals. This helps diversify the sources of their social support, increasing the availability and adequacy of the social support they need. Moreover, increased contact among internal migrants and the locals provides opportunities for them to develop mutual understanding, which contributes to positive intergroup attitudes and will thus increase internal migrants' local cultural identification. Last but not least, due to that social media use might increase internal migrants' acculturative stress, the government should strengthen the social media governance, carrying out regulations on the dissemination of information and opinions on social media to relieve the negative influence of social media on internal migrants' adaptation.

8.4 Contributions of the Present Study

China has been experiencing significant internal migration since its implementation of the reform and opening-up policy in

1978. Internal migration in China has become an important social issue which attracts a great deal of scholarly attention. Given the cultural diversity brought about by China's vast territory, internal migrants may face challenges when moving to new regions. Thus, the present study focuses on examining internal migrants' adaptation and factors affecting their adaptation. Additionally, in response to the context that social media has extended the traditional face-to-face communication pattern, the present study specifically focuses on the effects of social media use on the adaptation of internal migrants in China.

The present study is among the first endeavors to investigate the effects of social media use on internal migrants' adaptation using structural equation modeling(SEM). It has some contributions worthy of note:

First, the presents study supplements the existing theories on intercultural adaptation. As noted by Shuter(2012), the existing theories of intercultural adaptation are "grounded in a face-to-face paradigm"(p.233). As social media has changed the patterns of communication, it is necessary to "refine and expand"(Shuter, 2012, p.233) the existing theories of intercultural adaptation to incorporate the role of social media. Responding to the context that social media has dramatically changed patterns of human communication, this study examines the effects of social media use on the adaptation of internal migrants. By proposing and testing a hypothesized structural model featuring the relationships among social media use, social support, and key adaptation variables(acculturative stress, life satisfaction, and local cultural identification), this study has found some ways through which social media use affects the adaptation of internal migrants. The research results can update the existing theories and frameworks of intercultural adaptation, e.g., Berry's(1997) acculturation framework and Kim's(2001) integrative model of communication and cross-cultural adaptation by adding social media use as an important factor affecting adaption process and outcomes.

Second, the present study establishes the links between intercultural adaptation studies and internal migration studies in China. Intercultural adaptation studies have long been focusing on international migrant groups such as immigrants, international students, international scholars, and refugees. The present study represents a novel attempt to take internal migrants as subject of the research, yet still relies on theoretical frameworks(e.g., Berry, 1997; Kim, 2001) and concepts(e.g., acculturative stress) from intercultural adaptation literature to examine within-nation adaptation of internal migrants. According to Kim(2012), the concept of "intercultural" has been broadened from national cultural differences to include "essential patterns of cultural norms and practices in specific cultures and subcultures"(p.357). Gudykunst and Kim(2003) argued that "interculturalness" involves differences at intergroup, interethnic, and interracial levels. Therefore, intercultural adaptation theories have implications on the examination of with-nation adaptation in a large country like China, which is characterized by its cultural diversity and regional variations. By successfully extending intercultural adaptation literature to with-nation adaptation studies, this study suggests that there is a commonality of experience between internal and cross-border migrants.

Third, the measurements of the research variables which were developed for the present study has great value for future examination of the adaptation of internal migrants in China. The present study developed a perceived social support scale specifically designed for internal migrants in China. Through exploration factor analysis(EFA), three factors were extracted: emotional support, informational support, and occupational support. Then by conducting CFA, a second-order construct of social support comprising the first-order sub-constructs (emotional support, informational support, and occupational support) was derived and validated. What's more, the present study identified and tested a set of important in-

dicators that can be used in the future to assess internal migrants'
overall adaptation, including acculturative stress, life satisfaction,
and local cultural identification. Building on the literature, the author identified four dimensions of acculturative stress for internal
migrants: perceived discrimination, cultural discomfort, homesickness, and economic strain. Then, the author adapted established
scales to measure these variables and conducted confirmatory factor
analysis(CFA) to validate the adapted scales. A second-order construct of acculturative stress comprising four first-order sub-constructs (perceived discrimination, cultural discomfort, homesickness, and economic strain) was derived. The measurements of these
variables specifically designed to measure the adaptation of internal
migrants provide important reference for any future studies on topics related to the adaptation of internal migrants in China.

Finally, the present study enriches the available literature on
internal migration by examining the factors affecting internal
migrants' adaptation process and outcomes, as well as the effects of
social media use on their adaptation. Based on the findings of the
empirical research, the present study offers a few suggestions on
how to make the best use of social media to facilitate the adaptation
of internal migrants. For example, the government or relevant institutions could establish more official platforms via social media to
increase the efficiency of the dissemination of essential information
or the provision of support on migration-related issues such as
household registration policy, employment, house purchasing, and
education opportunities for internal migrants' children. In addition,
communities or some non-government organizations could provide
more "contact space"(Harwood, 2010, p.148) on social media plat-
forms(e.g., online forums) that involves both the locals and internal migrants, with an aim of diversifying the sources of social support needed by internal migrants. This could also facilitate communication between internal migrants and the locals, thereby increasing their mutual understanding towards each other, improving in-

tergroup relations and increasing internal migrants' cultural identification with the local society. Meanwhile, given that use of social media might expose internal migrants to more acculturative stress, the government should carry out some regulations to strengthen the governance of information dissemination or opinion expression on social media, and create a sound communication environment. In conclusion, these aforementioned suggestions could help the government or institutions concerned to formulate more "human-centered" policies on migration-related issues.

8.5　Research Limitations

The present study has several limitations that should be addressed. The first limitation lies in the measurement of social media use. The present study measured internal migrants' general use of social media. Some sample items included: "social media are part of my everyday life," and "I communicate with my family frequently via social media." However, due to a limited number of established scales measuring migrants' social media use, the present study did not measure internal migrants' specific use of social media related with their adaptation. It will deepen our understanding of the effects of social media use on adaptation if the scale of social media use is refined to incorporate items measuring internal migrants' specific use of social media related with adaptation issues, e.g., "I use social media to communicate with the locals."

A second research limitation is the data collection method. The respondents were recruited via the online survey website and they completed the online questionnaires. Despite the efficiency of the online survey, an actual random sample can't be obtained. The respondents recruited in the survey were people who were more active in participating in online activities. Some people who were less involved in online activities may be inaccessible. Others who were invited might not like to respond to online questionnaires. Therefore, online sampling limits the generalizability of the findings of the current research.

A third research limitation is the sample size. As the present study focuses on the social issue of the adaptation of internal migrants, a large sample size is more desirable. Also, a larger sample would be more suitable for conducting multigroup analysis to compare whether the research results vary from group to group. However, as a sample greater than 500 for SEM analysis is likely to yield undesirable model fit, the present study used 403 samples for SEM analysis. Despite the fact that the sample size met the criteria for SEM analysis and yielded a good mode fit, it was insufficient for multigroup analysis. The sample size for each group will be too small if multigroup analysis is conducted, which will affect the reliability of the results.

Fourth, the present study investigated internal migrants' social media use and its impact on their adaptation in a cross-sectional study. However, it should be noted that the adaptation variables in the present study(acculturative stress, life satisfaction, and local cultural identification) are related to internal migrants' length of stay and tend to change over time. Thus, cross-sectional studies cannot capture the dynamic nature of the overall adaptation process of internal migrants, and a longitudinal study should be conducted to measure these variables at certain intervals. In this way, we could better capture the direction of causality among these variables.

8.6   Directions for Future Research

The present study is a preliminary step towards examining the adaptation of internal migrants in China and the effects of social media use on their adaptation. There are several directions worth exploring in future research:

First, the present study used only the quantitative approach to examine internal migrants' social media use and their adaptation. In further research, some qualitative methods, such as case studies or interviews, should be conducted to supplement the survey data and provide a more rich and comprehensive perspective on this topic. Future research could utilize some in-depth or semi-structural interviews to learn more about internal migrants' specific use of social media. Also, future research could interview internal migrants on some issues in their adaptation process, such as the stress they experienced and the factors affecting their local cultural identification, which will better our understanding of the overall adaptation process of internal migrants.

Second, the present study used structural equation modeling (SEM) to test the effects of social media use on the adaptation of internal migrants in Shanghai. However, multigroup analysis was not conducted. Future research could divide the samples into different groups according to their age, gender, Hukou status (i. e., whether respondents have the Shanghai Hukou or not), and housing conditions(i.e., whether respondents have purchased their own house in Shanghai or not), and then conduct multigroup analysis to examine whether there are group-level differences concerning the effects of social media use on internal migrants' adaptation.

Third, as the adaptation variables are dynamic and develop over time, a longitudinal study should be conducted. The adaptation variables can be examined at certain intervals, for example, shortly after the respondents' arrival, one year later, and two or three years later. In this way, the change of internal migrants' adaptation can be captured, which can help to determine the direction of the effects of social media use on their adaptation.

Finally, the present study proposed and tested a hypothesized model regarding the effects of social media use on internal migrants' adaptation using the sample population of internal migrants living in Shanghai. Despite these respondents come from various regions of China, except Tibet, Qinghai, Hong Kong, and

Taiwan, there is no certainty that they represent the whole migration population in China. Future research could consider replicating the study in other cities with large migration population such as Beijing, Shenzhen, and Guangzhou to test the hypothesized model and attempt to generalize the research findings.

References

Adler, P. S., & Kwon, S.W.(2002). Social capital: Prospects for a new concept. *Academy of Management Review*, *27*(1), 17—40.

Adriaansen, J. J., van Leeuwen, C. M., Visser-Meily, J. M., van den Bos, G. A., & Post, M. W.(2011). Course of social support and relationships between social support and life satisfaction in spouses of patients with stroke in the chronic phase. *Patient Education and Counseling*, *85*(2), e48—e52.

Albrecht, T. L., & Adelman, M. B.(1987). *Communicating social support*. Thousand Oaks, CA: Sage.

Amit, K.(2010). Determinants of life satisfaction among immigrants from Western countries and from the FSU in Israel. *Social Indicators Research*, *96*(3), 515—534.

Anderson, J. C., & Gerbing, D. W.(1988). Structural equation modeling in practice: A review and recommended two-step approach. *Psychological Bulletin*, *103*(3),411—423.

Arango, J.(2000). Explaining migration: a critical view. *International Social Science Journal*, *52*(165), 283—296.

Ashton, M. C., Lee, K., & Paunonen, S. V.(2002). What is the central feature of extraversion? Social attention versus reward sensitivity. *Journal of Personality and Social Psychology*, *83*(1), 245—251.

Atterton, J.(2007). The "strength of weak ties": Social networking by business owners in the Highlands and Islands of Scotland. *Sociologia Ruralis*, *47*(3), 228—245.

Avolio, B. J., Yammarino, F. J., & Bass, B. M.(1991). Identifying common methods variance with data collected from a single

source: An unresolved sticky issue. *Journal of Management*, *17*(3),
571—587.

Aycan, Z., & Berry, J. W.(1996). Impact of employment-related experiences on immigrants' psychological well-being and adaptation to Canada. *Canadian Journal of Behavioural Science*, *28*(3), 240—251.

Ayoob, M., Singh, T., & Jan, M.(2011). Length of stay, acculturative stress, and health among Kashmiri students in central India. *Pakistan Journal of Social and Clinical Psychology*, *9*,11—15.

Bagozzi, R. P., & Yi, Y.(1988). On the evaluation of structural equation models. *Journal of the Academy of Marketing Science*, *16*(1), 74—94.

Baker, A. M., Soto, J. A., Perez, C. R., & Lee, E. A.(2012). Acculturative status and psychological well-being in an Asian American sample. *Asian American Journal of Psychology*, *3*(4), 275.

Bandalos, D. L.(2002). The effects of item parceling on goodness-of-fit and parameter estimate bias in structural equation modeling. *Structural Equation Modeling*, *9*(1), 78—102.

Baron, R. M., & Kenny, D. A.(1986). The moderator-mediator variable distinction in social psychological research: Conceptual, strategic, and statistical considerations. *Journal of Personality and Social Psychology*, *51*(6), 1173—1182.

Barrera Jr, M.(1986). Distinctions between social support concepts, measures, and models. *American Journal of Community Psychology*, *14*(4), 413—445.

Beiser, M., & Hou, F.(2001). Language acquisition, unemployment and depressive disorder among Southeast Asian refugees: a 10-year study. *Social Science & Medicine*, *53*(10), 1321—1334.

Benet-Martínez, V., & Haritatos, J.(2005). Bicultural identity integration(BII): Components and psychosocial antecedents. *Journal of Personality*, *73*(4), 1015—1050.

Benet-Martínez, V., Leu, J., Lee, F., & Morris, M. W.(2002). Negotiating biculturalism: Cultural frame switching in biculturals with oppositional versus compatible cultural identities. *Journal of Cross-cultural Psychology*, *33*(5), 492—516.

Bentler, P. M., & Chou, C. P.(1987). Practical issues in structural modeling. *Sociological Methods & Research*, *16*(1), 78—117.

Berkman, L. F.(1984). Assessing the physical health effects of social networks and social support. *Annual Review of Public Health*, *5*(1), 413—432.

Berkman, L. F., Glass, T., Brissette, I., & Seeman, T. E. (2000). From social integration to health: Durkheim in the new millennium. *Social Science & Medicine*, *51*(6), 843—857.

Bernstein, K. S., Park, S. Y., Shin, J., Cho, S., & Park, Y. (2011). Acculturation, discrimination and depressive symptoms among Korean immigrants in New York City. *Community Mental Health Journal*, *47*(1), 24—34.

Berry. J. W.(1980). Social and cultural change. In H. C. Triandis, & R. W. Brislin(Eds.), *Handbook of cross-cultural psychology*, *Vol.5*.(pp.211—279). Boston: Allyn & Bacon.

Berry, J. W.(1997). Immigration, acculturation, and adaptation. *Applied Psychology*, *46*(1), 5—34.

Berry, J. W.(2001). A psychology of immigration. *Journal of Social Issues*, *57*(3), 615—631.

Berry, J. W.(2005). Acculturation: Living successfully in two cultures. *International Journal of Intercultural Relations*, *29*(6), 697—712.

Berry, J. W., Kim, U., Minde, T., & Mok, D.(1987). Comparative studies of acculturative stress. *International Migration Review*, *21*(3), 491—511.

Berry, J. W., Phinney, J. S., Sam, D. L., & Vedder, P.(2006). Immigrant youth: Acculturation, identity, and adaptation. *Applied Psychology*, *55*(3), 303—332.

Berry, J. W., & Sam, D. L.(1997). Acculturation and adaptation. In J. W. Berry, Y. H. Poortinga, J. Pandey, M. H. Segall, & Ç. Kâğıtçıbaşı(Eds.), *Handbook of cross-cultural psychology: The-*

ory and method (*Vol .1*)(pp.291—326). London: Allyn & Bacon.

Bhugra, D.(2004). Migration and mental health. *Acta Psychiatrica Scandinavica*, *109*(4), 243—258.

Bolger, N., & Schilling, E. A.(1991). Personality and the problems of everyday life: The role of neuroticism in exposure and reactivity to daily stressors. *Journal of Personality*, *59*(3), 355—386.

Bollen, K. A.(1989). A new incremental fit index for general structural equation models. *Sociological Methods & Research*, *17*(3), 303—316.

Bourdieu, P.(2011). The forms of capital.(1986). *Cultural theory: An anthology*, *1*, 81—93.

Bourhis, R. Y., Moise, L. C., Perreault, S., & Senecal, S.(1997). Towards an interactive acculturation model: A social psychological approach. *International Journal of Psychology*, *32*(6), 369—386.

Braithwaite, D. O. & Baxter, L. A. 2008. Introduction: Metatheory and theory in interpersonal communication research. In L. A. Baxter & D. O. Braithwaite(Eds.), *Engaging theories in interpersonal communication: Multiple perspectives* (pp.1—18), Thousand Oaks, NY: Sage.

Brisset, C., Safdar, S., Lewis, J. R., & Sabatier, C.(2010). Psychological and sociocultural adaptation of university students in France: The case of Vietnamese international students. *International Journal of Intercultural Relations*, *34*(4), 413—426.

Browne, M. W.(1984). Asymptotically distribution-free methods for the analysis of covariance structures. *British Journal of Mathematical and Statistical Psychology*, *37*(1), 62—83.

Byrne, B. M.(2010). *Structural equation modeling with AMOS Basic concepts, applications, and programming (Multivariate Applications Series*) (2nd ed). New York, NY: Taylor & Francis Group.

Cai, H., & Cao, Z. G.[蔡禾、曹志刚],(2009),农民工的城市认

同及其影响因素——来自珠三角的实证分析,《中山大学学报(社会科学版)》,49(1):148—158。

Cao, L., & Zhang, T.(2012). Social networking sites and educational adaptation in higher education: A case study of Chinese international students in New Zealand. *The Scientific World Journal*, 1—5.

Caplan, G.(1976). The family as a support system. In G. Caplan & M. Killilea(Eds.), *Support system and mutual help: Multidisciplinary explorations* (pp. 19—36). New York, NY: Grune and Stratton.

Caplan, S.(2007). Latinos, acculturation, and acculturative stress: A dimensional concept analysis. *Policy, Politics, & Nursing Practice*, 8(2), 93—106.

Carver, C. S., & Connor-Smith, J.(2010). Personality and coping. *Annual Review of Psychology*, *61*(1), 679—704.

Castles, S.(2000). International migration at the beginning of the twenty-first century: global trends and issues. *International Social Science Journal*, *52*(165), 269—281.

Chae, M. H., & Foley, P. F.(2010). Relationship of ethnic identity, acculturation, and psychological well-being among Chinese, Japanese, and Korean Americans. *Journal of Counseling & Development*, *88*(4), 466—476.

Chan, K. W.(2012). Migration and development in China: Trends, geography and current issues. *Migration and Development*, *1*(2), 187—205.

Chan, K. W., & Zhang, L.(1999). The hukou system and rural-urban migration in China: Processes and changes. *The China Quarterly*, 160, 818—855.

Chang, S. J., Van Witteloostuijn, A., & Eden, L.(2010). From the editors: Common method variance in international business research. *Journal of International Business Studies 41*(2): 178—184.

Chen, C. H., & Zhu, L. [陈常花、朱力], (2008),知识型移民的

社会适应优势,《南方人口》,23(4):30—37。

Chen, G. M.(2012a). The impact of new media on intercultural communication in global context. *China Media Research*, 8(2), 1—10.

Chen, G. M. (2012b). Theorizing Intercultural Adaptation. InX. D. Dai & S. J. Kulich(Eds.) *Intercultural adaptation(Ⅰ): Theoretical explorations and empirical studies*(pp.51—73). Shanghai, SH: Shanghai Foreign Language Education Press.

Chen, J.(2011). Internal migration and health: re-examining the healthy migrant phenomenon in China. *Social Science & Medicine*, 72(8), 1294—1301.

Chen, L., & Yang, X.(2015). Nature and effectiveness of online social support for intercultural adaptation of Mainland Chinese international students. *International Journal of Communication*, 9, 2161—2181.

Chen, S. X., Benet-Martínez, V., & Harris Bond, M.(2008). Bicultural Identity, bilingualism, and psychological adjustment in multicultural societies: immigration-based and globalization-based acculturation. *Journal of Personality*, 76(4), 803—838.

Chen, W., & Choi, A. S. K.(2011). Internet and social support among Chinese migrants in Singapore. *New media & Society*, 13(7), 1067—1084.

Chen, X., Yu, B., Gong, J., Zeng, J., & MacDonell, K.(2015). The domestic migration stress questionnaire(DMSQ): development and psychometric assessment. *Journal of Social Science Studies*, 2(2), 117—133.

Chen, Y. B.[陈韵博],(2010),新一代农民工使用QQ建立的社会网络分析,《国际新闻界》,8:80—85。

Chen, Y. B.[陈韵博],(2011),新媒体赋权:新生代农民工对QQ的使用与满足研究,《当代青年研究》,8:22—25。

Chen, Y. F.[陈映芳],(2005),"农民工":制度安排与身份认同,《社会学研究》,3(9):119—132。

Chirkov, V. I., Safdar, S., De Guzman, J., & Playford, K.

(2008). Further examining the role motivation to study abroad plays in the adaptation of international students in Canada. *International Journal of Intercultural Relations*, *32*(5), 427—440.

Chou, H. T. G., & Edge, N.(2012). "They Are Happier and Having Better Lives than I Am": The Impact of Using Facebook on Perceptions of Others' Lives. *Cyberpsychology*, *Behavior*, *and Social Networking*, *15*(2), 117—121.

Chou, K. L.(2009). Pre-migration planning and depression among new migrants to Hong Kong: The moderating role of social support. *Journal of Affective Disorders*, *114*(1—3), 85—93.

Chou, K. L.(2012). Perceived discrimination and depression among new migrants to Hong Kong: The moderating role of social support and neighborhood collective efficacy. *Journal of Affective Disorders*, *138*(1—2), 63—70.

Chow, H. P.(2007). Sense of belonging and life satisfaction among Hong Kong adolescent immigrants in Canada. *Journal of Ethnic and Migration Studies*, *33*(3), 511—520.

Chung, R. H. G., Kim, B. S., & Abreu, J. M.(2004). Asian American multidimensional acculturation scale: development, factor analysis, reliability, and validity. *Cultural Diversity and Ethnic Minority Psychology*, *10*(1), 66—80.

Claudat, K., White, E. K., & Warren, C. S.(2016). Acculturative stress, self-esteem, and eating pathology in Latina and Asian American female college students. *Journal of Clinical Psychology*, *72*(1), 88—100.

Cobb, S.(1976). Social support as a moderator of life stress. *Psychosomatic Medicine*. *5*(38), 300—314.

Cohen, S., & McKay, G.(1984). Social support, stress and the buffering hypothesis: A theoretical analysis. *Handbook of Psychology and Health*, *4*, 253—267.

Cohen, S., & Wills, T. A.(1985). Stress, social support, and the buffering hypothesis. *Psychological Bulletin*, *98*(2), 310—357.

Cohen, S., Mermelstein, R., Kamarck, T., & Hoberman, H.

M.(1985). Measuring the functional components of social support. InI. G. Sarason(Ed.), *Social support: Theory, Research and Applications*(pp.73—94). New York, NY: Springer.

Connor-Smith, J. K., & Flachsbart, C.(2007). Relations between personality and coping: a meta-analysis. *Journal of Personality and Social Psychology*, *93*(6), 1080—1107.

Correa, T., Hinsley, A. W., & De Zuniga, H. G.(2010). Who interacts on the Web?: The intersection of users' personality and social media use. *Computers in Human Behavior*, *26*(2), 247—253.

Costa Jr, P. T., & McCrae, R. R.(1990). Personality disorders and the five-factor model of personality. *Journal of Personality Disorders*, *4*(4), 362—371.

Costello, A. B., & Osborne, J.(2005). Best practices in Exploratory Factor Analysis: Four recommendations for getting the most from your analysis. *Practical Assessment Research & Evaluation*, *10*(1), 1—9.

Crockett, L. J., Iturbide, M. I., Torres Stone, R. A., McGinley, M., Raffaelli, M., & Carlo, G.(2007). Acculturative stress, social support, and coping: Relations to psychological adjustment among Mexican American college students. *Cultural Diversity and Ethnic Minority Psychology*, *13*(4), 347—355.

Croucher, S. M.(2011). Social networking and cultural adaptation: A theoretical model. *Journal of International and Intercultural Communication*, *4*(4), 259—264.

Curran, P. J., West, S. G., & Finch, J. F.(1996). The robustness of test statistics to nonnormality and specification error in confirmatory factor analysis. *Psychological Methods*, *1*(1), 16—29.

Dalisay, F.(2012). Media use and acculturation of new immigrants in the United States. *Communication Research Reports*, *29*(2), 148—160.

De Jong, G. F., Chamratrithirong, A., & Tran, Q. G.(2002). For Better, For Worse: Life Satisfaction Consequences of Migration. *International Migration Review*, *36*(3), 838—863.

De Vroome, T., Verkuyten, M., & Martinovic, B. (2014). Host national identification of immigrants in the Netherlands. *International Migration Review*, 48(1), 1—27.

De Wind, J. & Holdaway, J. (2005) Internal and international migration in economic development. Paper presented to the Fourth Coordination Meeting on International Migration, Population Division of the UN, New York.

Dekker, R., & Engbersen, G. (2014). How social media transform migrant networks and facilitate migration. *Global Networks*, 14(4), 401—418.

Diddi, A., & LaRose, R. (2006). Getting hooked on news: Uses and gratifications and the formation of news habits among college students in an Internet environment. *Journal of Broadcasting & Electronic Media*, 50(2), 193—210.

Diener, E. D., Emmons, R. A., Larsen, R. J., & Griffin, S. (1985). The satisfaction with life scale. *Journal of Personality Assessment*, 49(1), 71—75.

Dong, J. Q., & Liu, S. [董金秋、刘爽],(2014),进城农民工:社会支持与城市融合,《华南农业大学学报:社会科学版》,13(2):41—48。

Dong, L. Q. [董立群],(2009),城市新移民的社会网络与社会融合——以宁波新移民为例,《淮南职业技术学院学报》,9(4):105—110。

Dong. M. W. [董明伟],(2008),城市农民工的自我社会认同分析,《云南财贸学院学报:社会科学版》,23(2):108—110。

Dorigo, G., & Tobler, W. (1983). Push-pull migration laws. *Annals of the Association of American Geographers*, 73(1), 1—17.

Doty, D. H., & Glick, W. H. (1998). Common methods bias: does common methods variance really bias results? *Organizational Research Methods*, 1(4), 374—406.

Dunne, Á., Lawlor, M. A., & Rowley, J. (2010). Young people's use of online social networking sites-a uses and gratifications perspective. *Journal of Research in Interactive Marketing*, 4(1), 46—58.

Duru, E., & Poyrazli, S. (2007). Personality dimensions, psychosocial-demographic variables, and English language competency in predicting level of acculturative stress among Turkish international students. *International Journal of Stress Management*, *14*(1), 99—110.

Edwards, L. M., & Lopez, S. J.(2006). Perceived family support, acculturation, and life satisfaction in Mexican American youth: A mixed-methods exploration. *Journal of Counseling Psychology*, *53*(3), 279—287.

Ellison, N. B., Steinfield, C., & Lampe, C.(2007). The benefits of Facebook "friends": Social capital and college students' use of online social network sites. *Journal of Computer-mediated Communication*, *12*(4), 1143—1168.

Eysenck, S. B. G., Eysenck, H. J., & Barrett, P. A.(1985). A revised version of the psychoticism scale. *Personality and Individual Differences*, *6*(1), 21—29.

Fan, C. C.(1996). Economic opportunities and internal migration: a case study of Guangdong Province, China. *The Professional Geographer*, *48*(1), 28—45.

Fields, G. S.(2004). Dualism in the labor market: a perspective on the Lewis model after half a century. *The Manchester School*, *72*(6), 724—735.

Finch, B. K., Hummer, R. A., Kol, B., & Vega, W. A. (2001). The role of discrimination and acculturative stress in the physical health of Mexican-origin adults. *Hispanic Journal of Behavioral Sciences*, *23*(4), 399—429.

Forbush, E., & Foucault-Welles, B.(2016). Social media use and adaptation among Chinese students beginning to study in the United States. *International Journal of Intercultural Relations*, *50*, 1—12.

Fornell, C., & Larcker, D. F.(1981). Structural equation models with unobservable variables and measurement error: Algebra and statistics. *Journal of Marketing Research*, *18*(3), 328—388.

Furnham, A., & Shiekh, S.(1993). Gender, generational and

social support correlates of mental health in Asian immigrants. *International Journal of Social Psychiatry*, *39*(1), 22—33.

Galchenko, I., & Van De Vijver, F. J.(2007). The role of perceived cultural distance in the acculturation of exchange students in Russia. *International Journal of Intercultural Relations*, *31* (2), 181—197.

Gallagher, D., Ting, L., & Palmer, A.(2008). A journey into the unknown: taking the fear out of structural equation modeling with AMOS for the first-time user. *The Marketing Review*, *8*(3), 255—275.

Gokdemir, O., & Dumludag, D. (2012). Life satisfaction among Turkish and Moroccan immigrants in the Netherlands: The role of absolute and relative income. *Social Indicators Research*, *106*(3), 407—417.

Gong, F., Xu, J., Fujishiro, K., & Takeuchi, D. T.(2011). A life course perspective on migration and mental health among Asian immigrants: The role of human agency. *Social Science & Medicine*, *73*(11), 1618—1626.

Gordon, M. M.(1964). *Assimilation in American Life: The Role of Race, Religion, and National Origins*. New York, NY: Oxford University Press.

Granovetter, M. S.(1973). The strength of weak ties. *American Journal of Sociology*, *78*(6), 1360—1380.

Granovetter, M. S.(1977). The strength of weak ties. In *Social networks*(pp.347—367). New York, NY: Academic Press.

Greenwood, M. J., & Hunt, G. L.(2003). The early history of migration research. *International Regional Science Review*, *26*(1), 3—37.

Grewal, R., Cote, J. A., & Baumgartner, H.(2004). Multicollinearity and measurement error in structural equation models: Implications for theory testing. *Marketing Science*, *23*(4), 519—529.

Grieve, R., Indian, M., Witteveen, K., Tolan, G. A., & Marrington, J.(2013). Face-to-face or Facebook: Can social con-

nectedness be derived online? *Computers in Human Behavior*, 29
(3), 604—609.

Gudykunst, W. B., & Kim, Y. Y.(2003). *Communicating With Strangers*(4th ed.). New York, NY: Mac Graw Hill.

Gunzler, D., Chen, T., Wu, P., & Zhang, H.(2013). Introduction to mediation analysis with structural equation modeling. *Shanghai Archives of Psychiatry*, 25(6), 390—395.

Guo, S., & Zhang, J.(2010). Language, work, and learning: exploring the urban experience of ethnic migrant workers in China. *Diaspora, Indigenous, and Minority Education*, 4(1), 47—63.

Guo, X. H., & Li, F.［郭星华、李飞］,(2009),漂泊与寻根:农民工社会认同的二重性,《人口研究》,33(6):74—84。

Guo, Y. J.［郭艳军］,(2017),城市新移民社交媒体使用与社会融合度研究——基于合肥个案网络数据分析,《东南传播》,1:52—54。

Guo, Y., Chen, X., Gong, J., Li, F., Zhu, C., Yan, Y., & Wang, L.(2016). Association between spouse/child separation and migration-related stress among a random sample of rural-to-urban migrants in Wuhan, China. *PLOS ONE*, 11(4), e0154252.

Guo, Y., Li, Y., & Ito, N.(2014). Exploring the predicted effect of social networking site use on perceived social capital and psychological well-being of Chinese international students in Japan. *Cyberpsychology, Behavior, and Social Networking*, 17(1), 52—58.

Hair, J. F., Black, W. C., Babin, B. J., & Anderson, R. E. (2010). *Multivariate Data Analysis*(7th ed.). New Jersey: Pearson Prentice Hall.

Hampton, K. N., Lu, W., & Shin, I.(2016). Digital media and stress: the cost of caring 2.0. *Information, Communication & Society*, 19(9), 1267—1286.

Han, H. R., Kim, M., Lee, H. B., Pistulka, G., & Kim, K. B.(2007). Correlates of depression in the Korean American elderly: Focusing on personal resources of social support. *Journal of Cross-cultural Gerontology*, 22(1), 115—127.

Hao, P., & Tang, S.(2018). Migration destinations in the urban hierarchy in China: Evidence from Jiangsu. *Population, Space and Place, 24*(2), 1—14.

Hare, D.(1999). 'Push' versus 'pull' factors in migration outflows and returns: Determinants of migration status and spell duration among China's rural population. *The Journal of Development Studies, 35*(3), 45—72.

Harris, J. R., & Todaro, M. P.(1970). Migration, unemployment and development: a two-sector analysis. *The American Economic Review, 60*(1), 126—142.

Harwood, J.(2010). The contact space: A novel framework for intergroup contact research. *Journal of Language and Social Psychology, 29*(2), 147—177.

Haviland, W. A.(2006), 瞿铁鹏、张钰译,《文化人类学》。上海: 上海社会科学院出版社。

Hayes, A. F.(2009). Beyond Baron and Kenny: Statistical mediation analysis in the new millennium. *Communication Monographs, 76*(4), 408—420.

Hayes, A. F., Preacher, K. J., & Myers, T. A.(2011). Mediation and the estimation of indirect effects in political communication research. *Sourcebook for Political Communication Research Methods, Measures, and Analytical Techniques, 23*(1), 434—465.

Haythornthwaite, C.(2002). Strong, weak, and latent ties and the impact of new media. *The Information Society, 18*(5), 385—401.

He, H. & Wang, S. [和红、王硕],(2016),不同流入地青年流动人口的社会支持与生活满意度,《人口研究》,40(3):45—57。

Hofstede, G., & McCrae, R. R.(2004). Personality and culture revisited: Linking traits and dimensions of culture. *Cross-cultural Research, 38*(1), 52—88.

Hombrados-Mendieta, M. I., Gomez-Jacinto, L., Dominguez-Fuentes, J. M., & Garcia-Leiva, P.(2013). Sense of community and satisfaction with life among immigrants and the native population. *Journal of Community Psychology, 41*(5), 601—614.

House, J. S.(1981). *Work stress and social support*. Reading,
MA: Addison-Wesley.

Hsu, T. C. K., Grant, A. E., & Huang, W. W.(1993). The influence of social networks on the acculturation behavior of foreign
students. *Connections*, *16*(1), 23—36.

Hu, H. [胡辉],(2018),珠三角新生代农民工媒体使用影响城市
融入研究,《中国市场》,(2)4:25—31。

Hu, L. T., & Bentler, P. M.(1999). Cutoff criteria for fit indexes in covariance structure analysis: Conventional criteria versus
new alternatives. *Structural Equation Modeling: A Multidisciplinary Journal*, *6*(1), 1—55.

Huang, K. S. [黄匡时],(2008),社会融合的心理建构理论研究,
《社会心理科学》,23(6):14—19。

Huang, P., & Zhan, S.(2005). Internal migration in China:
Linking it to development. In L. Frank & P. D. Ilse(Eds.), *Migration*, *Development and Poverty Reduction in Asia*(pp.65—84). Geneva, Switzerland: International Organization for Migration.

Huang, W. L., Zeng, T. D., & Zhu, S. Y. [黄文兰、曾天德、朱
淑英],(2013),新生代农民工社会支持、心理健康与主观幸福感的关
系研究,《漳州师范学院学报:自然科学版》,25(4):127—132。

Ifinedo, P.(2016). Applying uses and gratifications theory and
social influence processes to understand students' pervasive adoption of social networking sites: Perspectives from the Americas. *International Journal of Information Management*, *36*(2), 192—206.

Israel, B. A., & Rounds, K. A.(1987). Social networks and social support: A synthesis for health educators. *Advances in Health
Education and Promotion*, *2*(31), 1—35.

Jasinskaja-Lahti, I.(2008). Long-term immigrant adaptation:
Eight-year follow-up study among immigrants from Russia and Estonia living in Finland. *International Journal of Psychology*, *43*(1),
6—18.

Jasinskaja-Lahti, I., Liebkind, K., Jaakkola, M., & Reuter,
A.(2006). Perceived discrimination, social support networks, and

psychological well-being among three immigrant groups. *Journal of Cross-cultural Psychology*，37(3)，293—311.

Jia，Y.［贾毅］，(2012)，新生代农民工媒介接触的状况与反思，《新闻界》，8:8—11。

Jing，J. H.［荆建华］，(2013)，关于农民工主观幸福感与社会支持现状的研究——以河南省421名农民工为例，《河南教育学院学报：哲学社会科学版》，32(4)：57—61。

Jing，Z. Z.，& Guo，H.［景志铮、郭虹］，(2007)，城市新移民的社区融入与社会排斥——成都市社区个案研究，《西北人口》，28(2)：33—36。

Johnson，M. A.(1996). Latinas and television in the United States: Relationships among genre identification，acculturation，and acculturation stress. *Howard Journal of Communications*，7(4)，289—313.

Jorgenson，D. W.(1967). Surplus agricultural labour and the development of a dual economy. *Oxford Economic Papers*，19(3)，288—312.

Kaiser，H. F.(1960). The application of electronic computers to factor analysis. *Educational and Psychological Measurement*，20(1)，141—151.

Kalish，Y.，& Robins，G.(2006). Psychological predispositions and network structure: The relationship between individual predispositions，structural holes and network closure. *Social Networks*，28(1)，56—84.

Kang，L.［康岚］，(2007)，"谁是外地人"：大都市居民的地域身份意识及其影响因素——以上海为例，《华中科技大学学报(社会科学版)》，31(1):58—67。

Kaplan，A. M.，& Haenlein，M.(2010). Users of the world，unite! The challenges and opportunities of Social Media. *Business Horizons*，53(1)，59—68.

Katz，E.，Blumler，J. G.，& Gurevitch，M.(1974). Utilization of mass communication by the individual. In J. Blumler，& E. Katz (Eds.)，*The Uses of Mass Communications: Current Perspectives on*

Gratifications Research (pp.19—32). Beverly Hills, CA: Sage.

Kavanaugh, A. L., Reese, D. D., Carroll, J. M., & Rosson, M. B.(2005). Weak ties in networked communities. *The Information Society*, *21*(2), 119—131.

Kenneth, L. D.(2002). The social psychology of perceived prejudice and discrimination. *Canadian Psychology*, *43*, 1—10.

Kilinc, A., & Granello, P. F.(2003). Overall life satisfaction and help-seeking attitudes of Turkish college students in the United States: Implications for college counselors. *Journal of College Counseling*, *6*(1), 56—68.

Kim, E., Hogge, I., & Salvisberg, C.(2014). Effects of self-esteem and ethnic identity: Acculturative stress and psychological well-being among Mexican immigrants. *Hispanic Journal of Behavioral Sciences*, *36*(2), 144—163.

Kim, J., & Lee, J. E. R.(2011). The Facebook paths to happiness: Effects of the number of Facebook friends and self-presentation on subjective well-being. *Cyberpsychology*, *Behavior*, *and Social Networking*, *14*(6), 359—364.

Kim, K. H., Yun, H., & Yoon, Y.(2009). The Internet as a facilitator of cultural hybridization and interpersonal relationship management for Asian international students in South Korea. *Asian Journal of Communication*, *19*(2), 152—169.

Kim, L. S.(2016). *Social media and social support: A uses and gratifications examination of health 2.0* (Unpublished doctoral dissertation), Pepperdine University, California.

Kim, Y. Y.(1988). *Communication and cross-cultural adaptation: An integrative theory*. Clevedon: Multilingual Matters.

Kim, Y. Y.(2001). *Becoming intercultural: An integrative theory of communication and cross-cultural adaptation*. Thousand Oaks, CA: Sage.

Kim, Y. Y.(2012). Inquiry in intercultural and development communication. In Chen L.(Ed.), *Culture, Cultures and Intercultural Communication: A Cross Disciplinary Reader* (pp.355—385).

Shanghai, SH: Shanghai Foreign Language Education Press.

Kirkpatrick, C., & Barrientos, A.(2004). The Lewis model after 50 years. *The Manchester School*, 72(6), 679—690.

Kline, R. B.(2011). *Principles and Practice of Structural Equation Modeling*(3rd ed.). New York, NY: Guilford publications.

Ko, H., Cho, C. H., & Roberts, M. S.(2005). Internet uses and gratifications: A structural equation model of interactive advertising. *Journal of Advertising*, 34(2), 57—70.

Komito, L.(2011). Social media and migration: Virtual community 2.0. *Journal of the American Society for Information Science and Technology*, 62(6), 1075—1086.

Kong, X. X., & Zhang, X. S. [孔晓欣、张晓思],(2013),新生代农民工对微博的使用与评价情况——基于珠三角地区的实证研究,《东南传播》,10: 45—48。

Kontos, E. Z., Emmons, K. M., Puleo, E., & Viswanath, K.(2010). Communication inequalities and public health implications of adult social networking site use in the United States. *Journal of Health Communication*, 15(sup3), 216—235.

Kou, X. J. [寇学军],(2004),上海市民工对城市社会适应状况的调查,《社会》, 8:16—20。

Krahn, H., Derwing, T., Mulder, M., & Wilkinson, L.(2000). Educated and underemployed: Refugee integration into the Canadian labour market. *Journal of International Migration and Integration*, 1(1), 59—84.

Kulich, S. J.(2012). Reconstructing the histories and influences of 1970s intercultural leaders: Prelude to biographies. *International Journal of Intercultural Relations*, 36, 744—759.

Kulich, S. J. & Dai, X. D.(2012). Introduction. In X. D. Dai, & S. J. Kulich(Eds.), *Intercultural adaptation (Ⅰ): Theoretical explorations and empirical studies*(pp.12—27). Shanghai, SH: Shanghai Foreign Language Education Press.

Kulich, S. J., Weng, L. P., Tong, R. T., & DuBois, G.(2020). Interdisciplinary history of intercultural communication studies:

From roots to research and praxis. In D. Landis, & D. P. S. Bhawuk (Eds.), *Cambridge Handbook of Intercultural Training* (4th ed., pp.60—163). New York, NY: Cambridge University Press.

Kuo, B. C., & Roysircar, G.(2004). Predictors of acculturation for Chinese adolescents in Canada: Age of arrival, length of stay, social class, and English reading ability. *Journal of Multicultural Counseling and Development*, 32(3), 143—154.

Lakey, P. N.(2003). Acculturation: A review of the literature. *Intercultural communication studies*, 12(2), 103—118.

Landis, R. S., Beal, D. J., & Tesluk, P. E.(2000). A comparison of approaches to forming composite measures in structural equation models. *Organizational Research Methods*, 3(2), 186—207.

Larsen, R. J., & Ketelaar, T.(1989). Extraversion, neuroticism, and susceptibility to positive and negative mood induction procedures. *Personality and Individual Differences*, 10(12), 1221—1228.

Lee, E. S.(1966). A theory of migration. *Demography*, 3(1), 47—57.

Lee, J. S., Koeske, G. F., & Sales, E.(2004). Social support buffering of acculturative stress: A study of mental health symptoms among Korean international students. *International Journal of Intercultural Relations*, 28(5), 399—414.

Lee, K. S.(2006). Navigating between cultures: A new paradigm for Korean American cultural identification. *Pastoral Psychology*, 54(4), 289—311.

Lei, K. C. [雷开春], (2008), 白领新移民与本地居民的社会支持关系及影响因素, 《青年研究》, 9: 24—32。

Lev-On, A.(2012). Communication, community, crisis: Mapping uses and gratifications in the contemporary media environment. *New Media & Society*, 14(1), 98—116.

Lewis, W. A.(1954). Economic development with unlimited supplies of labour. *The Manchester School*, 22(2), 139—191.

Lewthwaite，M.(1996). A study of international students' perspectives on cross-cultural adaptation. *International Journal for the Advancement of Counselling*，19(2)，167—185.

Li，C.，& Tsai，W. H. S.(2015). Social media usage and acculturation: A test with Hispanics in the US. *Computers in Human Behavior*，45，204—212.

Li，P. L.［李培林］，(1996)，流动民工的社会网络和社会地位，《社会学研究》，4(50):43—43。

Li，P. L.［李培林］，(2003)，《农民工:中国进城农民工的经济社会分析》。北京:社会科学文献出版社。

Li，S. Z.，Yang，X. S.，Yue，Z. S.，& Jin，X. Y.［李树苗、杨绪松、悦中山、靳小怡］，(2007)，农民工社会支持网络的现状及其影响因素研究，《西安交通大学学报:社会科学版》，27(1):67—76。

Li，S. Z.，Ren，Y. K. & Jin，X. Y.［李树苗、任义科、靳小怡］，(2008)，中国农民工的社会融合及其影响因素研究——基于社会支持网络的分析，《人口与经济》，2:1—8。

Li，Y.，& Wu，S.(2010). Social networks and health among rural-urban migrants in China: a channel or a constraint? *Health Promotion International*，25(3)，371—380.

Liang，Z.，& Ma，Z.(2004). China's floating population: new evidence from the 2000 census. *Population and Development Review*，30(3)，467—488.

Liang，Z.，& White，M. J.(1996). Internal migration in China，1950—1988. *Demography*，33(3)，375—384.

Lim，S. S.，& Pham，B.(2016).'If you are a foreigner in a foreign country，you stick together': Technologically mediated communication and acculturation of migrant students. *New Media & Society*，18(10)，2171—2188.

Lin，N.(2008). A network theory of social capital. In Castiglione，D.，Deth，J. W. V.，& Wolleb，G.(Eds.)，*The Handbook of Social Capital* (pp.50—69). New York，NY: Oxford University Press.

Liu，C. Y.，& Yu，C. P.(2013). Can Facebook use induce well-

being? *Cyberpsychology*, *Behavior*, *and Social Networking*, *16*(9),
674—678.

Liu, J. E. [刘建娥], (2010), 乡—城移民(农民工)社会融入的实
证研究——基于五大城市的调查,《人口研究》,4:62—75。

Liu, Y. Q., Liu, Y., & Li, Z. G. [刘于琪、刘晔、李志刚],
(2014), 中国城市新移民的定居意愿及其影响机制,《地理科学》,
34(7):780—787。

Liu, Y., Li, Z., & Breitung, W.(2012). The social networks
of new-generation migrants in China's urbanized villages: A case
study of Guangzhou. *Habitat International*, *36*(1), 192—200.

Lowenstein, A., & Katz, R.(2005). Living arrangements,
family solidarity and life satisfaction of two generations of immigrants in Israel. *Ageing & Society*, *25*(5), 749—767.

Lu, S. Z., & Wei, W. Q. [陆淑珍、魏万青], (2011), 城市外来人
口社会融合的结构方程模型——基于珠三角地区的调查,《人口与经
济》,5:17—23。

Lysgaard, S.(1955). Adjustment in a foreign society: Norwe-
gian fulbright grantees visiting the United States. *International Social Science Bulletin*, *7*, 45—51.

Ma, D. F., & Li, F. X. [马德峰、李风啸], (2010), 近十年来我
国城市新移民问题研究述评,《学术界》,11:220—226。

MacKinnon, D. P., Lockwood, C. M., Hoffman, J. M.,
West, S. G., & Sheets, V.(2002). A comparison of methods to test
mediation and other intervening variable effects. *Psychological
Methods*, *7*(1), 83—118.

MacKinnon, D. P., Lockwood, C. M., & Williams, J.(2004).
Confidence limits for the indirect effect: Distribution of the product and resampling methods. *Multivariate Behavioral Research*,
39(1), 99—128.

Malinauskas, R.(2010). The associations among social support, stress, and life satisfaction as perceived by injured college
athletes. *Social Behavior and Personality*: *An International Journal*, *38*(6), 741—752.

Mallinckrodt, B., Abraham, W. T., Wei, M., & Russell, D. W.(2006). Advances in testing the statistical significance of mediation effects. *Journal of Counseling Psychology*, 53(3), 372—378.

Mangold, D. L., Veraza, R., Kinkler, L., & Kinney, N. A. (2007). Neuroticism predicts acculturative stress in Mexican American college students. *Hispanic Journal of Behavioral Sciences*, 29 (3), 366—383.

Mario, R., La Rosa, D., & Adrados, J. L. R.(1993). *Drug Abuse Among Minority Youth: Advances in Research and Methodology*. US Department of Health and Human Services, Public Health Service, Alcohol, Drug Abuse, and Mental Health Administration, National Institute on Drug Abuse.

Marsden, P. V., & Campbell, K. E. (1984). Measuring tie strength. *Social Forces*, 63(2), 482—501.

Marsiglia, F. F., Booth, J. M., Baldwin, A., & Ayers, S. (2013). Acculturation and life satisfaction among immigrant Mexican adults. *Advances in Social Work*, 14(1), 49.

Martin, J. N., & Nakayama, T. K.(2013). *Intercultural communication in contexts*. New York, NY: McGraw-Hill.

Massey, D. S.(1988). Economic development and international migration in comparative perspective. *The Population and Development Review*, 14(3), 383—413.

Massey, D. S., Arango, J., Hugo, G., Kouaouci, A., Pellegrino, A., & Taylor, J. E.(1993). Theories of international migration: A review and appraisal. *Population and Development Review*, 19(3), 431—466.

Matsunaga, M.(2008). Item parceling in structural equation modeling: A primer. *Communication Methods and Measures*, 2(4), 260—293.

Mayfield, A. (2008). What is social media? http://www. icrossing. co. uk/fileadmin/uploads/eBooks/What_is_Social_ Media _iCrossing_ebook. pdf.

McKay-Semmler, K., & Kim, Y. Y.(2014). Cross-cultural adaptation of Hispanic youth: A study of communication patterns, functional fitness, and psychological health. *Communication Monographs*, *81*(2), 133—156.

Miglietta, A., & Tartaglia, S.(2009). The influence of length of stay, linguistic competence, and media exposure in immigrants' adaptation. *Cross-Cultural Research*, *43*(1), 46—61.

Mikal, J. P., Rice, R. E., Abeyta, A., & DeVilbiss, J.(2013). Transition, stress and computer-mediated social support. *Computers in Human Behavior*, *29*(5), A40—A53.

Min, J. W., Moon, A., & Lubben, J. E.(2005). Determinants of psychological distress over time among older Korean immigrants and Non-Hispanic White elders: Evidence from a two-wave panel study. *Aging & Mental Health*, *9*(3), 210—222.

Moon, S. J., & Park, C. Y.(2007). Media effects on acculturation and biculturalism: A case study of Korean immigrants in Los Angeles' Koreatown. *Mass Communication & Society*, *10*(3), 319—343.

Mui, A. C., & Kang, S. Y.(2006). Acculturation stress and depression among Asian immigrant elders. *Social Work*, *51* (3), 243—255.

Nachtigall, C., Kroehne, U., Funke, F., & Steyer, R.(2003). (Why) Should we use SEM? Pros and cons of structural equation modeling. *Methods Psychological Research Online*, *8*(2), 1—22.

Nailevna, T. A.(2017). Acculturation and psychological adjustment of foreign students(the Experience of Elabuga Institute of Kazan Federal University). *Procedia-Social and Behavioral Sciences*, *237*, 1173—1178.

Nasirudeen, A. M. A., Josephine, K. W. N., Adeline, L. L. C., Seng, L. L., & Ling, H. A.(2014). Acculturative stress among Asian international students in Singapore. *Journal of International Students*, *4*(4), 363—373.

Nesterko, Y., Braehler, E., Grande, G., & Glaesmer, H. (2013). Life satisfaction and health-related quality of life in immigrants and native-born Germans: the role of immigration-related factors. *Quality of Life Research*, *22*(5), 1005—1013.

Nevitt, J., & Hancock, G. R.(2001). Performance of boot-strapping approaches to model test statistics and parameter standard error estimation in structural equation modeling. *Structural Equation Modeling*, *8*(3), 353—377.

Newman, A., Nielsen, I., Smyth, R., & Hooke, A.(2015). Examining the relationship between workplace support and life satisfaction: The mediating role of job satisfaction. *Social Indicators Research*, *120*(3), 769—781.

Ngo, H. Y., & Li, H.(2016). Cultural identity and adaptation of mainland Chinese immigrants in Hong Kong. *American Behavioral Scientist*, *60*(5—6), 730—749.

O'Dell, S.(2010). Opportunities and obligations for libraries in a social networking age: A survey of web 2.0 and networking sites. *Journal of Library Administration*, *50*(3), 237—251.

Oberg, K.(1960). Cultural shock: Adjustment to new cultural environments. *Practical Anthropology*,(4), 177—182.

Oetting, E. R.(1997). Orthogonal cultural identification theory: Theoretical links between cultural identification and substance use. *Substance Use & Misuse*, *32*(12—13), 1913—1918.

Oetting, E. R., & Beauvais, F.(1991). Orthogonal cultural identification theory: The cultural identification of minority adolescents. *International Journal of the Addictions*, *25*(sup5), 655—685.

Ogan, C. L., & Cagiltay, K.(2006). Confession, revelation and storytelling: patterns of use on a popular Turkish website. *New Media & Society*, *8*(5), 801—823.

Oh, H. J., Ozkaya, E., & LaRose, R.(2014). How does online social networking enhance life satisfaction? The relationships among online supportive interaction, affect, perceived social support, sense of community, and life satisfaction. *Computers in Human Behavior*, *30*, 69—78.

Oh, J. H.(2016). Immigration and social capital in a Korean-American women's online community: Supporting acculturation, cultural pluralism, and transnationalism. *New Media & Society*, *18* (10), 2224—2241.

Oh, Y., Koeske, G. F., & Sales, E.(2002). Acculturation, stress, and depressive symptoms among Korean immigrants in the United States. *The Journal of Social Psychology*, *142*(4), 511—526.

Olivas-Lujan, M. R., & Bondarouk, T.(2013). *Social media in human resources management*. Bingley: Emerald Group Publishing.

Olson, D. A., & Shultz, K. S.(1994). Gender differences in the dimensionality of social support[1]. *Journal of Applied Social Psychology*, *24*(14), 1221—1232.

Olson, D. A., Liu, J., & Shultz, K. S.(2012). The influence of Facebook usage on perceptions of social support, personal efficacy, and life satisfaction. *Journal of Organizational Psychology*, *12* (3/4), 133—144.

Ong, A. S., & Ward, C.(2005). The construction and validation of a social support measure for sojourners: The Index of Sojourner Social Support(ISSS) Scale. *Journal of Cross-Cultural Psychology*, *36*(6), 637—661.

Operario, D., & Fiske, S. T.(2001). Ethnic identity moderates perceptions of prejudice: Judgments of personal versus group discrimination and subtle versus blatant bias. *Personality and Social Psychology Bulletin*, *27*(5), 550—561.

Pan, J. Y., Wong, D. F. K., Joubert, L., & Chan, C. L. W. (2007). Acculturative stressor and meaning of life as predictors of negative affect in acculturation: A cross-cultural comparative study between Chinese international students in Australia and Hong Kong. *Australian & New Zealand Journal of Psychiatry*, *41* (9), 740—750.

Pan, J. Y., Wong, D. F. K., Joubert, L., & Chan, C. L. W. (2008). The protective function of meaning of life on life satisfaction among Chinese students in Australia and Hong Kong: A cross-cultural comparative study. *Journal of American College Health*, 57 (2), 221—232.

Pan, J. Y., Yue, X., & Chan, C. L. W.(2010). Development and validation of the Acculturative Hassles Scale for Chinese Students(AHSCS): An example of mainland Chinese university students in Hong Kong. *Psychologia*, 53(3), 163—178.

Park, H. S., & Rubin, A.(2012). The mediating role of acculturative stress in the relationship between acculturation level and depression among Korean immigrants in the U. S. *International Journal of Intercultural Relations*, 36(5), 611—623.

Park, N., Kee, K. F., & Valenzuela, S. (2009). Being immersed in social networking environment: Facebook groups, uses and gratifications, and social outcomes. *Cyberpsychology & Behavior*, 12(6), 729—733.

Park, N., Song, H., & Lee, K. M.(2014). Social networking sites and other media use, acculturation stress, and psychological well-being among East Asian college students in the United States. *Computers in Human Behavior*, 36, 138—146.

Pembecioğlu, N. (2012). Building Identities: Living in the Hybrid Society. *Scientific Journal of Humanistic Studies*, 4 (7), 46—59.

Pfister, D. S., & Soliz, J.(2011).(Re) conceptualizing intercultural communication in a networked society. *Journal of International and Intercultural Communication*, 4(4), 246—251.

Phinney, J. S.(1996). When we talk about American ethnic groups, what do we mean? *American Psychologist*, 51 (9), 918—927.

Phinney, J. S., Horenczyk, G., Liebkind, K., & Vedder, P.(2001). Ethnic identity, immigration, and well-being: An interactional perspective. *Journal of Social Issues*, 57(3), 493—510.

Podsakoff, P. M., MacKenzie, S. B., Lee, J. Y., & Podsakoff, N. P.(2003). Common method biases in behavioral research: A critical review of the literature and recommended remedies.

Journal of Applied Psychology, *88*(5), 879.

Portes, A.(1998). Social capital: Its origins and applications in modern sociology. *Annual Review of Sociology*, *24*(1), 1—24.

Poyrazli, S., Thukral, R. K., & Duru, E.(2010). International students' race-ethnicity, personality and acculturative stress. *International Journal of Psychology and Counselling*, *2*(2), 25—32.

Preacher, K. J., & Hayes, A. F.(2004). SPSS and SAS procedures for estimating indirect effects in simple mediation models. *Behavior Research Methods*, *Instruments*, *& Computers*, *36*(4), 717—731.

Procidano, M. E., & Heller, K.(1983). Measures of perceived social support from friends and from family: Three validation studies. *American Journal of Community Psychology*, *11*(1), 1—24.

Prosser, M. H.(2012). K. S. Sitaram, an early interculturalist: Founding the field May 6, 1970. *International Journal of Intercultural Relations*, *36*(6), 857—868.

Putnam, R.(2001). Social capital: Measurement and consequences. *Canadian Journal of Policy Research*, *2*(1), 41—51.

Qian, M. Y., Wu, G. C., Zhu, R. C., & Zhang, X.［钱铭怡、武国城、朱荣春、张莘］,（2000），艾森克人格问卷简式量表中国版（EPQ-RSC)的修订,《心理学报》,32(3):317—323。

Qin, M. X.［覃明兴］,（2005），移民的身份建构研究,《浙江社会科学》,1:88—94。

Quan-Haase, A., & Young, A. L.(2010). Uses and gratifications of social media: A comparison of Facebook and instant messaging. *Bulletin of Science*, *Technology & Society*, *30*(5), 350—361.

Raacke, J., & Bonds-Raacke, J.(2008). MySpace and Facebook: Applying the uses and gratifications theory to exploring friend-networking sites. *Cyberpsychology & Behavior*, *11*(2), 169—174.

Rasool, F., Botha, C. J., & Bisschoff, C. A.(2012). Push and pull factors in relation to skills shortages in South Africa. *Journal of Social Sciences*, *30*(1), 11—20.

Ravenstein, E. G.(1885). The laws of migration. *Journal of the Statistical Society of London*, 48(2), 167—235.

Reich, S. M., Subrahmanyam, K., & Espinoza, G. (2012). Friending, IMing, and hanging out face-to-face: overlap in adolescents' online and offline social networks. *Developmental Psychology*, 48(2), 356.

Ren, Y., & Qiao, N. [任远、乔楠],(2010),城市流动人口社会融合的过程、测量及影响因素,《人口研究》,34(2):11—20。

Ren, Y., & Tao, L. [任远、陶力],(2012),本地化的社会资本与促进流动人口的社会融合,《人口研究》,36(5):47—57。

Ren, Y., & Wu, M. L. [任远、邬民乐],(2006),城市流动人口的社会融合:文献述评,《人口研究》,30(3):87—94。

Richardson, H. A., Simmering, M. J., & Sturman, M. C. (2009). A tale of three perspectives: Examining post hoc statistical techniques for detection and correction of common method variance. *Organizational Research Methods*, 12(4), 762—800.

Richmond, A. H.(1993). Reactive migration: Sociological perspectives on refugee movements. *Journal of Refugee Studies*, 6(1), 7—24.

Roberts, K. D.(1997). China's "tidal wave" of migrant labor: What can we learn from Mexican undocumented migration to the United States? *International Migration Review*, 31(2), 249—293.

Roberts, R. E., Phinney, J. S., Masse, L. C., Chen, Y. R., Roberts, C. R., & Romero, A.(1999). The structure of ethnic identity of young adolescents from diverse ethnocultural groups. *The Journal of Early Adolescence*, 19(3), 301—322.

Roesch, S. C., Wee, C., & Vaughn, A. A.(2006). Relations between the Big Five personality traits and dispositional coping in Korean Americans: Acculturation as a moderating factor. *International Journal of Psychology*, 41(02), 85—96.

Romero, A. J., Martinez, D., & Carvajal, S. C.(2007). Bicultural stress and adolescent risk behaviors in a community sample of Latinos and non-Latino European Americans. *Ethnicity and*

Health, 12(5), 443—463.

Rucker, D. D., Preacher, K. J., Tormala, Z. L., & Petty, R. E.(2011). Mediation analysis in social psychology: Current practices and new recommendations. *Social and Personality Psychology Compass*, 5(6), 359—371.

Russell, D. W., Booth, B., Reed, D., & Laughlin, P. R. (1997). Personality, social networks, and perceived social support among alcoholics: A structural equation analysis. *Journal of Personality*, 65(3), 649—692.

Ryder, A. G., Alden, L. E., & Paulhus, D.(2000). Is acculturation unidimensional or bidimensional? A head-to-head comparison in the prediction of personality, self-identity, and adjustment. *Journal of Personality and Social Psychology*, 79(1), 49—65.

Salgado, H., Castañeda, S. F., Talavera, G. A., & Lindsay, S. P.(2012). The role of social support and acculturative stress in health-related quality of life among day laborers in Northern San Diego. *Journal of Immigrant and Minority Health*, 14(3), 379—385.

Sam, D. L. (2000). Psychological adaptation of adolescents with immigrant backgrounds. *The Journal of Social Psychology*, 140(1), 5—25.

Sam, D. L., & Berry, J. W.(1995). Acculturative stress among young immigrants in Norway. *Scandinavian Journal of Psychology*, 36(1), 10—24.

Sandhu, D. S., & Asrabadi, B. R.(1994). Development of an acculturative stress scale for international students: Preliminary findings. *Psychological Reports*, 75(1), 435—448.

Sarason, I. G., Levine, H. M., Basham, R. B., & Sarason, B. R.(1983). Assessing social support: the social support questionnaire. *Journal of Personality and Social Psychology*, 44(1), 127—139.

Sawyer, R. & Chen, G. M.(2012). The Impact of Social Media on Intercultural Adaptation. *Intercultural Communication Studies*,

21(2)，151—169.

Schiller，N. G.，Basch，L.，& Blanc，C. S.(1995). From immigrant to transmigrant：Theorizing transnational migration. *Anthropological Quarterly*，*68*(1)，48—63.

Schumacker，R. E.，& Lomax，R. G.(2010). A Beginner's Guide to. *Structural Equation Modeling*(3rd ed.)，New York，NY：Taylor & Francis Group.

Schwartz，S. J.，Unger，J. B.，Zamboanga，B. L.，& Szapocznik，J.(2010). Rethinking the concept of acculturation：implications for theory and research. *American Psychologist*，*65*(4)，237.

Searle，W.，& Ward，C.(1990). The prediction of psychological and sociocultural adjustment during cross-cultural transitions. *International Journal of Intercultural Relations*，*14*(4)，449—464.

Segal，U. A.，Mayadas，N. S.，& Elliott，D.(2006). A framework for immigration. *Journal of Immigrant & Refugee Studies*，*4*(1)，3—24.

Shao，G.(2009). Understanding the appeal of user-generated media：a uses and gratification perspective. *Internet Research*，*19*(1)，7—25.

Shao，Y. L.，& Fu，X. H.［邵雅利、傅晓华］，(2014)，新生代农民工的社会支持与主观幸福感研究，《四川理工学院学报（社会科学版）》，4：8—15。

Sheldon，P.(2008). The relationship between unwillingness-to-communicate and students' Facebook use. *Journal of Media Psychology*，*20*(2)，67—75.

Shen，B. J.，& Takeuchi，D. T.(2001). A structural model of acculturation and mental health status among Chinese Americans. *American Journal of Community Psychology*，*29*(3)，387—418.

Sherbourne，C. D.，& Stewart，A. L.(1991). The MOS social support survey. *Social Science & Medicine*，*32*(6)，705—714.

Shi，L.(2008). *Rural migrant workers in China：scenario，challenges and public policy*. Geneva：ILO.

Shin，D. C.，& Johnson，D. M.(1978). Avowed happiness as an

overall assessment of the quality of life. *Social Indicators Research*,
5(1—4), 475—492.

Shrout, P. E., & Bolger, N.(2002). Mediation in experimental
and nonexperimental studies: new procedures and recommendations. *Psychological methods*, 7(4), 422.

Shumaker, S. A., & Brownell, A.(1984). Toward a theory of
social support: Closing conceptual gaps. *Journal of Social Issues*, 40
(4), 11—36.

Shuter, R.(2012). Intercultural new media studies: The next
frontier in intercultural communication. *Journal of Intercultural
Communication Research*, 41(3), 219—237.

Sin, S. C. J., & Kim, K. S.(2013). International students' everyday life information seeking: The informational value of social
networking sites. *Library & Information Science Research*, 35(2),
107—116.

Sjaastad, L. A.(1962). The costs and returns of human migration. *Journal of Political Economy*, 70(5, Part 2), 80—93.

Smith, R. A., & Khawaja, N. G.(2011). A review of the acculturation experiences of international students. *International Journal of Intercultural Relations*, 35(6), 699—713.

Sobel, M. E.(1982). Asymptotic confidence intervals for indirect effects in structural equation models. *Sociological Methodology*,
13, 290—312.

Sodowsky, G. R., & Plake, B. S.(1992). A study of acculturation differences among international people and suggestions for sensitivity to within—group differences. *Journal of Counseling & Development*, 71(1), 53—59.

Spier, S.(2011). Collective Action 2.0: The impact of ICT—
based social media on Collective Action—difference in degree or
difference in kind? SSRN Electronic Journal.

Stark, O.(1984). Rural-to-urban migration in LDCs: a relative
deprivation approach. *Economic Development and Cultural Change*,
32(3), 475—486.

Stark, O., & Bloom, D. E.(1985). The new economics of labor migration. *The American Economic Review*, 75(2), 173—178.

Stark, O., & Taylor, J. E.(1989). Relative deprivation and international migration. *Demography*, 26(1), 1—14.

Streeter, C. L., & Franklin, C.(1992). Defining and measuring social support: Guidelines for social work practitioners. *Research on Social Work Practice*, 2(1), 81—98.

Sun, L.(2019). Introduction. In L. Sun,(2019), *Rural urban migration and policy intervention in China: Migrant workers' coping strategies*(pp.1—9). New York, NY: Springer.

Sussman, N. M.(2000). The dynamic nature of cultural identity throughout cultural transitions: Why home is not so sweet. *Personality and Social Psychology Review*, 4(4), 355—373.

Swagler, M. A., & Jome, L. M.(2005). The effects of personality and acculturation on the adjustment of North American sojourners in Taiwan. *Journal of Counseling Psychology*, 52(4), 527.

Swickert, R. J., Hittner, J. B., & Foster, A.(2010). Big Five traits interact to predict perceived social support. *Personality and Individual Differences*, 48(6), 736—741.

Swickert, R. J., Hittner, J. B., Harris, J. L., & Herring, J. A. (2002). Relationships among Internet use, personality, and social support. *Computers in Human Behavior*, 18(4), 437—451.

Tabachnick, B. G., Fidell, L. S., & Ullman, J. B.(2007). *Using Multivariate Statistics(Vol.5)*. Boston, MA: Pearson.

Tartakovsky, E.(2009). Cultural identities of adolescent immigrants: A three-year longitudinal study including the pre-migration period. *Journal of Youth and Adolescence*, 38(5), 654—671.

Taylor, E. J.(1999). The new economics of labour migration and the role of remittances in the migration process. *International Migration*, 37(1), 63—88.

Thoits, P. A.(1985). Social support and psychological well-being: Theoretical possibilities. In Sarason I. G.(Ed.), *Social Support: Theory, Research and Applications* (pp.51—72). Dordrecht:

Springer.

Thoits, P. A.(1995). Identity-relevant events and psychological symptoms: A cautionary tale. *Journal of Health and Social Behavior*, *36*(1), 72—82.

Thomas, M., & Choi, J. B.(2006). Acculturative stress and social support among Korean and Indian immigrant adolescents in the United States. *Journal of Sociology & Social Welfare*, *33*(2), 123—144.

Thurber, C. A., & Walton, E. A.(2012). Homesickness and adjustment in university students. *Journal of American College Health*, *60*(5), 415—419.

Todaro, M. P.(1969). A model of labor migration and urban unemployment in less developed countries. *The American Economic Review*, *59*(1), 138—148.

Todaro, M. P.(1980). Internal migration in developing countries: a survey. In R. A. Easterlin(Ed.), *Population and Economic Change in Developing Countries* (pp.361—402). Chicago: University of Chicago Press.

Tong, X., & Ma, X. H. [童星、马西恒],(2008),"敦睦他者"与 "化整为零"——城市新移民的社区融合,《社会科学研究》,1:77—83。

Tonsing, K. N., Tse, S., & Tonsing, J. C.(2016). Acculturation, perceived discrimination, and psychological distress: Experiences of South Asians in Hong Kong. *Transcultural Psychiatry*, *53*(1), 124—144.

Trepte, S., Dienlin, T., & Reinecke, L.(2015). Influence of social support received in online and offline contexts on satisfaction with social support and satisfaction with life: A longitudinal study. *Media Psychology*, *18*(1), 74—105.

Uchino, B. N.(2004). *Social support and physical health: Understanding the health consequences of relationships*. London: Yale University Press.

Uchino, B. N., Uno, D., & Holt-Lunstad, J.(1999). Social support, physiological processes, and health. *Current Directions in*

Psychological Science, *8*(5), 145—148.

Ullman, C., & Tatar, M.(2001). Psychological adjustment among Israeli adolescent immigrants: A report on life satisfaction, self-concept, and self-esteem. *Journal of Youth and Adolescence*, *30*(4), 449—463.

Valenzuela, S., Park, N., & Kee, K. F.(2009). Is there social capital in a social network site?: Facebook use and college students' life satisfaction, trust, and participation. *Journal of Computer-mediated Communication*, *14*(4), 875—901.

Vergara, M. B., Smith, N., & Keele, B.(2010). Emotional intelligence, coping responses, and length of stay as correlates of acculturative stress among international university students in Thailand. *Procedia-Social and Behavioral Sciences*, *5*, 1498—1504.

Verkuyten, M.(2011). Assimilation ideology and outgroup attitudes among ethnic majority members. *Group Processes & Intergroup Relations*, *14*(6), 789—806.

Virk, A.(2011). Twitter: The strength of weak ties. *University of Auckland Business Review*, *13*(1), 19—21.

Virta, E., Sam, D. L., & Westin, C.(2004). Adolescents with Turkish background in Norway and Sweden: A comparative study of their psychological adaptation. *Scandinavian Journal of Psychology*, *45*(1), 15—25.

Vohra, N., & Adair, J.(2000). Life satisfaction of Indian immigrants in Canada. *Psychology and Developing Societies*, *12*(2), 109—138.

Wadsworth, M. E., & Compas, B. E.(2002). Coping with family conflict and economic strain: The adolescent perspective. *Journal of Research on Adolescence*, *12*(2), 243—274.

Walker, K. N., MacBride, A., & Vachon, M. L.(1977). Social support networks and the crisis of bereavement. *Social Science & Medicine*, *11*(1), 35—41.

Wang, C. [王诚],(2005),劳动力供求"拐点"与中国二元经济转型,《中国人口科学》,6:2—10。

Wang，G. H.［汪国华］,（2009），新生代农民工文化适应的内在逻辑：系统抑或构架?《调研世界》,10：9—11。

Wang，J.，& Wang，X.（2012）. *Structural equation modeling：Applications using mplus*. New Jersey，NJ：John Wiley & Sons.

Wang，K. T.，Heppner，P. P.，Fu，C. C.，Zhao，R.，Li，F.，& Chuang，C. C.（2012）. Profiles of acculturative adjustment patterns among Chinese international students. *Journal of Counseling Psychology*，*59*（3），424—436.

Wang，L. L.［汪琳岚］,（2014），知识型移民的总体特征及结构性分化——以北京市为例,《理论月刊》,（6）：151—155。

Wang，M. C.［王孟成］,（2018）,《潜变量建模与 Mplus 应用：基础篇》。重庆：重庆大学出版社。

Wang，W. W.，& Fan，C. C.（2012）. Migrant workers' integration in urban China：Experiences in employment，social adaptation，and self-identity. *Eurasian Geography and Economics*，*53*（6），731—749.

Wang，D/T. L.，Liu，B. J.，& Lou，S. P.［王佃利、刘保军、楼苏萍］,（2011），新生代农民工的城市融入——框架建构与调研分析,《中国行政管理》,2：111—115。

Wang，Y. J.，& Tong，X.［王毅杰、童星］,（2004），流动农民社会支持网探析,《社会学研究》,2：42—48。

Wang，Z.，Tchernev，J. M.，& Solloway，T.（2012）. A dynamic longitudinal examination of social media use，needs，and gratifications among college students. *Computers in Human Behavior*，*28*（5），1829—1839.

Wang. D.［王东］,（2005），农民工社会支持系统的研究——一个社会工作理论研究的视角,《西南民族大学学报：人文社会科学版》,26（1）：77—79。

Ward，C.，Leong，C. H.，& Low，M.（2004）. Personality and sojourner adjustment：An exploration of the Big Five and the cultural fit proposition. *Journal of Cross-Cultural Psychology*，*35*（2），137—151.

Ward，C.，& Kennedy，A.（1992）. Locus of control，mood disturbance, and social difficulty during cross-cultural transitions. *International Journal of Intercultural Relations*, *16*(2), 175—194.

Ward, C., & Kennedy, A.(1999). The measurement of sociocultural adaptation. *International journal of intercultural relations*, *23*(4), 659—677.

Ward, C., & Rana-Deuba, A.(1999). Acculturation and adaptation revisited. *Journal of Cross-cultural Psychology*, *30*(4), 422—442.

Ward, C., & Rana-Deuba, A.(2000). Home and host culture influences on sojourner adjustment. *International Journal of Intercultural Relations*, *24*(3), 291—306.

Ward, C., & Searle, W.(1991). The impact of value discrepancies and cultural identity on psychological and sociocultural adjustment of sojourners. *International Journal of Intercultural Relations*, *15*(2), 209—224.

Watson, D., & Hubbard, B.(1996). Adaptational style and dispositional structure: Coping in the context of the Five-Factor model. *Journal of personality*, *64*(4), 737—774.

Wei, L., & Chen, W. ［韦路、陈稳］,(2015),城市新移民社交媒体使用与主观幸福感研究,《国际新闻界》,37(1):114—130。

Wei, M., Heppner, P. P., Mallen, M. J., Ku, T. Y., Liao, K. Y. H., & Wu, T. F.(2007). Acculturative stress, perfectionism, years in the United States, and depression among Chinese international students. *Journal of Counseling Psychology*, *54*(4), 385.

Wei, M., Ku, T. Y., Russell, D. W., Mallinckrodt, B., & Liao, K. Y. H.(2008). Moderating effects of three coping strategies and self-esteem on perceived discrimination and depressive symptoms: A minority stress model for Asian international students. *Journal of Counseling Psychology*, *55*(4), 451.

Wei, M., Wang, K. T., Heppner, P. P., & Du, Y.(2012). Ethnic and mainstream social connectedness, perceived racial discrimination, and posttraumatic stress symptoms. *Journal of Counseling Psychology*, *59*(3), 486—493.

Wei，X. P.，& Yang，L.［位秀平、杨磊］,（2014），国际移民理论综述.《黑河学刊》,1:3—5。

Wellman，B.，& Wortley，S.（1990）. Different strokes from different folks：Community ties and social support. *American Journal of Sociology*，*96*（3），558—588.

Wellmann，B.（1992）. Which types of ties and networks give what kinds of social report? *Advances in Group Processes*，*9*（1），207—235.

Wen，M.，& Wang，G.（2009）. Demographic，psychological，and social environmental factors of loneliness and satisfaction among rural-to-urban migrants in Shanghai，China. *International Journal of Comparative Sociology*，*50*（2），155—182.

West，S. G.，Finch，J. F.，& Curran，P. J.（1995）. Structural equation models with non-normal variables：Problems and remedies. In R. H. Hoyle（Ed.），*Structural equation modeling：Concepts，issues，and applications*（pp.56—75）. Thousand Oaks，CA：Sage.

Weston，R.，& Gore Jr，P. A.（2006）. A brief guide to structural equation modeling. *The Counseling Psychologist*，*34*（5），719—751.

Williams，B.，Onsman，A.，& Brown，T.（2010）. Exploratory factor analysis：A five-step guide for novices. *Australasian Journal of Paramedicine*，*8*（3），1—13

Wilson，R. E.，Gosling，S. D.，& Graham，L. T.（2012）. A review of Facebook research in the social sciences. *Perspectives on Psychological Science*，*7*（3），203—220.

Wilton，L.，& Constantine，M. G.（2003）. Length of residence，cultural adjustment difficulties，and psychological distress symptoms in Asian and Latin American international college students. *Journal of College Counseling*，*6*（2），177—186.

Wong，D. F. K.，He，X.，Leung，G.，Lau，Y.，& Chang，Y.（2008）. Mental health of migrant workers in China：prevalence and correlates. *Social Psychiatry and Psychiatric Epidemiology*，*43*（6），483—489.

Wong，D. F. K.，& Song，H. X.（2008）. The resilience of migrant workers in Shanghai China: the roles of migration stress and meaning of migration. *International Journal of Social Psychiatry*, 54(2), 131—143.

Wong, W. K., Chou, K. L., & Chow, N. W.(2012). Correlates of quality of life in new migrants to Hong Kong from Mainland China. *Social Indicators Research*, 107(2), 373—391.

Wu, M. L.［吴明隆］,(2010),《问卷统计分析实务：SPSS 操作与应用》。重庆:重庆大学出版社。

Xiao, S. Y.［肖水源］,(1999),社会支持评定量表,见:汪向东、王希林、马弘编著,心理卫生评定量表手册(增刊),《中国心理卫生杂志》,127—131。

Xu, C. X.［许传新］,(2007),新生代农民工的身份认同及影响因素分析,《学术探索》,3:58—62。

Yako, R. M., & Biswas, B.(2014). "We came to this country for the future of our children. We have no future": Acculturative stress among Iraqi refugees in the United States. *International Journal of Intercultural Relations*, 38, 133—141.

Yalçın, İ.(2011). Social support and optimism as predictors of life satisfaction of college students. *International Journal for the Advancement of Counselling*, 33(2), 79—87.

Yang, J. H.［杨菊华］,(2009),从隔离、选择融入到融合:流动人口社会融入问题的理论思考,《人口研究》,33(1):17—29。

Yang, P.［杨萍］,(2010),论 SNS 社交网站的传播价值:基于社会资本理论的视角,《东南传播》,9:95—97。

Yang, S. Y.［杨淑芸］,(2014),新生代农民工社会支持的多元线性回归分析.《社会科学论坛》,11:216—221。

Yang, T. Y.［杨天宇］,(2018),判断劳动力短缺的两种理论之区别——马克思产业后备军理论与刘易斯二元经济理论的比较,《贵州社会科学》,10:107—111。

Yang, T., Xu, X., Li, M., Rockett, I. R., Zhu, W., & Ellison-Barnes, A.(2012). Mental health status and related characteristics of Chinese male rural-urban migrant workers. *Community Mental Health Journal*, 48(3), 342—351.

Yang. X. S., Jin, X. Y., Xiao, Q. Y., & Bai. M. [杨绪松、靳小怡、肖群鹰、白萌],(2006),农民工社会支持与社会融合的现状及政策研究——以深圳市为例.《中国软科学》,12:18—26。

Ye, J.(2006a). An examination of acculturative stress, interpersonal social support, and use of online ethnic social groups among Chinese international students. *Howard Journal of Communications*, *17*(1), 1—20.

Ye, J.(2006b). Traditional and online support networks in the cross-cultural adaptation of Chinese international students in the United States. *Journal of Computer-Mediated Communication*, *11*(3), 863—876.

Yoder, C., & Stutzman, F.(2011, May). Identifying social capital in the Facebook interface. In *Proceedings of the SIGCHI Conference on Human Factors in Computing Systems*(pp.585—588). New York, NY: ACM.

Yong, A. G., & Pearce, S.(2013). A beginner's guide to factor analysis: Focusing on exploratory factor analysis. *Tutorials in Quantitative Methods for Psychology*, *9*(2), 79—94.

Young, M. Y.(2001). Moderators of stress in salvadoran refugees: the role of social and personal resources. *International Migration Review*, *35*(3), 840—869.

Yu, S. & Kak, S.(2012). A survey of prediction using social media. http://arxiv. org/ftp/arxiv/papers/1203/1203.1647.pdf.

Yu, Y. J., Gao, X. D., & Guo, Q. [余运江、高向东、郭庆],(2012),新生代乡-城流动人口社会融合研究——基于上海的调查分析,《人口与经济》,(1):57—64。

Yuan, H. [袁浩],(2015),上海新白领移民的社会网络构成、相对剥夺感与主观幸福感——以上海市为例,《福建论坛:人文社会科学版》,(4):186—192。

Yue, Z. S., Li, S. Z., & Jin, X. Y. [悦中山、李树茁、靳小怡],(2011),从"先赋"到"后致":农民工的社会网络与社会融合,《社会》,31(6):130—152。

Zhai, X. H. [翟秀海],(2009),制度视角下农民工身份认同困境问题研究,《农业经济》,(4):62—63。

Zhang, J. H.［张结海］,(2011),外地白领移民上海文化适应影响因素研究,《社会科学》,(11):73—80。

Zhang, J., Mandl, H., & Wang, E.(2010). Personality, acculturation, and psychosocial adjustment of Chinese international students in Germany. *Psychological Reports*, *107*(2), 511—525.

Zhang, L. B.［张丽彬］,(2015),全球化时代国际移民理论综述,《新西部(理论版)》,(8):163—164。

Zhang, L., & Wang, G. X.(2010). Urban citizenship of rural migrants in reform-era China. *Citizenship Studies*, *14*(2), 145—166.

Zhang, W. H., & Lei, K. C.［张文宏、雷开春］,(2008),城市新移民社会融合的结构、现状与影响因素分析,《社会学研究》,(5):117—141。

Zhang, W. H., & Lei, K. C.［张文宏、雷开春］,(2009),城市新移民社会认同的结构模型,《社会学研究》,(4):61—87。

Zhao, L., Liu, S., & Zhang, W.(2018). New trends in internal migration in China: Profiles of the New-generation migrants. *China & World Economy*, *26*(1), 18—41.

Zhao, X. G., & Li, Z. G.［赵向光、李志刚］,(2013),中国大城市新移民的地方认同与融入,《城市规划》,(12):22—29。

Zhen, Y. Q., Zhang, Y., & Zhu. R. H.［甄月桥、张圆、朱茹华］,(2015),社会支持对新生代农民工心理健康的影响——以杭州新生代农民工调查为例,《发展研究》,(6):93—97。

Zheng, X.［郑欣］,(2011),新生代农民工的城市适应——基于传播社会学的视角,《南京社会科学》,(3):71—77。

Zheng, X., & Berry, J. W.(1991). Psychological adaptation of Chinese sojourners in Canada. *International Journal of Psychology*, *26*(4), 451—470.

Zhong, B. L., Liu, T. B., Huang, J. X., Fung, H. H., Chan, S. S., Conwell, Y., & Chiu, H. F.(2016). Acculturative stress of Chinese rural-to-urban migrant workers: a qualitative study. *PLOS ONE*, *11*(6), e0157530.

Zhou, B. H., & Lv, S. N.［周葆华、吕舒宁］,(2011),上海市新

生代农民工新媒体使用与评价的实证研究,《新闻大学》,(2):145—
150。

Zhou, D. M. [周大鸣], (2014),《城市新移民问题及其对策研
究》。北京:经济科学出版社。

Zhou, P. [周萍], (2011),城市移民就业歧视的个人成本分析,
《技术与市场》,18(1):34—35。

Zhu, G. D., Liu, H., & Chen, Zh, Q. [朱国栋、刘红、陈志强],
(2008),上海移民。上海:上海财经大学出版社。

Zhu, K. J., & Liu, R. Q. [朱考金、刘瑞清], (2007),青年农民工
的社会支持网与城市融入研究——以南京市为例,《青年研究》,(8):
9—13。

Zhu, L., Zhao, L. L., & Wu, J. G. [朱力、赵璐璐、邬金刚],
(2010),"半主动性适应"与"建构型适应"——新生代农民工的城市适
应模型,《甘肃行政学院学报》,4:4—10。

Zhu, X., Woo, S. E., Porter, C., & Brzezinski, M.(2013).
Pathways to happiness: From personality to social networks and
perceived support. *Social Networks*, 35(3), 382—393.

Zimet, G. D., Dahlem, N. W., Zimet, S. G., & Farley, G. K.
(1988). The multidimensional scale of perceived social support.
Journal of Personality Assessment, 52(1), 30—41.

Appendix 1：Chinese Questionnaire

上海国内移民适应情况的问卷调查

您好！感谢您参与本问卷调查。本问卷调查旨在了解上海国内移民的适应情况,分析移民社交媒介使用与其文化适应之间的关系。

本问卷采用匿名作答的方式进行,调查结果会受到严格保密。我们郑重保证不会将您个人的填写结果透漏给任何第三方。另外,本调查旨在对国内移民的社交媒介使用与其文化适应的关系进行总体分析,并不关注某一个体的填写结果。因此,您不必有任何顾虑,请根据您的实际情况如实填写。您所填写的一切资料仅用于纯学术研究,不用于任何商业目的。

一、个人基本情况

1. 您的性别：[单选题]*

○男　　　　○女

2. 您的年龄段：[单选题]*

○18 岁以下　○18～25　○26～30　○31～40　○41～50

○51～60　　○60 以上

3. 您的家乡：[单选题]*

○安徽　○北京　○重庆　○福建　○甘肃　○广东

○广西　○贵州　○海南　○河北　○黑龙江　○河南

○香港　○湖北　○湖南　○江苏　○江西　○吉林

○辽宁　○澳门　○内蒙古　○宁夏　○青海　○山东

○上海　○山西　○陕西　○四川　○台湾　○天津

○新疆　○西藏　○云南　○浙江　○海外

4. 您的婚姻状况：[单选题]*

○已婚　　　○未婚

5. 您的受教育程度：[单选题]*

○初中及以下　　○高中或中专　　○大学专科

○大学本科　　　○硕士　　　　　○博士/博士后

6. 您在上海生活多久了？　＿＿年＿＿月[填空题]*

7. 您当初选择来上海的主要原因是？[单选题]*

○读书　　　　　○工作　　　　　○随迁

○投资经营　　　○其他

8. 您目前的职业是：[单选题]*

○各级政府部门、企事业单位、党政机关和公众团体的领导者

○专业技术人员（教师、医生、工程技术人员、作家等专业人员）

○公务员、事业单位/政府工作人员

○公司职员

○工人（如工厂工人/建筑工人/城市环卫工人等）

○从事农林牧副渔的劳动者

○私营企业主/个体经营者

○自由职业者

○军人

○家庭主妇

○学生

○离退休人员

○失业人员

○其他（如志愿者）

9. 您目前在上海的户籍状况是：[单选题]*

○常住户口　　○居住证　　○集体户口　　○其他

10. 您目前在上海的居住方式是：[单选题]*

○自购住房

○租赁住房

○借住在亲戚或朋友家

○单位（学校）集体宿舍

○其他

11. 在过去一年中,您每个月的平均收入是多少元?[单选题]*

○5000 以下　　　　　○5000～10000　　　　○10001～15000

○15001～20000　　　○20000 以上

12. 您能听懂上海话吗?[单选题]*

○完全听不懂　　　　　○听懂一些

○听懂大部分　　　　　○全部听懂

13. 您会讲上海话吗?[单选题]*

○不会讲　　　　　　　○会讲一些

○大部分会讲　　　　　○全部会讲

14. 您是否有在上海长期定居的打算（5 年以上）?[单选题]*

○是　　　　　○否

二、社交媒体使用

1. 您使用最频繁的社交媒体有哪些?[多选题]*

□微信　　　□腾讯 QQ　　　□新浪微博　　　□豆瓣

□人人网　　□知乎网　　　　□百度贴吧　　　□天涯论坛

□领英　　　□开心网　　　　□Skype　　　　□其他

2. 过去一周,您平均每天花多少时间使用社交媒体?[单选题]*

○30 分钟以下　　○31～60 分钟　　○1～2 小时

○2～3 小时　　　○3 小时以上

3. 请根据您的实际情况,从 1～9 中选择最符合的数字:1 → 9 表示强烈反对→强烈同意。[矩阵量表题]*

	1	2	3	4	5	6	7	8	9
(1) 使用社交媒体是我日常生活的一部分。	○	○	○	○	○	○	○	○	○
(2) 如果不使用社交媒体,我感觉与外界失去了联系。	○	○	○	○	○	○	○	○	○
(3) 我愿意在社交媒体上分享一些信息。	○	○	○	○	○	○	○	○	○
(4) 我使用社交媒体寻求帮助。	○	○	○	○	○	○	○	○	○
(5) 我和我的家人在社交媒体上交流频繁。	○	○	○	○	○	○	○	○	○
(6) 我通过社交媒体和朋友保持密切联系。	○	○	○	○	○	○	○	○	○

三、性格

请仔细阅读以下问题，根据自身情况做出是或否的判断。[矩阵量表题]*

	是	否
1. 你的情绪是否时起时落？	○	○
2. 你是个健谈的人吗？	○	○
3. 你是否会无缘无故地感到"很惨"？	○	○
4. 你是个生机勃勃的人吗？	○	○
5. 你是个容易被激怒的人吗？	○	○
6. 你愿意认识陌生人吗？	○	○
7. 你的感情容易受伤害吗？	○	○
8. 在热闹的聚会中你能使自己放得开，使自己玩得开心吗？	○	○
9. 你是否时常感到"极其厌倦"？	○	○
10. 在结交新朋友时，你经常是积极主动的吗？	○	○
11. 你认为自己是一个胆怯不安的人吗？	○	○
12. 你能否很容易地给一个沉闷的聚会注入活力？	○	○
13. 你是个忧心忡忡的人吗？	○	○
14. 在社交场合你是否倾向于待在不显眼的地方？	○	○
15. 你认为自己是个神经紧张或"弦绷得过紧"的人吗？	○	○
16. 你是否喜欢和人们相处在一起？	○	○
17. 在经历了一次令人难堪的事之后，你是否会为此烦恼很长时间？	○	○
18. 你是否喜欢在自己周围有许多热闹和令人兴奋的事情？	○	○
19. 你是否因自己的"神经过敏"而感到痛苦？	○	○
20. 你是否喜欢说笑话和谈论有趣的事？	○	○
21. 你是否时常感到孤独？	○	○
22. 在别人眼里你总是充满活力的吗？	○	○
23. 你是否时常被负疚感所困扰？	○	○
24. 你能使一个聚会顺利进行下去吗？	○	○

四、社会支持

请根据您的实际情况,从 1～9 中选择最符合的数字:1→9 表示强烈反对→强烈同意。[矩阵量表题]*

	1	2	3	4	5	6	7	8	9
1. 当我求职时,会有人帮我推荐一些职位。	○	○	○	○	○	○	○	○	○
2. 当我需要倾诉时,我能找到人倾听我的烦恼。	○	○	○	○	○	○	○	○	○
3. 会有人分享我的快乐。	○	○	○	○	○	○	○	○	○
4. 我能找到人和我聚在一起消遣一下。	○	○	○	○	○	○	○	○	○
5. 会有人给我提供一些有用的资讯,帮我融入上海的生活。	○	○	○	○	○	○	○	○	○
6. 会有人帮我熟悉上海的文化习俗。	○	○	○	○	○	○	○	○	○
7. 我可以找到值得信赖的人来讨论私人问题。	○	○	○	○	○	○	○	○	○
8. 会有人给我一些意见,帮我认清我的处境。	○	○	○	○	○	○	○	○	○
9. 会有人帮我了解当地的规章制度。	○	○	○	○	○	○	○	○	○
10. 当我需要去看医生时,会有人愿意陪我。	○	○	○	○	○	○	○	○	○
11. 会有人愿意陪我做一些事情,帮我摆脱烦恼。	○	○	○	○	○	○	○	○	○
12. 当我身处困境时,会有人给我好的建议。	○	○	○	○	○	○	○	○	○
13. 我能找到人分担我的忧愁。	○	○	○	○	○	○	○	○	○
14. 当我找工作时,会有人给我提供一些求职信息。	○	○	○	○	○	○	○	○	○
15. 会有人为我的职业发展提供一些建议。	○	○	○	○	○	○	○	○	○

五、适应压力

请结合您移居上海后的经历,从 1～9 中选出一个反映您自身情况的数字,1→9 表示强烈反对→强烈同意。[矩阵量表题]*

	1	2	3	4	5	6	7	8	9
1. 因为我是外地人,我在社会上受到区别对待。	○	○	○	○	○	○	○	○	○
2. 因为我是外地人,有很多机会我得不到。	○	○	○	○	○	○	○	○	○
3. 因为我是外地人,别人对我有偏见。	○	○	○	○	○	○	○	○	○
4. 因为我是外地人,我受到不公平的对待。	○	○	○	○	○	○	○	○	○

continued

	1	2	3	4	5	6	7	8	9
5. 因为我是外地人,一些应得的待遇我得不到。	○	○	○	○	○	○	○	○	○
6. 我觉得外地人在上海受到歧视。	○	○	○	○	○	○	○	○	○
7. 因为想家,我觉得苦恼。	○	○	○	○	○	○	○	○	○
8. 生活在不熟悉的环境里,我感到难过。	○	○	○	○	○	○	○	○	○
9. 我想念家乡和家乡的亲人。	○	○	○	○	○	○	○	○	○
10. 远离家乡的亲人,我感到难过。	○	○	○	○	○	○	○	○	○
11. 我不太适应上海的饮食。	○	○	○	○	○	○	○	○	○
12. 我不太适应上海本地人的文化价值观。	○	○	○	○	○	○	○	○	○
13. 当有人用上海话和我交流时,我会紧张。	○	○	○	○	○	○	○	○	○
14. 当别人不理解我的文化价值观时,我感觉痛苦。	○	○	○	○	○	○	○	○	○
15. 我每月会为要支付的账单发愁。	○	○	○	○	○	○	○	○	○
16. 如果家里要添置一辆小轿车,我要积攒好几个月的收入。	○	○	○	○	○	○	○	○	○
17. 我有多余的钱供自己和家人每年出国旅游一次。	○	○	○	○	○	○	○	○	○
18a. 房贷占我每个月家庭收入的很大比重。	○	○	○	○	○	○	○	○	○
18b. 房租占我每个月家庭收入的很大比重。	○	○	○	○	○	○	○	○	○

六、生活满意度

请根据您的实际情况,从 1~9 中选择最符合的数字:1 → 9 表示强烈反对 → 强烈同意。[矩阵量表题]*

	1	2	3	4	5	6	7	8	9
1. 我在上海的生活基本接近于我的理想状态。	○	○	○	○	○	○	○	○	○
2. 我在上海的生活状况很好。	○	○	○	○	○	○	○	○	○
3. 我对自己在上海的生活感到满意。	○	○	○	○	○	○	○	○	○
4. 目前为止,我得到了生活中想要的重要东西。	○	○	○	○	○	○	○	○	○
5. 我不想对我在上海的生活做任何改变。	○	○	○	○	○	○	○	○	○

七、文化认同

请根据您的实际情况,从 1~9 中选择最符合的数字:1 → 9 表示强烈反对 → 强烈同意。[矩阵量表题]*

	1	2	3	4	5	6	7	8	9
1. 我愿意结交上海人。	○	○	○	○	○	○	○	○	○
2. 我觉得我与上海人有许多共同点。	○	○	○	○	○	○	○	○	○
3. 我认为自己是上海人。	○	○	○	○	○	○	○	○	○
4. 我愿意学说上海话。	○	○	○	○	○	○	○	○	○
5. 我愿意遵循上海的风俗习惯。	○	○	○	○	○	○	○	○	○

Appendix 2: English Questionnaire

A Questionnaire on Adaptation of Internal Migrants in Shanghai

Thanks for your participation in the survey. The purpose of this survey is to learn about the adaptation of internal migrants in Shanghai and examine the relationships between their social media use and their adaptation.

The questionnaire is anonymous, and the survey results are strictly confidential. The researcher solemnly promises that the survey results will not be revealed to any third party. Moreover, the researcher will focus on analyzing the overall relationship between social media use and adaptation, rather than the answers of any individual respondent. So, you do not have to have any concern and please give your true answers. The questionnaire is used for academic studies, and will not be used for any business purpose.

I. Personal Information

1. Your gender: [Single Choice]*

○Male   ○Female

2. Your age:[Single Choice]*

○Below 18   ○18~25   ○26~30   ○31~40

○41~50   ○51~60   ○Above 60

3. Your hometown:[Single Choice]*

○Anhui   ○Beijing   ○Chongqing   ○Fujian

○Ganshu   ○Guangdong   ○Guangxi   ○Guizhou

○Hainan   ○Hebei   ○Heilongjiang ○Henan

○Hong Kong   ○Hubei   ○Hunan   ○Jiangsu

○Jiangxi   ○Jilin   ○Liaoning   ○Macau

○Inner Mongolia ○Ningxia   ○Qinghai   ○Shandong

○Shanghai   ○Shanxi   ○Shaanxi   ○Sichuan

○Taiwan   ○Tianjin   ○Xinjiang   ○Tibet

○Yunnan   ○Zhejiang   ○Abroad

4. Your marital status: [Single Choice] *

○Married   ○Single

5. Your educational background: [Single Choice] *

○Junior high or lower

○Senior high or vocational and technical schools

○College diplo

○Bachelor

○M. A.

○Ph. D. /Post-Doc

6. How long have you been in Shanghai? ____ years ____
months. [Fill in the blank] *

7. What are the main reasons for you to choose to come to
Shanghai? [Single Choice] *

○Pursuit of study   ○Working   ○Family migration

○Investment/Running my business   ○Other

8. Your present occupation: [Single Choice] *

○Leaders of all levels of the government, enterprise and public institutions, Party and government offices, and public organizations

○Professionals(e.g., teachers, doctors, engineering and technical personnel, lawyers and accountants)

○Public servant, staff at enterprise and public institutions or
   the government

○Workers(e.g., factory workers, construction workers, and urban sanitary workers)

○Personnel in business and service industry(e.g., salesclerks, waiters/waitress, and hotel clerks)

○Labors in farming, forestry, animal husbandry, side-line production and fishery

○Private business owners/individual operators

○Self-employed

○Soldier

○Housewives

○Student

○Retired

○Unemployed

○Other(e.g., volunteers)

9. Your current household registration status in Shanghai: [Single Choice]*

○Registered Shanghai Hukou

○Residence Permit

○Registered Corporate Hukou

○Other

10. Your housing condition: [Single Choice]*

○Self-owned housing

○Renting

○Lodging with relatives or friends

○Dormitory provided by the employer

○Other

11. Your average monthly income of the past year (unit: RMB): [Single Choice]*

○Below 5000   ○5000~10000   ○10001~15000

○15001~20000   ○Above 20000

12. Can you understand the Shanghai dialect? [Single Choice]*

○Can not understand at all.   ○Can understand only a little.

○Can understand most of it.   ○Can fully understand it.

13. Can you speak the Shanghai dialect? [Single Choice]*

○Can not speak at all.   ○Can speak only a little.

○Can speak most of it.   ○Can speak it.

14. Do you plan to stay in Shanghai for a long time(say, more than 5 years)? [Single Choice]*

○Yes   ○No

II. Social Media Use

1. What types of social media did you use most often in your daily life? [Check all that apply]*

☐WeChat   ☐Tencent QQ   ☐Sina Weibo   ☐Douban

☐Renren   ☐Zhihu   ☐Baidu Tieba   ☐Tianya BBS

☐LinkedIn   ☐Kaixin   ☐Skype   ☐Other

2. On average, approximately how much time per day have you spent on social media in the past week? [Single Choice]*

○Below 30 min.   ○31~60 min.   ○1~2 hours

○2~3 hours   ○Above 3 hours

3. Choose ONE number from 1 to 9 that best indicates how much each statement applies to you. Here, 1 — 9 represents the range of strongly disagree — strongly agree. [Matrix Scale Question]*

	1	2	3	4	5	6	7	8	9
(1) Using social media is part of my everyday activity.	○	○	○	○	○	○	○	○	○
(2) I feel out of touch when I do not use social media.	○	○	○	○	○	○	○	○	○
(3) I am willing to share some information on social media.	○	○	○	○	○	○	○	○	○
(4) I use social media to seek help.	○	○	○	○	○	○	○	○	○
(5) I communicate with my family frequently via social media.	○	○	○	○	○	○	○	○	○
(6) I maintain close contact with my friends via social media.	○	○	○	○	○	○	○	○	○

III. Personality

Read the following questions carefully. According to your actual situation, please choose Yes or No to answer the questions. [Matrix Scale Question]*

	Yes	No
1. Does your mood often go up and down?	○	○
2. Are you a talkative person?	○	○
3. Do you ever feel "just miserable" for no reason?	○	○
4. Are you rather lively?	○	○
5. Are you an irritable person?	○	○
6. Do you enjoy meeting new people?	○	○
7. Are your feelings easily hurt?	○	○
8. Do you usually let yourself go and enjoy yourself at a lively party?	○	○
9. Do you often feel "fed-up"?	○	○
10. Do you usually take the initiative in making new friends?	○	○
11. Would you call yourself a nervous person?	○	○
12. Can you easily get some life into a rather dull party?	○	○
13. Are you a worrier?	○	○
14. Do you tend to keep in the background on social occasions?	○	○
15. Would you call yourself tense or "highly-strung"?	○	○
16. Do you like mixing with people?	○	○
17. Do you worry too long after an embarrassing experience?	○	○
18. Do you like plenty of bustle and excitement around you?	○	○
19. Do you suffer from "nerves"?	○	○
20. Do you like telling jokes and funny stories?	○	○
21. Do you often feel lonely?	○	○
22. Do other people think of you as being very lively?	○	○
23. Are you often troubled about feelings of guilt?	○	○
24. Can you get a party going?	○	○

IV. Social Support

Please choose ONE number from 1 to 9 that best indicates how much each statement applies to you. Here, 1 → 9 represents the range of strongly disagree → strongly agree. [Matrix Scale Question]*

	1	2	3	4	5	6	7	8	9
1. There is someone to recommend me for some positions when I seek jobs.	○	○	○	○	○	○	○	○	○
2. There is someone I can count on to listen to me when I need to talk.	○	○	○	○	○	○	○	○	○
3. There is someone to share my good times.	○	○	○	○	○	○	○	○	○
4. There is someone to get together with for relaxation.	○	○	○	○	○	○	○	○	○
5. There is someone to provide necessary information to help orient me to the surroundings of Shanghai.	○	○	○	○	○	○	○	○	○
6. There is someone to explain and help me understand the local culture.	○	○	○	○	○	○	○	○	○
7. There is someone to confide in or talk to about myself or my problems	○	○	○	○	○	○	○	○	○
8. There is someone to give me information to help me understand a situation.	○	○	○	○	○	○	○	○	○
9. There is someone to help me learn about some local institutions' official rules and regulations.	○	○	○	○	○	○	○	○	○
10. There is someone to take me to the doctor if I need it.	○	○	○	○	○	○	○	○	○
11. There is someone to do things with to help me get my mind off things	○	○	○	○	○	○	○	○	○
12. There is someone to give me good advice about a crisis	○	○	○	○	○	○	○	○	○
13. There is someone to share my most private worries and fears with.	○	○	○	○	○	○	○	○	○
14. There is someone to give me necessary information to help me find jobs.	○	○	○	○	○	○	○	○	○
15. There is someone to give me suggestions to help me with my career development.	○	○	○	○	○	○	○	○	○

V. Acculturative Stress

Think of your life experience after you moved to Shanghai. Choose ONE number from 1 to 9 that best indicates how much each statement applies to you. Here, 1 → 9 represents the range of strongly disagree → strongly agree.   [Matrix Scale Question]*

	1	2	3	4	5	6	7	8	9
1. I am treated differently in social situations because I am from outside Shanghai.	○	○	○	○	○	○	○	○	○
2. Many opportunities are denied to me because I am from outside Shanghai.	○	○	○	○	○	○	○	○	○
3. Others are biased toward me because I am from outside Shanghai.	○	○	○	○	○	○	○	○	○
4. I feel that I receive unequal treatment because I am from outside Shanghai.	○	○	○	○	○	○	○	○	○
5. I am denied what I deserve because I am from outside Shanghai.	○	○	○	○	○	○	○	○	○
6. I feel that people from outside Shanghai are discriminated against.	○	○	○	○	○	○	○	○	○
7. Homesickness bothers me.	○	○	○	○	○	○	○	○	○
8. I feel sad living in unfamiliar surroundings.	○	○	○	○	○	○	○	○	○
9. I miss my hometown and the people at my hometown.	○	○	○	○	○	○	○	○	○
10. I feel sad leaving my relatives behind.	○	○	○	○	○	○	○	○	○
11. I feel uncomfortable adjusting to Shanghai foods.	○	○	○	○	○	○	○	○	○
12. I feel uncomfortable to adjusting to the values of the local Shanghai culture.	○	○	○	○	○	○	○	○	○
13. I feel nervous when people speak Shanghai dialect around me.	○	○	○	○	○	○	○	○	○
14. It hurts when people don't understand my cultural values.	○	○	○	○	○	○	○	○	○
15. I worry about having money to pay the bills each month.	○	○	○	○	○	○	○	○	○
16. I have to save the salaries of several months to purchase a car.	○	○	○	○	○	○	○	○	○
17. I have extra money to afford my family and me to travel abroad once every year.	○	○	○	○	○	○	○	○	○
18a. The mortgage accounts for a large percentage of my household income.	○	○	○	○	○	○	○	○	○
18b. The rent accounts for a large percentage of my household income.	○	○	○	○	○	○	○	○	○

VI. Life Satisfaction

Please read the following statements carefully. Choose ONE number from 1 to 9 that best indicates how much each statement applies to you. Here, 1 -- 9 represents the range of strongly disagree -- strongly agree.[Matrix Scale Question]*

	1	2	3	4	5	6	7	8	9
1. In most ways my life in Shanghai is close to my ideal.	○	○	○	○	○	○	○	○	○
2. The conditions of my life in Shanghai are excellent.	○	○	○	○	○	○	○	○	○
3. I am satisfied with life here in Shanghai.	○	○	○	○	○	○	○	○	○
4. So far I have gotten the important things I want in life here.	○	○	○	○	○	○	○	○	○
5. I do not want to change anything about my life in Shanghai.	○	○	○	○	○	○	○	○	○

VII. Local Cultural Identification

Please read the following statements carefully. Choose ONE number from 1 to 9 that best indicates how much each statement applies to you. Here, 1 -- 9 represents the range of strongly disagree -- strongly agree.[Matrix Scale Question]*

	1	2	3	4	5	6	7	8	9
1. I like to associate with the Shanghainese.	○	○	○	○	○	○	○	○	○
2. I feel I have much in common with the Shanghainese.	○	○	○	○	○	○	○	○	○
3. I identify with the Shanghainese.	○	○	○	○	○	○	○	○	○
4. I would like to learn Shanghai dialect.	○	○	○	○	○	○	○	○	○
5. I would like to follow the customs of Shanghai.	○	○	○	○	○	○	○	○	○

Appendix 3: Pearson's Correlation Matrix(N=703)

	time	SMU	extro	neuro	SS	PD	HS	CD	ES	AS	LS	LCI
length of stay(time)	1											
mean of social media use(SMU)	-0.003	1										
extroversion(extro)	0.017	.200**	1									
neuroticism(neuro)	-0.045	-.113**	-.706**	1								
mean of social support(SS)	0.051	.468**	.442**	-.452**	1							
mean of perceived discrimination(PD)	-.128**	-0.069	-.164**	.154**	-.113**	1						
mean of homesickness(HS)	-.124**	0.042	-.150**	.190**	-.074*	.360**	1					
mean of cultural Discomfort(CD)	-.177**	-0.040	-.168**	.174**	-.157**	.529**	.388**	1				
mean of economic strain(ES)	-.168**	-0.036	-.281**	.252**	-.235**	.254**	.273**	.271**	1			
mean of acculturative stress(AS)	-.201**	-0.043	-.257**	.258**	-.192**	.828**	.681**	.747**	.575**	1		
mean of life satisfaction(LS)	.177**	.266**	.299**	-.311**	.477**	-.135**	-0.063	-0.067	-.415**	-.224**	1	
mean of local cultural identification(LCI)	.296**	.246**	.245**	-.232**	.432**	-.215**	-.113**	-.287**	-.229**	-.290**	.476**	1

Note: 1. ** at the 0.01 level(double-tailed), the correlation was significant.
2. * at the 0.05 level(double-tailed), the correlation was significant.

图书在版编目（CIP）数据

社交媒体视域下中国国内移民适应研究/孟娇娇著
.—上海：上海三联书店,2022.9
ISBN 978 - 7 - 5426 - 7718 - 1

Ⅰ.①社… Ⅱ.①孟… Ⅲ.①移民-适应性-研究-
中国 Ⅳ.①D632.4

中国版本图书馆 CIP 数据核字(2022)第 097760 号

社交媒体视域下中国国内移民适应研究

著　　者 / 孟娇娇

责任编辑 / 殷亚平
装帧设计 / 一本好书
监　　制 / 姚　军
责任校对 / 王凌霄

出版发行 / 上海三联书店
　　　　　(200030)中国上海市漕溪北路 331 号 A 座 6 楼
邮　　箱 / sdxsanlian@sina.com
邮购电话 / 021 - 22895540
印　　刷 / 上海惠敦印务科技有限公司

版　　次 / 2022 年 9 月第 1 版
印　　次 / 2022 年 9 月第 1 次印刷
开　　本 / 640mm×960mm　1/16
字　　数 / 310 千字
印　　张 / 23
书　　号 / ISBN 978 - 7 - 5426 - 7718 - 1/D·536
定　　价 / 98.00 元

敬启读者,如发现本书有印装质量问题,请与印刷厂联系 021 - 63779028